Utilitarianism and Malthus's Virtue Ethics

T0270765

The die-hard image of Malthus the ogre has not completely disappeared yet. And yet, Malthus showed no less concern than Adam Smith for the labouring poor. In order to make full sense of such expression of concern and to appraise their relevance in Malthus's work, we need to know what moral philosophy, what view of natural science, and what view of the 'moral and political science' Malthus endorsed.

This book reconstructs Malthus's meta-ethics, his normative ethics and his applied ethics on such topics as population, poverty, sexuality and war and slavery. It shows how Malthus's understanding of his own population theory and political economy was that of sub-disciplines of moral and political philosophy, empirical enquiries required in order to be able to pronounce justified value-judgements on such matters as the Poor Laws. But Malthus's population theory and political economy were no value-free science and his non-utilitarian policy advice resulted from his overall system of ideas and was explicitly based on a set of familiar moral assumptions.

It is mistaken to claim that Malthus's explanation of disharmony by reference to Divine Wisdom is extraneous to analysis and without influence on the theory of policy; it is true instead that theological consequentialist considerations were appealed to in order to provide a justification for received moral rules, but these were meant to justify a rather traditional normative ethics, quite far from Benthamite 'new morality'.

Sergio Cremaschi is a Professor of Moral Philosophy at the Department of Humanities, Amedeo Avogadro University of Eastern Piedmont, Italy.

Routledge Studies in the History of Economics

Utilitarianism and Malthus's Virtue Ethics

Respectable, virtuous and happy

Sergio Cremaschi

Routledge
Taylor & Francis Group

LONDON AND NEW YORK

First published 2014
by Routledge
2 Park Square, Milton Park, Abingdon, Oxon OX14 4RN

and by Routledge
52 Vanderbilt Avenue, New York, NY 10017

First issued in paperback 2020

Routledge is an imprint of the Taylor & Francis Group, an informa business

British Library Cataloguing in Publication Data
A catalogue record for this book is available from the British Library

Library of Congress Cataloging in Publication Data
Cremaschi, Sergio, 1949-
Utilitarianism and Malthus' virtue ethics : respectable, virtuous and happy / Sergio Cremaschi.
    pages cm. – (Routledge studies in the history of economics)
1. Population policy–Moral and ethical aspects. 2. Population–Moral and ethical aspects. 3. Malthus, T. R. (Thomas Robert), 1766-1834. 4. Virtue. 5. Utilitarianism. I. Title.
    HQ766.15.C74 2014
    179'.9–dc23
            2014001680

ISBN 13: 978-0-367-66949-2 (pbk)
ISBN 13: 978-0-415-73536-0 (hbk)
ISBN 13: 978-1-315-81923-5 (ebk)

Typeset in Times New Roman
by Taylor & Francis Books

Contents

Preface

Donald Winch (1993) argued that Malthus did have strong value-judgements on the British society of his time and these, a die-hard tradition notwithstanding, starting with those among Malthus's contemporaries who depicted him as an ogre, were far from going in the direction of political economy as an amoral science. Such die-hard misreading is indeed still around in rather recent literature (Himmelfarb 1995, p. 246–247). Winch contended that Malthus showed no less concern than Adam Smith for the labouring poor's lot, adding that, without 'some idea of the character of the intellectual and moral framework which licensed such individual evaluative judgments, however, the exercise [of listing them] would be inconclusive [...] one needs to ask what a systematic moral philosophy Malthus endorsed, what view of science, natural or moral, did he accept?' (p. 247). He concluded that a full answer would require 'at least an article'.

Such 'at least an article' is what I am trying to provide here. What I try to do is a reconstruction of Malthus's system of ideas *in its own terms*. That is, I try to reconstruct the meaning and context of doctrines he either vindicated in press or endorsed in manuscript documents about such topics as natural and revealed theology, the problem of evil, ethics, both theoretical and applied, politics, and then population, poverty, agriculture, commerce, freedom of trade, rent, profit and salaries. The point is not adding one more chapter to the history of opinions by famous past characters about rather trifling matters but, quite on the contrary, trying to put first what comes first. In our case, this is not Malthus's having been a great demographer and economist but, on the contrary, his having been a moral and political philosopher/theologian who aimed at working out a comprehensive answer to such questions as how is a benevolent Deity compatible with suffering in the world, and how are we to deal with poverty, how is liberty related with population and poverty, and how can human beings cope with an imperfect world. The wealth of technical tools Malthus worked out for answering such questions in a realistic way that would take hard facts into account was a side-effect of his quest for comprehensive treatment of such issues. It goes without saying that we can neatly separate analytic tools from theology, politics and ethics, and this is indeed the right thing to do when we want to compare formulations of such analytic tools by Malthus with those by, say, Ricardo, Say, Sismondi, but the possibility of such separation cannot be the subject of a triumphant announcement of some historical discovery, since it is simply true by fiat.

The point is that even *internal* history of science – a fully legitimate pursuit – can be seriously misled by lack of a parallel wider history, which need not be based on an outright *externalist* sociological approach, but should try nonetheless to read texts against the background of their context and co-test. By *context* I mean events, such as the Napoleonic wars, fluctuations in external trade and the confrontation between alignments in British politics. By *co-text* I mean published and unpublished documents that may contribute in reconstructing the full meaning of what is being said in the *primary text*, that is Malthus's writings. Accordingly, such a wider history should not ignore, for example, that Adam Smith was a close friend of Hume but also of moderate Presbyterian clergymen and that he wrote the *History of Astronomy* before *The Wealth of Nations*, or that Malthus was a Cambridge-educated Anglican divine who had met the idea of the 'test of utility' in John Gay's and Thomas Brown's consequentialist-voluntarist doctrines while a student at Cambridge and never read instead Jeremy Bentham's *Principles of Morals and Legislation*, or that he did not discover the doctrine of proportions while musing on *Nichomachean Ethics*, or worse while forerunning future developments in mathematical economics, but instead studied this doctrine in Colin MacLaurin's textbooks in mathematics and physics that were part of Cambridge reading lists.

The present attempt at reading Malthus in some kind of a 'stereoscopic' way is the application of approaches and methodologies that have been discovered in such different fields as the French tradition of historical epistemology, the history of science, the history of ideas, the history of political concepts, which I tried to put to work while carrying out research on Adam Smith in the 1970s and 1980s. In the meanwhile Marcelo Dascal, while working together on the controversy between Malthus and Ricardo, was trying to teach me how Gricean pragmatics may be a tool for interpreting scientific texts and the study of controversy a key to the comprehension of theory change. Daniel Diatkine, the discussant of a draft of Chapters 1–3 at the 10th ESHET conference (Porto, April 2006), made useful comments. Maria Luisa Pesante, Terenzio Maccabelli and Pierluigi Porta made useful suggestions on Malthus and his context, Marco Guidi, Massimo Reichlin, James Crimmins and Gianfranco Pellegrino added more suggestions on classical utilitarianism. A draft of Chapter 7, presented as a Public Lecture at the School of Education, Aarhus University (Copenhagen, April 2012) as well as a contributed paper at the School on Philosophy and Social Sciences (Prague, May 2012) has been published in the *Bulletin Prague College Research Centre* 2013 under the title 'Malthus's war on poverty as moral reform'. The greatest debt yet is with Anthony Waterman, who, besides commenting more than one version of the manuscript, performed the miracle of defeating my 'natural indolence' in persuading me that writing this book was the right thing to do.

Bibliography

Himmelfarb, G. (1995) *The De-Moralization of Society: From Victorian Virtues to Modern Values.* London: IEA Health and Welfare Unit.

Winch, D. (1993) 'Robert Malthus: Christian moral scientist, arch-demoralizer or implicit secular utilitarian?' *Utilitas* 5(2), pp. 239–254.

1 Malthus the Utilitarian vs. Malthus the Christian moral thinker

Malthus was believed by several historians of economic thought to have been a utilitarian. In fact he frequently mentioned 'utility' as a *test* for moral laws, and the greatest sum of happiness for his creatures as the *goal* the Creator had in mind. On the other hand, he was the target of James Mill's scorn for his priest-like nonsense, and he did, in fact, mention more than once 'laws of nature', 'virtue' and 'rights', that is, precisely the kind of ideas Bentham believed to be 'nonsense upon stilts'. The alternative between Malthus the Utilitarian and Malthus the Christian Moral Thinker has emerged again in a recent dispute between Hollander and Winch. Settling the dispute is not the main aim in this book, which aims instead at reconstructing a 'stereoscopic' view of Malthus's social science qua applied ethics, but at least I will try to do also that, and, in case I succeed, this will be one useful side-effect.

Malthus understood his own contributions as belonging neither to demography nor to economics – the later labels for two still non-existing disciplines – but instead to the 'moral and political science'. Note that 'political economy' was becoming the name for a discipline precisely in those years, while for Adam Smith it still conveyed the flavour of the rhetorical figure through which Antoine de Montchrétien had launched the expression in 1615, a label for the management of the resources of the nation *as if* they were those of a private household. Besides, in cases he used the expression to denote those systems which he criticized, and not just a part of 'the science of a legislator', he tended to associate it with the word 'systems', one with a rather derogatory connotation hinting at an aprioristic way of thinking which tends to bend facts to theory instead of correcting theory in the light of facts, like the Cartesian theory of vortexes (Cremaschi 1981; 1984, pp. 11–72; 1989; 2000). This is why Malthus claimed that political economy is a science that 'bears a nearer resemblance to the science of morals and politics' (Malthus 1820, vol. 1, p. 2) than to mathematics, and that his own contribution to the field might be of use to those who were interested in 'moral and political questions' (Malthus 1803, vol. 1, p. 3). Given such self-image of his work, singling out 'the philosophic tradition to which Malthus belongs' (Paglin 1961, p. 15) is no matter of idle curiosity; Paglin went on complaining of confusion lingering in the literature regarding this point, and added that:

Bonar as well as more recent authors such as Lionel Robbins and Plamenatz have tended to consider Malthus as a participant in the utilitarian
tradition. This was based on the fact that Malthus occasionally used the
principle or utility in his reasoning on economic problems. But as we
shall see, this is not a sufficient reason for considering him as a utilitarian
at a time when utilitarianism had crystallized into a complete theory of
government and a definite body of policy prescriptions.

(p. 16)

Unfortunately Paglin added of his own to the confusion existing, by enlisting
him instead in the current of 'conservative traditionalism espoused by Burke'
(p. 16). Several later commentators – the most recent among them is Samuel
Hollander – seem to believe that Malthus, who never met Bentham and
apparently never read anything of his and had a rather distant and occasionally conflictive relationship with James Mill (Cremaschi and Dascal forthcoming), was nonetheless simply a Utilitarian in ethics and politics. I believe
that this sounds a bit strange to anybody who has any familiarity with the
climate of opinion in early nineteenth-century Britain. In these decades there was
an increasingly raging confrontation going on between several alignments,
namely conservative-conservative Tories and conservative-humanitarian
Tories, Whigs, an older petty-bourgeois radicalism that had Godwin as its
spokesman, and an emerging new middle-class radicalism that found its
spokesmen in the Philosophic Radicals (Fetter 1965). This confrontation
became increasingly polarized around the two poles that survived natural
selection. The two currents fit for survival were the Whigs and the Philosophic Radicals (later called Utilitarians) and the alternative was defined by a
number of oppositions: Church of England vs. irreligion, the British Constitution
vs. democracy, the interests of the gentry vs. those of the urban middle class,
the soft version of principle of population vs. its hard version (Lively and
Rees 1978; Cremaschi and Dascal forthcoming).

   In ethics and politics, Whigs had either Paley or Dugald Stewart as their
mentors. In the first three decades the principle of utility was not a debated
issue or a source of dispute between the Whigs and the Philosophic Radicals.
In fact, Bentham's more abstract theories still had scant circulation and it was
about the practical agenda that cooperation was established between real
Benthamite (amounting perhaps, strange as it may sound, to Bentham himself and James Mill – not a large group) and other friends of reason, first
among them Unitarians, like John Bowring or David Ricardo. It was perhaps
in the Thirties and Forties, when an inductivist idea of the 'Noble science of
Politics' was vindicated against Bentham's aprioristic approach by Thomas
Babington Macaulay (1829) that the difference between Whig liberalism and
Utilitarian technocracy was denounced (Lively and Rees 1978), and Paley's
authority was first contested within Anglicanism while an Intuitionist
alternative emerged to both Paleyite and Benthamite ethics (Whewell 1845;
Cremaschi 2006; 2008).

This does not amount to assuming that Paleyite and Benthamite ethics and politics were basically the same. Indeed they were different; for example Paleyite politics made room for innate rights, and it legitimized the institution of monarchy, and Paleyite ethics accepted the traditional set of duties and virtues as had been taught by the Anglican and the Ciceronian humanist traditions without any concession to Bentham's 'new morality'. It was just the presence of something called the 'principle of utility' that made for a similarity between both schools, a similarity by which Albee (1901) was later seduced into dreaming of an alleged school of religious Utilitarians as a forerunner of the school of secular utilitarianism. But the principle played a different function in each system; for Paley and his followers it was a test of laws that may be assumed to be sanctioned by divine will; for Bentham it was instead a normative criterion to be applied directly to real-world cases. Bonar's claim, uncritically followed by others, that Malthus had been basically a 'utilitarian' is accordingly either irreparably vacuous or blatantly false. In a thin sense, being a utilitarian could be read as implying accepting the principle of utility as playing some role, and this was what Malthus clearly did, as several others had done before him. But if the function of the principle is accounting for God's choice of one given set of moral laws, this is fully compatible with adhesion to one version of the same moral and political system that Bentham believed to be his mission to attack (Crimmins 1998). In a thicker sense, if the word Utilitarian denotes a follower of the family of doctrines that was being promoted by the group called the Philosophic Radicals, or the Benthamite, or later on, the Utilitarians, it is clear enough that Malthus was no Utilitarian and that he was precisely one of the enemies the Bentham–Mill coterie wanted to fight. In fact, this family of doctrines included democracy, atheism, psychological associationism, sociological individualism, *Laissez-Faire* economic liberalism somehow supported by a simplified version of Ricardianism, and the 'new morality', in turn consisting of hedonism, the harmony between self-interest and general interest, and the war on prejudice. The right answers then is that, first, the utilitarians in the first decades of the nineteenth century were the 'Philosophic radicals', and it is clear beyond any doubt that Malthus did not belong to the group; second, that 'the utilitarian tradition has always seen itself as a broad church' (Chappell and Crisp 1998, p. 552) and accordingly tended to present almost everybody as its own 'forerunner' (indeed John Stuart Mill went so far as to enlist Jesus and the Stoics in the category), and accordingly also the Anglican consequentialist voluntarism – a current that will be discussed in the next chapter – as soon as Paley, the last of its proponents, lost any influence and ceased being a dangerous competitor, was reclassified under the fuzzy label 'forerunners'.

On the basis of these considerations, we could start making sense of two apparently inconsistent facts, first, that Malthus was no 'utilitarian' in matters of normative ethics and even less in matters of political doctrines, since what he contended for on most issues was the opposite of what Bentham's followers wanted; second, that the Malthusian system of ideas has one intersection with the Benthamite one. A reasonable way of making sense of these facts may be assuming that (i) Malthus's ethical theory shared important elements with Bentham's utilitarianism simply because Bentham was less original than utilitarian hagiography has always been preaching, and indeed had borrowed those elements from the same sources as Malthus; (ii) Bentham's followers adopted so enthusiastically Malthus's population theory and found it so powerful a weapon for fighting their own battles that they ignored everything Malthus had to add from 1803 on, sticking to its early cruder version; (iii) after 1820, in order to bring some order into their mixed pro- and anti-Malthus attitude, they adopted the doctrine formulated by John Ramsey McCulloch (1820) according to which there are 'two Malthuses': the 'progressive' one, that is, the population theorist, and the 'reactionary' one, that is, the political economist.

As to the shared sources in ethical theory, these were the proponents of the doctrine that I have proposed to name – as a token for a better word – 'consequentialist voluntarism' (Cremaschi 2008), that is, the Anglican divines Richard Cumberland, John Gay, Thomas Brown and David Hartley and, obviously enough, Paley. Bentham's revolution in ethical theory consisted simply in taking their doctrine and cutting its head – namely God – off, thus leaving the moral agent alone in *judging*. The important difficulty implied was that the moral agent was left to himself also as far as *sanctioning* was concerned, but without the Creator's alleged omnipotence that made such a task supposedly easier to carry out. Bentham's effort at finding a solution for this problem in the *Deontology*, decades after the *Introduction*, testifies as to his awareness of the conundrum any non-theological consequentialism unavoidably ends with.

The conclusion is that Malthus was simply a follower of this school, whose doctrine he had been taught at Cambridge, and which – far from being *not-yet-fully-secularized-utilitarianism* or better *atheism-for-clergymen* – was instead a doctrinal system on his own, with its own inner logic and – unsavoury as it may prove to any post-Kantian (or post-Barthian, or post-Bonhoefferian) palate including that of the present writer – more consistent than Benthamite utilitarianism. If any surviving Utilitarian is unconvinced, he may look at Sidgwick's reflections on the conclusions reached in his own *Methods of Ethics*, namely that 'we are limited to merely mundane sanctions, owing to the inevitable divergence, in this imperfect world, between the individual's Duty and his Happiness' (Sidgwick 1906, p. 472).

In order to make my conclusion more precise, let me start with current definitions of utilitarianism. These (Chappell and Crisp 1998; Smart 1967; Lyons 2001; Sinnot-Armstrong 2006) suggest that a utilitarian theory implies:

i   a definition of the good in terms of welfare;
ii an assumption that we can compare welfare across different people's lives;

iii   a definition of the right in terms of the good, or consequentialism.

I would like to add two more conditions, spelling out what is already in the former, namely:

iv   impartiality as a criterion for the allocation of such good;
v   identification of the judging subject with the agent.

I assume the five above conditions to be necessary and sufficient ones. One more condition is required for inclusion into a stricter kind of utilitarianism, that is, act-utilitarianism, namely:

vi   individual acts, not classes of acts, are considered.

On the basis of such a definition, Jeremy Bentham, James Mill and John Stuart Mill may be safely classified as utilitarian philosophers, albeit the younger Mill does not comply with requirement (vi), while this is not true of William Paley, who fails to comply with requirement (v), even though he does with (vi); Malthus does somewhat worse than Paley, since – as I argue in what follows – he fails to comply with requirements (v) and (vi) and limits the scope of (iii) to the point that it does apply to the spectator but does not to the agent.

So, who was properly a utilitarian? 'Theological utilitarianism' has been used for almost one century as a label for such theories as Paley's. I suggest instead that, even though everybody has a right to paste any label he likes upon any pot he chooses, theological utilitarianism sounds too much of an oxymoron and it was invented by secular utilitarians in order to provide a pigeon-hole for those second-rank utilitarians who forgot to abjure their Christian faith. But Paley's doctrine was not a sweetened version of Bentham's (and indeed Bentham's appeared *after* Paley), but instead a not-too-original systematization of claims that had been first advanced, and then step by step elaborated on, by quite orthodox and non-Calvinist members of the Anglican clergy who stressed the role of natural theology. Was this line of thinking in any sense utilitarian? The answer is that this school adopted claims (i) and (ii), but rejected claims from (iii) to (v). The resulting system of ideas was a kind of consequentialism in meta-ethics combined with a different normative ethic, a virtue ethic turning around love as the chief precept and virtue; even though their consequentialist meta-ethics was similar to utilitarianism (or better, even though Bentham's pillaged their works), their normative ethics was worlds apart from the 'new morality' announced by Bentham, and was instead believed to be fully compatible with the familiar Ciceronian system of duties and natural laws that had been for some time the staple for the European elite education. All this may be found in Malthus's works, and indeed the second *Essay* includes a generally overlooked but rather systematic treatment of ethics.

I mentioned that Hollander's hasty conclusion about the utilitarian character of Malthus's policy advice was not his own invention. Indeed, in Malthus scholarship there has been a remarkable degree of uncertainty as to his relationship to utilitarianism. The original sin was perhaps committed by William Empson, who told a joke in a somewhat infelicitous way. After Malthus's death he wrote that the latter had chosen to dedicate his talents to useful pursuits, having in mind that a scholar's aim should be contributing to those fields of learning that may prove useful in bettering man's lot, and thus:

> in his view of life and in his management of himself, he was a Utilitarian *of the right sort* [...] His quarrel with the followers of Bentham was only in their narrow conception of utility, and in their apparent ignorance of human nature.
>
> (Empson 1837, p. 478; italics added)

This comment, written in the 1830s, precisely when utilitarianism was approaching its zenith, comes as a conclusion to a description of Malthus's intellectual career, emphasizing how, after what he describes as a 'general education' at Cambridge, Malthus choose for himself a well-defined intellectual vocation and pursued it without deviations, hoping that his intellectual efforts would be useful to mankind (and accordingly agreeing with the Utilitarians in a 'philanthropic' interpretation of his intellectual vocation), and then goes on clarifying that he was at odds with the Utilitarians on everything else, that is on *philosophical* issues. As a result, what Empson actually *wanted to* say is that Malthus was a philosophical opponent of utilitarianism but he was read the other way round. The first who got it wrong was James Bonar who wrote that Malthus was 'nominally a utilitarian' (Bonar 1885, p. 337) but, not unsurprisingly, the adverb 'nominally' is never given a precise meaning throughout his monograph, by showing where and how Malthus had manifested his adhesion to utilitarian principles and where and how he eventually deviated from his professed creed. Instead, after such a 'proof' of Malthus's nominal utilitarianism, Bonar proceeds to prove that the latter did differ at some points not from Bentham and James Mill but from William Paley. Malthus allegedly disagreed with Paley 'by refusing to allow moral value to action done from wither fear of punishment or hope of reward' (p. 39; cf. Malthus 1798, p. 135), and the main difference from Paley is in the definition of virtue. Thus:

> the ethical system of both is a utilitarianism which is narrow and personal in its motive (the private happiness of the individual in another world), but broad and catholic in its end (the general happiness of human beings in the present world) [...] Malthus took a larger view, and thought rather of the development of the human faculties than of mere satisfaction of desires, both in this world and in the next; but he nowhere distinctly breaks with Paley, and his division of passions into self-love (or

prudence) and benevolence is taken straightly from that theologian. (Principles, viii, 10)

(Bonar 1885, p. 331)

Bonar added also – how far consistently I do not dare to say – that Malthus, far from not being utilitarian enough, 'was a utilitarian of the old school', in so far as he believed in spontaneous harmony of private and public interests, and 'the greatest happiness of the great body of the people seemed to him to be best secured by the devotion of the individual members of it, each to his own permanent and real happiness' (p. 213). This is to Bonar's eyes 'the only course open to the older Utilitarians'; namely they should 'have shown that the individual best secures his own happiness by securing that of his fellows; but that is not shown by Bentham, who in fact rather takes his maxim for granted than proves it in any way. Even though they had taken this course, there would have been a difficulty, that is, if each man is his own best judge, how can another (Bentham or any other legislator) judge for him' (p. 227). Thus, Malthus was a Utilitarian on principle, even a more consequent Utilitarian than Bentham, but he adopted different views on such individual issues as moral motivation and the definition of virtue. Bonar insisted also on the influence of Abraham Tucker, a rather eclectic philosopher who had in fact some influence on Paley and with whom Malthus was surely familiar. What Bonar seems to have missed is the fact that both Tucker and Paley came after one century of consequentialist voluntarism, a school whose conclusions were brilliantly systematized in Paley's *Principles*. One would expect to find in Bonar's work some conclusion about precise philosophical affiliations of Malthus' work; instead, Bonar limited himself to jump to a kind of apology for Malthus's flirtations with philosophy, as if the latter were some kind of absurd vice, a rather common idea in the age of positivism, but a strange idea for any eighteenth-century thinker. Bonar's conclusion is that it is true that Malthus 'had not risen above the *metaphysical superstition* of his age' (p. 338, italics added), but also that at least he was not 'behind them'. This foolish comment may encourage in reading also the previous phrase 'nominally utilitarian' as nonsensical chatter of the same positivist kind.

This would have been not too bad, had not Bonar's eulogy been quoted by others as a serious scholar's comment. The first to do so was Leslie Stephen, the author of a monumental work on *The English Utilitarians* (1900). His work was heavily biased by his being some kind of idealist who wanted to come to a *redde rationem* with utilitarianism. Concerning Malthus he follows the path inadvertently opened by Empson and trampled on by Bonar. He mentions his utilitarianism in connection with the idea of a 'moral' restraint while asking 'what precisely is meant by "moral" in this connection?', and answering that 'Malthus takes his ethical philosophy pretty much for granted' and adding that 'he is clearly a utilitarian according to the version of Paley' (Stephen 1900, vol. 1, p. 156). In a footnote he adds: 'Mr. Bonar thinks that Malthus followed Paley's predecessor, Abraham Tucker, rather than Paley.

The difference is not for my purpose important. In any case, Malthus's references are to Paley' (p. 156 fn.). Let me note that Stephen's statement that 'Malthus's references are to Paley' is true if taken literally, but the implications are not those Stephen believed to be. Yet, after such a lapidary statement, no one dared to check Malthus's own references any more. Stephen goes on saying that Malthus agrees with Paley on the idea that 'virtue evidently consists in educing from the materials which the Creator has placed under our guidance the greatest sum of human happiness' (p. 156). Here the remark is in order that such a definition of virtue is in any event John Gay's, not Paley's, and the fact that Paley repeats it does not imply that Malthus found it in Paley. Stephen adds also that Malthus declares that our 'natural impulses are, abstractly considered, good, and only to be distinguished by their consequences' (p. 217) and that Malthus agreed with Godwin that 'morality means the "calculation of consequences"' (p. 217). In these matters Malthus 'was entirely at one with the utilitarians proper, and seems to regard their doctrine as self-evident' (p. 157). The remark is in order here that Stephen, before baldly declaring that Malthus took his ethics 'for granted' and that he had learned it from the Utilitarians, should have spent some time in reading chapters 1 and 2 in book IV of the second *Essay*, where Malthus presents his own ethics. In fact, Stephen's clumsy anachronism anticipates the birth of a Utilitarian school to the last decades of the eighteenth century. The reason for such a blunder were clearly the facts of being blinded by the weight utilitarianism had in England *after* the 1830s and having confused notions about the kind of ideas entertained by eighteenth-century Anglican divines, whose writings he apparently did not bother to read and thus he was left with the vague notion that there were, between 1798 and 1803, some *proper* utilitarians and a number of *sputniks*, mainly *shy-utilitarian clergymen* among whom Malthus might fit. Stephen's entry on Malthus in the *Dictionary of National Biography* adds something to what he had written in his book, albeit remaining as vague as ever. He says that '[t]hough a utilitarian he did not, any more than Bentham, accept the abstract principle of laissez-faire which became the creed of Bentham's followers' (Stephen 1882, p. 888).

Ernest Albee, who produced an accurate reconstruction of the doctrines of Cumberland, Gay, Brown and Paley, for whom he adopted the label 'theological Utilitarian' (Albee 1901, p. xvii–ix), sensed that there was something stinking in Stephen's story of the utilitarian parson, and adopted the safer escape-way of just omitting any mention of Malthus. Half a century later, John Plamenatz, who had missed Albee's book while compiling his own on *The English Utilitarians* (or who apparently did so, since the book carries no bibliography) takes it as a matter of course that Malthus was 'another utilitarian clergyman' (Plamenatz 1949, p. 115), no less than 'the classical economists, especially the three most famous of them, Adam Smith, Malthus and Ricardo', who were 'all of them Utilitarians. They believed that the proper end of government is the greatest happiness of the governed' (p. 111). One would look in vain for any citation from any of the three mentioned economists and should content himself with the somewhat odd argument that classical political economy 'was the theory behind the advice given by Utilitarians to the successive government of their country' (p. 111). William Petersen, who wrote a modest biography of Malthus, seems to share the belief that discussion of moral philosophy at the turn of eighteenth century was becoming unfashionable in the social disciplines and was thus reverting to the religious tracts (Petersen 1979, p. 17), that Malthus was a wholehearted utilitarian (p. 38, 214, 239), but also, surprisingly enough, that he seemed to be an unfaithful utilitarian 'in his own analysis' (p. 214), and that he believed in 'individual responsibility as the key to his ethical system' (p. 239), a belief that is unclear whether made him a Utilitarian, but at least alienated him from 'conventional Christians' (p. 239) who – needless to say – do not make room for individual responsibility!

Patricia James, who wrote a pretty biography, doing some kind of contextual historiography that gives the reader a flavour of everyday life as if seen from inside, as if he was reading one of Jane Austen's novels, is taken too far yet by her enthusiasm for her own fascinating approach, and tends to see Malthus's life more from the perspective of the drawing room than from that of the classroom, the library or the chapel; the final output smells a little bit of '*surtout, pas des idées*'; she treats Malthus's education in nine pages (James 1979, p. 25–29), leaving the reader with the impression that Malthus neither studied theology nor philosophy. She writes only that he 'admired' Paley's *Principles* (p. 32) and does not take the pain of describing the contents of Malthus's studies, particularly those he did in 1788, the year between his BA and holy orders (p. 3–34); besides, she deals with the theodicy of the first *Essay* in one page (p. 66–67) and ignores the second *Essay*'s two chapters on ethics (but this is not James's special fault). At least she treats the ensuing debate on religion and sexual morality in detail (p. 116–126) and is roughly right in remarking that Malthus in 1803 did not reject his own 1798 theological views but just omitted their treatment as unnecessary (p. 119).

Samuel Hollander, in an article of 1989 and then in his monumental monograph of 1997, seems in his final outcome to coagulate the results of almost two centuries cross-purpose by adding the catalyst of the logical-empiricist dichotomy between science and ethics. He argues that Lionel Robbins had been right in claiming, several decades ago (Robbins 1952, 28 fn.), that 'Malthus's explanation of disharmony by reference to Divine Wisdom is extraneous to analysis and without influence on the theory of policy' (Hollander 1989, p. 171), and that he was a Utilitarian in his appraisal of policies, albeit a Utilitarian afflicted with 'damaging vagueness'. Hollander is aware that the last two chapters in the 1798 *Essay* turn out to be an embarrassment for a Utilitarian such as the one Malthus was trying to become, but this is easily explained away by the consideration that 'the apologia for the benevolent Deity is radically altered in later editions' (p. 171), without enquiring into such alterations. And finally he adds that Malthus should obviously have rejected 'reliance upon the supernatural revelation or scriptural authority'

(p. 74 fn.). The objection is obvious that he did have recourse to Scriptural authority as late as 1824 in *A Summary View of the Principle of Population* (Malthus 1824). In his monograph he adds that Robbins was right in his claim that 'the test of policy is to be its effect on human happiness' and Malthus's discussion of policies concerning population is the best proof thereof, his case against communism showing a 'paramount case of adoption of the utilitarian perspective on social organization – the evaluation of institutions only by their consequences rather than as "good" or "bad" per se' (Hollander 1997, p. 910), but he adds also that communism was undesirable for Malthus because it would have implied legal limitations to individual freedoms which would be 'unnatural, immoral, or cruel' (Malthus 1803, vol. 2, p. 285). I would have noted that Malthus writes 'unnatural, immoral, or cruel', not 'un-felicific, un-felicific, un-felicific', and drawn the conclusion that such an argument, far from being utilitarian, implies adoption of a *pluralist* moral ontology incompatible with utilitarianism.

Hollander does note the non-utilitarian character of the definition of virtue in the first *Essay* (Hollander 1997, p. 927), but then immediately mistakes the eudemonistic doctrine presented in the same essay for a utilitarian doctrine (pp. 927–928). He also notes Malthus's distinction between general tendency of actions to produce good effects as the criterion of morality in general and the immediate effect of one action, which might be good without exempting the action in itself from being judged immoral (pp. 937–938). In the following, Hollander constantly tends to assume without discussion that amendments in following editions of the second *Essay* go towards secular utilitarianism, while on the contrary – as I show in what follows – they constantly tend to pave objections from Anglican critics by stressing the voluntarist foundation of the system as a whole as well as emphasizing focus on *rules* instead of *acts*. The points at which Hollander successfully singles out convergences between Malthus and the secular Utilitarian John Stuart Mill are in fact not points where the dogmatic divine gives way to the secular Utilitarian but those where a maximizing criterion is fully justified for Malthus the theologian in his own terms. The fact is that they concern the only fields where a maximizing criterion may be adopted not only by the legislator, i.e. God, but also by the agent, i.e. Man, namely justice and benevolence. Thus, a plausible 'utilitarian' argument noted by Hollander in Malthus is his plea for high wages (p. 912), where the reason given is that a greater number of individuals would be happier; no doubt this would be plausible for a utilitarian, but it is also Adam Smith's argument, and it could be endorsed by thinkers of different descriptions since it needs no specifically utilitarian premise. As far as all other virtues are concerned, such as chastity, respect for rights, love for equality, God as a legislator follows a maximizing criterion but men have to comply with God's laws in an unconditional way.

Donald Winch has defended in several contributions an approach to the history of economic thought as well as an overall view of Malthus that are almost opposite to Hollander's. Winch's reading has been inspired by a desire to read authors in their own terms, paying attention to 'languages', that is the existing background of shared meanings and the existing sets of rhetorical *topoi* shared by the time's audience, and avoiding strained modernization or, even worse, pseudo-history that sorts the wheat from the chaff and gives grades to past authors according to the amount of modern economic analysis they have been able to 'forerun'. Accordingly, Winch has insisted on the intellectual background of Malthus's work, provided by eighteenth-century experimental natural philosophy and Anglican natural theology, stressing that Malthus's explanations should be reconstructed according to his own standards of what was supposed to hold as satisfying explanation, thus leaving the Deity safely in the place where Malthus had put it, and leaving economic analysis as entrenched in theology as before. In *Malthus* he insists that a view of Malthus's 'trajectory' like the one taken for granted by Hollander is still Keynes's description, the one that most economists have gratefully accepted, an evolution 'from a caterpillar of a moral scientist and chrysalis of an historian' to a 'winged economist who could gaily survey the world from the heights of economic science' (Winch 1987, p. 98), while reminding us that, on the opposite, Malthus had always been committed 'to the enterprise of constructing and applying a science of politics and morals' (p. 98). He recalls that one among several reasons why the questions addressed in Malthus's *Essay* were explosive ones was 'the major question of how belief in a benevolent deity could be squared with the existence of widespread poverty and misery that was only loosely or problematically connected with sinful conduct' (p. 4). He wisely reminds that the depuration of science from theology, metaphysics and similar cant wished for by the Bonar–Robbins–Hollander alignment is a hasty enterprise since 'Malthus should also be regarded as a seeker after scientific truth because of, rather than despite, his clear theological commitments' (p. 18), and also that Malthus did not abandon in the second *Essay* the theological and metaphysical 'residues' still present in the first *Essay*, but on the contrary 'this work reveals a great deal about his later work, despite the changes that were later to be made to Malthus's opinions on population and related matters of political economy' (p. 18) precisely because Malthus's quest for a middle way between opposed doctrines, his search for the golden mean, his desire for a balance between abstract theory and experience derived from the intellectual legacy of the eighteenth-century Anglican *via media* whose stronghold was Cambridge. Yet, Winch does not go into a deep enough analysis of Malthus's own moral theory and he fails to clarify in detail how, for so-called theological utilitarians in general and Malthus in particular, the supreme criterion for judging individual actions and policies was 'the greatest surplus of virtue and happiness over vice and misery' (p. 7).

In the already mentioned 'Robert Malthus: Christian moral scientist, archdemoralizer or implicit secular utilitarian?' Winch suggests that: (a) Malthus does not provide a full-blown moral system as Adam Smith had done; (b) he does make use of providentialist arguments and these are marked unambiguously by a clearly theistic and Christian sense; (c) Mandeville's system is refuted more drastically by Malthus than by Smith; (d) he makes a much less extensive use than Smith of the ideas of Nature's deceit and unintended consequences (Winch 1993, p. 247). Thus, the basic problem for human beings is the existence of 'partial evil' in the world God has created and the basic moral question is how 'humankind should best comport itself so as to minimize pain and evil, or maximize happiness and virtue in such a universe' (p. 248). The answer to such a question is provided by a combination of 'Newtonian science with theological utilitarianism' (p. 248), and indeed 'Paleyite utilitarianism provided a basis for the moral cost/benefit analysis Malthus conducted on moral restraint as a remedy for poverty in an imperfect world' (p. 248).

In the meanwhile another development has taken place in Malthus scholarship, namely the rediscovery of Malthus's theology and theodicy (Levin 1976; Bowler 1976; LeMahieu 1979; Santurri 1982; Pullen 1981; Waterman 1983; Harvey-Phillips 1984; Rashid 1984; Stradley 1993) that proved that: (a) Malthus's theological connection was something more than an embarrassment; (b) it was not confined to his early career; (c) his theological and philosophical views were more complex than the usual qualification as a Paleyite theological utilitarian implies, since a significant part of his legacy came from the Platonic tradition (Stradley 1993) whose main ideas were the 'chain of beings' and the 'principle of plenitude'. Anthony Waterman (1991) gave the most remarkable contribution to such rescue of Malthus the theologian. He proved that (a) the theological issue of theodicy at large was directly related with the issue of 'social theodicy', namely, the question about the causes of social evil and the possibility and duty of correcting such evil; (b) this was the very *raison d'être* of Malthus's work as a social theorist; (c) Malthus's work was the starting point of two distinct lines of thinking, namely the classical political economy of David Ricardo, James Mill, Robert Torrens, William Nassau Senior, John Stuart Mill, and the Christian political economy of Thomas Chalmers, John Bird Sumner, Edward Copleston and Richard Whately.

The present book, while trying to provide the study of Malthus's theology and philosophy called forth by Winch, tries also to fill a blank in Waterman's reconstruction. In more detail, he concentrates on theodicy and then goes on showing how Malthus's attempt was continued by others giving birth to the current of Christian Political Economy, and how in 1803 he modified his own theodicy in order to make it compatible with orthodoxy by incorporating ideas from Paley's *Natural Theology*, and then further modified in 1817 by incorporating Sumner's theological elaboration on Paley and Malthus himself. I add something to Waterman's conclusions, first by showing how in 1803 Paley's *Natural Theology* (Paley 1802) provided suggestions on which Malthus grafted his own 'social theodicy', a theodicy different from the one presented in 1798 in so far as it tried to discover an acceptable balance of evil and good *within* society. In more detail, in the 1803 social theodicy partial evil was proved to be unavoidable in a world governed by general rules. Then I proceed to show how Sumner's *Treatise on the Records of the Creation* (Sumner 1816) provided the staple by which Malthus worked out the second version of his own social theodicy, a version that proved how partial evil could be limited by generalized practice of prudence and the other virtues to the point that, even though the danger of population pressure with the ensuing amount of vice and misery was always pending, a *decent* – not an equalitarian and idyllic – society could be achieved and kept in stable albeit precarious existence. In more detail, I contend, first, that Malthus in 1803 did find not only a more orthodox, but also a more convincing answer to questions left open by his own theodicy by transforming it into a *social* theodicy; second, that the answer was given by adding a systematic treatment of morality in general and of the morality of sex, marriage and procreation in particular in those chapters that replace the two theodicy chapters of the first *Essay*; third, that his solution, once it was made less inhumane by the discovery of self-correcting devices in partial evils carried by general laws, also gave flesh and bones to a programme for a decent society where the middle classes would be more numerous and the condition of the poor not so destitute and abject. And let me anticipate at least one particular conclusion: this programme for a decent society is – *pace* Hollander – quite compatible with the claim (in turn questionable and questioned, but actually held by Malthus) that the effects of moral restraint were virtually absent *in the past*, since this does not rule out the possibility of their influence *in the future*.

Bibliography

Albee, E. (1901 [2002]) *A History of English Utilitarianism*. London: Allen & Unwin.
Bonar, J. (1885 [1924]) *Malthus and his Work*. London: Cass.
Bowler, P.J. (1976) 'Malthus, Darwin and the concept of struggle'. *Journal of the History of Ideas* 37(4), pp. 631–650.
Chappell, T. and Crisp, R. (1998) Utilitarianism. In *Routledge Encyclopedia of Philosophy*. Volume 9. Ed. by Craig, E. Abingdon: Routledge.
Cremaschi, S. (1981) 'Adam Smith, Newtonianism and political economy'. *Manuscrito. Revista de Filosofia* 5(1), pp. 117–134.
Cremaschi, S. (1984) *Il sistema della ricchezza. Economia politica e problema del metodo in Adam Smith*. Milan: Angeli.
Cremaschi, S. (1989) Adam Smith. Sceptical Newtonianism, disenchanted republicanism, and the birth of social science. In Dascal, M. and Gruengard, O. (eds) *Knowledge and Politics: Case Studies on the Relationship between Epistemology and Political Philosophy*. Boulder, CO: Westview Press.
Cremaschi, S. (2000) Les Lumières Écossaises et le roman philosophique de Descartes. In Senderowicz, Y. and Wahl, J. (eds) *Descartes: Reception and Disenchantment*. Tel Aviv: University Publishing Projects.
Cremaschi, S. (2006) The Mill-Whewell controversy on ethics and its bequest to analytic philosophy. In Baccarini, E. and Prijić Samaržja, S. (eds) *Rationality in Belief and Action*. Rijeka: University of Rijeka, Faculty of Arts and Sciences and Croatian Society for Analytic Philosophy.
Cremaschi, S. (2008) 'Utilitarianism and its nineteenth-century critics'. *Notizie di Politeia* 24(90), pp. 31–49.

Cremaschi, S. and Dascal, M. (forthcoming) *The Malthus-Ricardo Controversy. From a Pragma-Rhetoric Point of View*. The Hague: Benjamins.

Crimmins, J. (1998) Introduction. Religious advocates of the utility principle. In *Utilitarianism and Religion*. Ed. by Crimmins, J. Bristol: Thoemmes.

Empson, W. (1837) 'Life, writings and character of Mr. Malthus'. *Edinburgh Review* 64(80), pp. 469–506.

Fetter, F.W. (1965) 'Economic Controversy in the British Reviews, 1802–1850.' *Economica* 32(128), pp. 424–437.

Harvey-Phillips, M.B. (1984) 'Malthus' theodicy: the intellectual background of his contribution to political economy'. *History of Political Economy* 16(4), pp. 591–608.

Hollander, S. (1989) 'Malthus and Utilitarianism with special reference to the Essay on Population'. *Utilitas* 1(2), pp. 170–210.

Hollander, S. (1997) *The Economics of Thomas Robert Malthus*. Toronto: University of Toronto Press.

James, P. (1979) *Population Malthus. His Life and Time*. London: Routledge.

LeMahieu, D.L. (1979) 'Malthus and the theology of scarcity'. *Journal of the History of Ideas* 40(3), pp. 467–474.

Levin, S.M. (1976) 'Malthus and the idea of progress'. *Journal of the History of Ideas* 27(1), pp. 92–108.

Lively, J. and Rees, J. (1978) Introduction. In *Utilitarian Logic and Politics*. Ed. by Lively, J. and Rees, J. Oxford: Clarendon Press.

Lyons, D. (2001) Utilitarianism. In *Encyclopedia of Ethics*, Second edn, Volume 3 P-W. Ed. by Becker, L.C. and Becker, Ch.L. London: Routledge.

Macaulay, T.B. (1829 [1978]) Mill's Essay on Government: Utilitarian logic and politics. In *Utilitarian Logic and Politics*. Ed. by Lively, J. and Rees, J. Oxford: Clarendon Press.

Malthus, Th.R. (1798 [1986]) An Essay on the Principle of Population. In *The Works of Thomas Robert Malthus*. Volume 1. Ed. by Wrigley, E.A. and Souden, D. London: Pickering.

Malthus, Th.R. (1803 [1989]) *An Essay on the Principle of Population. The Version Published in 1803, with the Variora of 1806, 1807, 1817 and 1826*. Ed. by James, P. Cambridge: Cambridge University Press.

Malthus, Th.R. (1820 [1989]). *Principles of Political Economy*. Ed. by Pullen, J. Cambridge: Cambridge University Press.

Malthus, Th.R. (1824 [1986]) Population. In *The Works of Thomas Robert Malthus*. Volume 4. Ed. by Wrigley, E.A. and Souden, D. London: Pickering.

McCulloch, J.M.R. (1820) 'Review of Malthus's Principles of Political Economy'. *The Scotsman, or Edinburgh Political and Literary Journal* April 29 (171).

Paglin, M. (1961 [1973]) *Malthus and Lauderdale. The anti-Ricardian Tradition*. Clifton: Kelley.

Paley, W. (1785 [2002]) *The Principles of Moral and Political Philosophy*. Ed. by Le Mahieu, D.L. Indianapolis, IN: Liberty Fund.

Paley, W. (1802 [1970]) *Natural Theology: or: Evidences of the Existence and Attributes of the Deity, Collected from the Appearances of Nature*. Westmead: Gregg.

Petersen, W. (1979) *Malthus. Founder of Modern Demography*. Second edn. New Brunswick, NJ: Transaction Books.

Plamenatz, J. (1949) *The English Utilitarians*. Oxford: Blackwell.

Pullen, J.M. (1981) 'Malthus' theological ideas and their influence on his principle of population'. *History of Political Economy* 13(1), pp. 39–54.

Rashid, S. (1984) 'Malthus' theology; an overlooked letter and some comments'. *History of Political Economy* 16(1), pp. 135–138.

Robbins, L.C. (1952) *The Theory of Economic Policy in English Classical Political Economy.* London: Macmillan.

Santurri, E.N. (1982) 'Theodicy and social policy in Malthus' thought'. *Journal of the History of Ideas* 43(2), pp. 315–330.

Sidgwick, H. (1906 [1996]) *Henry Sidgwick: a Memoir.* Ed. by Sidgwick, A. and Sidgwick, E.M. Bristol: Thoemmes.

Sinnot-Armstrong, W. (2006) Consequentialism. In *The Stanford Encyclopedia of Philosophy.* Ed. by Zalta, E.N. (Winter 2012 Edition). http://plato.stanford.edu/archives/win2012/entries/consequentialism (4 Oct. 2013).

Smart, J.J.C. (1967) Utilitarianism. In *The Encyclopedia of Philosophy.* Ed. by Edwards, P. New York: Macmillan.

Stephen, L. (1882) Malthus, Thomas Robert. In *The Dictionary of National Biography.* Volume 12 LLWYD-MASON. Ed. by Stephen, L. and Lee, S. Oxford: Oxford University Press.

Stephen, L. (1900 [1950]) *The English Utilitarians.* London: The London School of Economics.

Stradley, S.A. (1993) The Great Chain of Being: a possible source of Malthus's metaphysics. In *Themes on Economic Discourse, Method, Money and Trade: Selected Papers from the History of Economics Conference 1991.* Perspectives on the History of Economic Thought Volume 9. Ed. by Hebert, R.F. Aldershot: Elgar.

Sumner, J.B. (1816) *A Treatise on the Records of the Creation, and on the moral attributes of the creator; with particular reference to the Jewish history, and to the consistency of the principle of population with the wisdom and goodness of the deity.* London: Hatchard.

Waterman, A.M.C. (1983) 'The ideological alliance of Christian theology and political economy, 1798–1833'. *The Journal of Ecclesiastical History* 34(2), pp. 231–244.

Waterman, A.M.C. (1991) *Revolution, Economics and Religion. Christian Political Economy, 1798–1833.* Cambridge: Cambridge University Press.

Whewell, W. (1845) *Elements of Morality.* London: Parker.

Winch, D. (1987) *Malthus.* Oxford: Oxford University Press.

Winch, D. (1992) *Introduction to Essay on Population.* Cambridge: Cambridge University Press.

Winch, D. (1993) 'Robert Malthus: Christian moral scientist, arch-demoralizer or implicit secular utilitarian?' *Utilitas* 5(2), pp. 239–254.

2   Eighteenth-century Anglican ethics

Ethics in the context of Cambridge education

Before textual reconstructions, let me reconstruct the background. When carrying out such tasks, familiar blunders are mistaking effects for causes, equating succession or concomitance with causality, and singling out authors who have enjoyed a period of later notoriousness as obvious sources, while disregarding highly influential non-entities of the time. Such alleged non-entities, in Malthus's case, are the Cambridge Professors of Divinity of the Eighties and Nineties, his two remarkable tutors Gilbert Wakefield and William Frend, and his East India College colleagues, first among them Bewick Bridge.

Let me first describe what a Cambridge education used to be. All undergraduates were required to attend College lectures on Scripture, Latin and Greek Classics as well as Moral and Political Philosophy. Students reading for an Honours degree were required also to learn some mathematics on MacLaurin's handbook and to read Newton's *Principia* and *Opticks* with the help of MacLaurin's introduction to Newton (Cremaschi 2010, p. 13–16). Every student was expected to engage in five public Scholastic *disputationes* in Latin on topics assigned by tutors, and basically drawn from their reading lists, making use of the kind of proofs allowed by Aristotelian logic. For example, a disputation William Paley had to stand up to was on the reconciliation of God's goodness with the presence of evil in the world (Watson 1818, p. 19–20; Gascoigne 1989, p. 241).

There were three main careers open to graduates who did or could not just aspire to the condition of an educated country gentleman. The first was Holy Orders, the second was the Bar, and the third was the practice of medicine. For the second and third, the training required was based outside the University, and indeed access to the Medical profession was possible also without a university degree, so that there were among physicians also Dissenters and Jews. Preparation for Orders amounted to one more year residence after graduation during which candidates were encouraged to read Watson's *Theological Tracts*, that is, a compilation renowned, or controversial, because of its broad views making room, besides Anglican divines, also for tracts by

Dissenters. From 1780 on, they were invited also to attend John Hey's divinity lectures, whose attendance was encouraged but not required until the end of the century (Winstanley 1977, pp. 174–176).

A few words are in order here on Cambridge professorships. These were a few chairs endowed either by the Crown or by private legacies with varying (and most of the time neglected) duties and election according to disparate procedures, boiling down to one decisive factor, that is, patronage. Such chairs covered mathematics and natural philosophy, classical languages and literatures, Natural Divinity, with the additional oddment of a chair of Arabic with virtually no students. Toward the end of the century, a need was felt to give revealed theology more weight. The malaise originated from the circumstance that in the eighteenth century the Anglican clergy's education, as a result of shift in the age for admission to University, had been virtually reduced to attendance of the programme of Arts, which in the seventeenth century was still meant to be an introduction to a theological course of study. Proposals were agitated of founding separate theological seminars for the clergy, and such concessions as the institution of chairs of revealed theology were felt by the academic body to be a lesser evil when compared with the prospect of separation between lay students and candidates to Orders, a separation potentially weakening the university's weight through loss of an important part of their students. This led to the institution of the Norrisonian Professorship for Revealed Theology to which Hey was appointed in the Eighties.

It is worth noting that the average Anglican clergyman, especially so if he came from Cambridge, had little formal training in 'divinity' as understood nowadays, having been taught basically Natural Theology, that is a philosophical discussion of the existence of God and his relationship with his creatures. In our times something analogous is considered to belong to philosophy of religion or to an intersection between philosophy and theology going under the label 'fundamental theology'. Only during the final year before Orders candidates were expected to undertake a plan of reading in divinity properly understood and to attend a lecture course in Divinity. Later on, within the context of the early nineteenth-century evangelical revival, there were proposals, looked at as strange kind of innovations, to import from Germany the kind of historical and philological Biblical Studies with which Lutheran theological faculties were familiar (Gascoigne 1989, pp. 237–269).

In order to make sense of such education one has to look back at what happened in English universities after the 1688 settlement. The shared enemy was for almost everybody Calvinism. In ethics the latter had been teaching a morality of God's command or a kind of extreme voluntarism. This meant in practice no room for *natural morality*, that is, morality based on reason before revelation, or morality shared by followers of different religions or different confessions. From doctrinal premises two opposite and mutually contradictory normative doctrines derived: the first was antinomianism, that is the refusal of the Law in the name of freedom from the Law itself allegedly announced by the New Testament – an alternative that lived a short life during the first years of the Reformation in Germany – and the second was rigorism, that is, an extremely ascetic approach to life justified by human nature's depravity – the alternative adopted by the Calvinists (Schneewind 1998, pp. 15–36; Cremaschi 2007, pp. 15–18).

At Oxford, not as heavily compromised with Cromwell's Commonwealth as Cambridge had been, need for innovation after the fall of English Calvinism was felt too, albeit in a rather lukewarm way, yielding a watered-down copy of the official philosophy of Lutheranism, that is, Melanchtonian Aristotelianism, basically Thomism without Thomas Aquinas. The textbook adopted at Oxford was Daniel Whitby's *Ethices compendium* (1724).This was the ethics still taught in the Sixties, when a boy named Jeremy Bentham was a student at Oxford, and Benthamite utilitarianism, needless to say, would have been perhaps somewhat different had young Bentham been offered some more appetizing starter than such unsavoury moral philosophy.

Cambridge, having been instead heavily involved with Calvinism, saw a more marked reaction after the fall of the Commonwealth, carrying the rise of Natural Theology, that is, a doctrinal system based on the assumption of concordance between Reason and Revelation (the quintessence of deprecated Roman Catholic theology). Newtonian natural philosophy was at the basis of such a system of doctrines. In ethics, the Cambridge Platonists Benjamin Whichcote, John Smith, Henry More, Ralph Cudworth, and their fellow-traveller Samuel Clarke defended an ethic of love with some Platonic flavour and a natural morality based on evidence accessible to human Reason unassisted by Revelation.

A non-Calvinist ethical tradition

Richard Cumberland started a line of enquiry alternative to that of the Cambridge Platonists. He adopted Grotius's claim of the existence of universal natural laws evident to the reason of any man, independent of his belief in the existence of God but nonetheless combined with a voluntarist understanding of the moral law. For this doctrine, a not too bad label may be 'consequentialist voluntarism'. Cumberland's concerns were on the one hand that of avoiding Grotius's intellectualism in order not to come too close to Roman Catholic Thomism, and, on the other, drawing from voluntarism implications opposite to the those of the Calvinists and more similar to William of Ockham's, that is, a justification of a set of universal prescriptions that makes room, yet, for God's omnipotence. In fact, Cumberland did what other Catholic or Lutheran writers (Nicholas Malebranche and Gottfried Wilhelm Leibniz) were doing: taking Ockham's idea of *imposed* law (as opposed to Aquinas's *immanent* law) and then having it proclaimed by God, but not on the basis of his inscrutable will, but instead on the basis of his perfect intellect, including unlimited factual knowledge and ability to predict consequences. In other words, they assumed that God had chosen, out of the infinite number of possible sets of laws he could have enacted, the one whose enforcement would yield the greatest amount of positive consequences for his creatures (Schneewind 1998, pp. 101–117; Cremaschi 2007, pp. 73–76).

Butler adopted a way intermediate between the Cambridge Platonists and Cumberland. Not unlike Catholic Nicholas Malebranche, he made enlightened self-love ultimately coincident with virtue (Butler 1726, p. 113; 1736, p. 182), contended that there is a special moral faculty and that moral truths are self-evident, thus rejecting voluntarism by the argument that moral laws do not need to be proclaimed in order to be valid (p. 231); besides, he refuted selfishness by the argument that in certain cases the moral duty is still obliging, even though it contradicts self-love, in the name of motives such as benevolence and the pursuit of public good that command at least as much respect as the former (pp. 115–116).

John Gay, a clergyman and a Cambridge fellow, was the author of a short essay *Concerning the Fundamental Principle of Virtue or Morality* (Gay 1731), published as a preface to the English version of John King's treatise on theodicy *De origine mali* of 1706 (Schneewind 1998, pp. 405–8; Cremaschi 2007, pp. 76–78). Such an apparently odd collocation turns out at a closer look, as I argue in what follows, to be rather apropos. His main claim is that different accounts for the criterion of virtue turn out to be extensionally equivalent and thus equivalent *in practice*; that is, they do nothing else than sorting out the same instances of actions as right and wrong, or asserting just the same criterion in different words. Gay even notes (apparently 'forerunning' Henry Sidgwick – but in fact it is the latter who was less original than he made us believe) that the consequentialist criterion in particular is untenable, since choosing on the basis of a calculus of consequences would yield sub-optimal choices in the very terms of desirable consequences and the choices yielding optimal consequences are those made on some non-consequentialist criterion. The question on the motive of action is answered by dissolving it, arguing that the end of action is happiness, and 'to expect a reason, i.e., an end, to be assigned for an ultimate end, is absurd. To ask why I pursue happiness, will admit of no other answer than an explanation of the terms' (Gay 1731, p. 278). Moral rules arise through mechanisms illustrated by the Lockean theory of knowledge, particularly the principle of association that makes so that virtue is a 'mixed idea', arising from perception of usefulness of certain behaviour and then winning independent life. The source of moral obligation lies in a combination of self-interest and God's will; if we were to make 'the immediate criterion of virtue to be the good of mankind' while excluding the will of God, we should allow either that virtue is not in all cases obligatory or that the good of mankind is a sufficient source of obligation. But – he asks – how can this 'be an obligation to me, when perhaps in particular cases, such as laying down my life [...] it is contrary to my happiness?' (p. 275).

Thomas Brown was the author of the *Essays on the Characteristics of the Earl of Shaftesbury*, a sustained criticism of Shaftesbury's Platonic philosophy (Cremaschi 2007, p. 78). The second of such essays, 'On the motives to virtue', argues that there is in human beings a tendency to happiness and that conformity of our actions to this end is the 'very essence of moral rectitude'. He contends that motives are always 'selfish' in a sense, in so far as a motive is always a prospect of our private happiness, but all this is tautological. In fact, no affection 'can be more or less selfish or disinterested than another; because [...] the Affection itself is still no other than a Mode either of Pleasure or Pain'; the only motive human beings may have to virtue or to the production of public happiness is the:

> belief in an all-seeing and all-powerful God, who will hereafter make them happy or miserable, according as they designedly promote or violate the happiness of their fellow creatures [...] And this is the essence of religion.
>
> (Brown 1751, p. 210)

Cambridge moral philosophy in Malthus's time

Malthus had apparently no opportunity to attend lecture courses in philosophical ethics during his course of study. The theological teaching to which he was exposed probably did not offer very much in the field. Its contents amounted to: (i) occasional discussion of the main problems of natural theology within the courses of Natural Philosophy such as the treatment of the argument from Design, that is, of the proof of the existence of God starting with the world order at the end of one of Malthus's textbooks, namely Colin MacLaurin's *Introduction to Newton's Natural Philosophy*; (ii) a lecture course in Divinity by Richard Watson that he may have attended during the year between graduation and orders; (iii) the course of 50 lectures a year of the Norrisonian Professorship in Revealed Religion held by John Hey, established at about 1777, which Malthus may also have attended in this very year. The only course where ethics was treated to some extent was (iv) the lecture course of the Knightsbrige Professorship of Moral Theology or Casuistical Divinity which existed since 1770 and lasted under this description for about seventy years. Note that when William Whewell was elected to this Professorship in 1838 he declared that he should understand his office as a 'Professorship of Moral philosophy' (Whewell 1846, p. 1), adding that, even though the lectures to be delivered were at least four each term, he was not aware that any if his predecessors had ever lectured.

An idea of the plan of reading in theological subjects that Malthus was expected to carry out may be gained by looking at *A Collection of Theological Tracts* edited by Richard Watson (Watson 1785) as core reading for candidates to Orders. Some conjectures on possible further reading might be made on the basis of the Malthus Library Catalogue (Jesus College 1983) and of the Registrar of borrowed books at Jesus College Library for year 1788. Unfortunately, we have no letters dating from this year whence some information about his reading could be obtained (Waterman 1991a, pp. 82–96).

Hey

John Hey (1734–1815), a tutor at Sidney Sussex from 1760 to 1779, lectured on Greek, Hebrew and algebra, and in the 1770s also on moral and political philosophy, attracting voluntary attendance by undergraduates from other colleges (Waterman 2004). Following Cumberland, Butler, Gay and Brown, Hey believes that morality has something to do with happiness, that a virtuous act is one agreeable to God, and that the will of God can be recognized on the basis of the fact that an action promotes the happiness of mankind.

In the *Lectures on moral philosophy*, Hey denies the existence of natural rights. What lies behind such apparent rights is the widespread experience of the fact that a certain practice was likely 'to make men happier' (Hey unpublished, vol. 3, p. 957). The fact is remarkable that the lectures include a treatment of contracts, the exchange of goods or services (pp. 1273–1300), value, price, money (vol. 4, pp. 1301–1334) and loans (pp. 1359–1372). It is worth noting also that the lectures refer several times to Hume's *Essays*, even though – not surprisingly since the manuscript lectures bear dates (then deleted) referring to November 1776 – references to Adam Smith are lacking. A few remarks may be striking for Malthus scholars, for example a sharp distinction between imaginary and real value. He says that:

> every thing is valuable as it gratifies some appetite or passions; that thing has a real value which gratifies some appetite or passion given us for necessary continuance of life, or which procures enjoyment of its some lower conveniences; that thing has an imaginary value, which we live without and not badly, but which gratifies some of our finer perceptions and affords some of the pleasures of the Imagination such as arise from poetry, imitation, truth, beauty, vanity, superiority and painting, music, but it may be difficult to draw the line between them. Hence we may see why Imaginary value must be more constant.
>
> (p. 1333)

In this passage Hey formulates a doctrine concerning the importance of luxury and unproductive consumption in the economy which 'foreruns' Malthus's *Principles*. And also mention of lotteries, and of the reasons why a lottery may be fair even to those who draw a blank, since they had 'bought a probability' (p. 1287) may be striking for Malthus scholars as a possible source for Malthus's idea, illustrated in the *Essay*, that society is a lottery where some draw a blank and yet have no *right* to complain of unfairness. Did Malthus get in touch with these lectures or with some of their contents, possibly through oral sources? It is a question that admits of no answer, and it is as well to keep in mind that sources for Malthus's ideas were multiple and in turn influencing each other.

In 1780 Hey was elected to the Norrisonian Professorship of Divinity, which he resigned in 1794. In his *Lectures on Revealed Religion* (Hey 1796–98), he often refers to the previous lectures while repeating the main claims he had presented there on morality. Most of the lectures consist of discussion of the 39 articles, that is, the doctrinal basis of the Church of England (Winstanley 1935, pp. 175–176; Gascoigne 1989, pp. 244–169; Waterman 1991b, pp. 75–76) and, far from delivering Unitarianism in disguise as implied by Stephen (1881, vol. 1, p. 426), they provide precisely an argument for acceptance of these articles according to their plain meaning even in those cases in which they are impossible for us to understand. The argument is based on the Cambridge *via media*, that is, an attitude rejecting both scepticism and 'system'. Hey starts declaring that, facing unintelligible propositions we 'may run into two faulty extremes about them: too easily receiving them leads to error, and fruitless controversy [...] too easily rejecting them, tends to ignorance and disorder' (Hey 1796–98, vol. 2, p. 48), and arguing that in certain cases we ought to assent not for the sake of truth but for the sake of utility, in order to avoid some evil or attain some good or in order not to throw away something which has pleased God to reveal to mankind (Waterman 1991b, pp. 75–76). There is no evidence that Malthus ever attended Hey's lectures on morality or read their manuscript version, for they were College lectures, but we can be fairly sure that he did attend those on revealed religion, since they were intended for all candidates to Orders. Here, when Hey mentions morality, he repeats the main points from the *Lectures on moral philosophy*. For example he discusses the role for consequences in morality, that is, still the issue debated by Cumberland, Gay and Brown, and writes that it:

> has been matter of dispute, whether *Morality* is capable of Demonstration; I suppose all that is meant, in such dispute, by demonstration, is shewing, that good *consequences* follow from Virtue: but as consequences are only matter of *experience* ad *analogy*, that is only *probable* proof.
>
> (Hey 1796–98, vol. 1, p. 88)

He then proves the existence of a natural morality prior to Revelation, and discusses the question how men could improve without Revelation. He answers that:

> as morality is nothing but a set of rules, adapted to promote happiness, social and private, established and recognized by the moral sense; and as these rules must arise from experience, the observation must extend to morality. The constitution of our nature, with regard to habits, must help forward improvement, both in things natural and moral; for, as arts and moral duties grow easier by becoming habitual, the faculties of body and mind can enter upon new fields of action, and multiply the objects, on which they may exercise themselves, as well as increase their own efficacy by such exercise.
>
> (p. 316)

Besides, revealed morality is not the last word, and what really matters is natural morality, since morality not only varies but is also improving, and revealed morality admits too of improvement. Hey writes:

It is in the nature of morality to keep constantly improving, if men make a right use of their experience [...] I suppose that Scripture-morality may, in some sense, be considered as imperfect. It is not systematical, it does not describe limits, &c. of rights and obligations; it rather inforces what it takes for granted, than teaches what is perfectly new. But this is not any reason against its divine original. Why should moral philosophy be revealed all at once, rather than natural? We improve gradually in making natural bodies promote our happiness, why should we not improve gradually in making our own conduct promote happiness?

(vol. 2, pp. 465–66)

Such a vindication of *natural* vis-à-vis *revealed* morality has obvious non-Calvinist implications. In order to dispel any possible doubts to this effect, Hey adds that – the doctrine of divine justification notwithstanding – virtue or good works are not something secondary but are instead still strictly requested.

Since it consists of such set of rules, morality may vary from place to place and time to time without implying variation in the ideal of perfect virtue. In fact rules vary in time and space, and:

men do really go by established rules in *morality*, though they may not always be aware of it; the best of these rules are far short of perfect virtue; and the rules differ much in different ages and countries. *Conscience* also seems to follow established virtue.

(vol. 1, p. 435)

Hey was committed, as mentioned, to eudemonism and consequentialism. It may be noted that Calvinists affirmed almost opposite doctrines, and that any hint in this sense is clearly absent from the 39 articles, but this – he warns us – should not upset us too much, since the 39 articles should not be considered to be 'inconsistent with any doctrines which were unknown to the compilers of them', and it is conceivable:

that our Reformers, though excellently well skilled in the Scriptures, might not attend sufficiently to morality, nor see how the study of it is conspired with Scripture to make men good and happy; nor perceive that improvements in morality afforded additional internal evidence of the truth of Christianity.

(p. 89)

Watson

Richard Watson (1737–1816), a Trinity College fellow from 1760 and a Professor of Chemistry from 1764 to 1773 (Scott 1981; Brain 1999), was elected in 1771, after Thomas Rutherford's death, to the Regius Professorship of Divinity, and in 1782 to the Episcopal see of Llandaff that he accepted without renouncing the professorship (Hole 2004b, pp. 647–648; Thompson 2008, pp. 13–25). He was a Lockean Whig in politics and a latitudinarian in theology who, in *A letter by a Christian Whig* (1772), argued the case for abolition of subscription to the 39 articles by the clergy. His 1776 Restoration Day Sermon (Watson 1776b), in other years 'would have been seen as an unexceptionable restatement of Locke's Whig doctrine, but with the Americans on the brink of declaring independence it was perceived by many as bold support of the rebels' doctrine' (Hole 2004b, p. 647). His *Apology for Christianity* (1776a), being a rejoinder to Edward Gibbon, won remarkable popularity, and his *Apology for the Bible* (1796), a rejoinder to Thomas Paine, went through several editions (Thompson 2008, pp. 13–25). Even after his moderate turn of the Ninctics, he consistently advocated full civil rights for Dissenters as well as for Roman Catholics. Not unlike Paley and Hey, he redefined his own former radicalism facing developments of the French Revolution and war with France (Waterman 1991b, pp. 72–75). In fact, in 1798 he published *An Address to the People of Great Britain* (Watson 1798) justifying war to France, which was the occasion for a reply by Gilbert Wakefield, Malthus's former tutor at Warrington Academy, a reply paid with two years imprisonment for seditious libel.

Watson was the last proponent of Cambridge theological rationalism, defending a view of natural theology as confirmed by revealed theology. He declared that he intended to reduce theology to 'that which the father of the universe has written with the hand of what is called Nature [and] that which he hath declared to a peculiar people, by the mouth of his Son' (Watson 1818, p. 377). In a vein similar to Hey's, he declared more than once his own 'extreme aversion' to public controversy on theological issues, since such subjects are so obscure that we understand too little about them as to be in a position to engage in controversy; he declared that for all divines 'their Bible is the only foundation upon which they ought to build every article of the faith which they profess. All the other foundations [...] ought to be considered by them as sandy and unsafe' (Watson 1785, p. xii). Such foundations were supposedly 'the opinions of councils, fathers, churches, bishops, and other men, as little inspired as myself' (Watson 1818, p. 39). In the same vein it is important to remind that, in the Preface to vol. 1 of the *Chemical Essays*, he repeats what he declared in all his theological writings, namely that God speaks to us in two voices, Nature and Revelation, and 'the book of Nature and Revelation equally elevate our conceptions and incite our piety; they mutually illustrate each other; they have an equal claim to our regard, for they are both written by the finger of one *eternal incomprehensible God*' (Watson 1781–1787, vol. 1, p. vii).

Watson seems to have shared the kind of theological consequentialism taught in the Cumberland–Paley tradition. He declares that he believes, on philosophical grounds, 'that God not only primarily formed, but that he has through all ages, executed, the laws of nature; and that he will through all eternity, administer them, for the general happiness of his creatures' (Watson

1796a, p. 18). And, not surprisingly, he also professes the current claims about the just, albeit incomprehensible, moral government of the world and the happiness widespread in the universe. He adds an interesting side-argument inspired perhaps by the Great Chain of Being doctrine. According to this argument, even though God's goodness may be unequal, it is not imperfect, for:

> it must be estimated from the whole, and not from a part. Every order of beings is so sufficient for its own happiness, and so conducive at the same time to the happiness of every other, that in one view it seems to be made for itself alone, and in another not for himself, but for every other.
>
> (Watson 1796a, p. 125)

Two key ideas may also be found that were echoed in Paley's *Natural Theology* of 1802 and then in Malthus's second *Essay*, namely that Christianity is not inimical to *happiness* and that Christian morality consists in *regulation of the passions*. He writes:

> It is a trite objection, and grounded on a misapprehension of the design of Christianity, which would represent an intolerable yoke, so opposite to the propensities, as to be utterly destructive of the felicity of the human mind. It is, in truth, quite the reverse; there is not a single precept in the Gospel, without excepting either that which command every one to possess his vessel in sanctification and honour, which is not calculated to promote our happiness. Christianity regulates, but does not extinguish our affections; and in the regulation of our affections consists our happiness as reasonable beings.
>
> (Watson 1785, p. x)

In the *Chemical Essays* he also illustrates the idea of an epistemological *via media* between the Cartesian dogmatizing attitude and untutored inductivism. The third way or the new mode of philosophizing carried by the Newtonian philosophy lies instead in cautious introduction of such principles as may prove useful in accounting for phenomena, and the lesson we learn from all our attempts to investigate the works of God is that such attempts are 'weak and ineffectual', for 'we cannot apprehend the nature of his agency any where' (Watson 1781, vol. 1, p. 90). The practice of this modest approach, wary of 'systematic distinctions' with no 'real foundation in nature' (p. 129) will teach us an attitude to be adopted in theology too, for 'it will cure us of all attachment to system, whether it be a system of bigotry or infidelity' (p. 90).

Watson's collection of theological tracts is in Malthus's Library (Jesus College 1983, p. 180), even though Malthus acquired it one year after ordination and apparently had not borrowed it from Jesus College Library in the year before (Waterman 1991a, p. 94). This collection met with enormous popularity, selling one thousand copies in three months, but was 'very ill received by the bishops' since it included 'some tracts originally written by Dissenters'

(Watson 1818, p. 136). It included 22 works, among others by Samuel Clarke, John Locke, David Hartley, Joseph Addison, and also a few by Dissenters such as George Benson, Samuel Chandler, Nathaniel Lardner and John Taylor. The works collected deal with the authenticity of Scripture, such as Lardner's *Argument for the Truth of Christianity* and *The Reasonableness of Christianity*, or Locke's tract bearing the same title, Clarke's *Discourse Concerning the Unchangeable Obligations of Natural Religion and Certainties of Christian Revelation*, and Hartley's *Truth of the Christian Religion* (Thompson 2008, pp. 13–20). In Watson's preface the reader is presented with a handful of familiar Cambridge methodological claims, for example a warning against 'blind attachment to system' that has often been an unnecessary obstacle for unbelievers, since their objections were frequently 'against what is not Christianity, but mere human system' (Watson 1785, p. xiv). Watson adds that in Christian faith there are a few certain truths, first among them the existence of a 'moral government of the world' and the rest is made of uncertain truths, such as the questions which relate to 'the materiality or immateriality of the human soul; the state of the dead before the general resurrection; the resurrection of the same body; the duration of future punishment' (p. xvi).

Concerning the first of these unsettled issues, the immateriality of the soul, Watson suggests a more precise answer, namely that what is usually called the soul is just a bunch of properties with which man's body is endowed. He writes:

> The essential properties of extension, solidity, mobility, divisibility, and inactivity, are common properties belonging equally to the table, the tree, the oyster, and the man; but to these common properties are added [...] to that of man, life, perceptivity, and thought.
>
> (Watson 1818, p. 17)

A similar theme emerges in the *Chemical Essays* in connection with the idea of the Great Chain of Being. Watson suggests that the conjecture might be not so extravagant 'that all matter is, or hath been organized, enlivened, animated' and that 'it may appear probable' that God 'hath established an uninterrupted concatenation in all his works' (Watson 1781, vol. 1, p. 169). The implication would be that matter and mind constitute a continuum, and the distinguishing trait of human beings should be better understood not to be their possessing a spiritual soul but, more modestly, their being a 'class of animals' that is 'capable of forming a moral character' (p. 173), or their being 'at the top of the scale' or 'the first term of a series, descending indefinitely by imperceptible gradations' (p. 175). As a conclusion:

> Different kingdoms he has distinguished, perhaps, but by lines of division too minute for our observation, This strong analogy, by which men and minerals, and all intermediate existences, are bound together in a common chain, and thence, it would seem, naturally subjected to a common

fate, may appear humiliating to such as have been wont to entertain high notions of the physical dignity of human nature: but it cannot offend nor disquiet those, who feel within themselves faculties essential to the constitution of moral agency, and who from thence become capable at least of retribution, of punishment, or reward, in another state.

(p. 175)

Needless to say, when facing the first *Essay*'s final chapters discussing the production of mind out of matter, the reader may feel that he does not need to go too far in order to find sources for Malthus's heterodox ideas on the soul, since some of these ideas were already there in the writings of a Cambridge professor of divinity.

After 1787, Watson retired on ill-health and appointed – as it was then customary – Thomas Kipling as a deputy, so that it is probable that Malthus attended the latter's lectures. As one more piece of evidence to Destiny's cruel irony, as Watson had contributed to pave the way to jail for Gilbert Wakefield, Malthus's Warrington tutor, Kipling played a leading part in the expulsion of William Frend, Malthus's Jesus College tutor, from the University on unorthodox religious views (Hole 2004a; Knight 1971; Gascoigne 1989, pp. 228–234; Waterman 1991b, pp. 420–425). His scholarly career yielded the edition of a Latin and Greek New Testament Code (Kipling 1793), 'marred by a Latin preface which Kipling wrote, littered with linguistic errors' (Hole 2004a, p. 757).

Paley

William Paley, once the tutor of Malthus's own tutor William Frend, was no more in residence when Malthus went to Cambridge, but he published works adopted as textbooks. Two of them, namely the *Principles of Moral and Political Philosophy* (1785) and the *Natural Theology* (1802) are in Malthus's Library (Jesus College 1983, p. 128–129). The *Principles* were adopted as a textbook in 1786 and kept their place in reading lists up to 1845, when Whewell published his *Elements of Morality* in order to provide an alternative textbook. Paley elaborates on Gay's and Brown's ideas assuming that the moral quality of actions is assessed on the basis of the total quantity of happiness they may bring about (Schneewind 1998, p. 409–413; Cremaschi 2007, p. 78–81). Happiness is understood as a state of the nervous systems when faced with pleasant stimuli of the senses (Paley 1785, p. 18). The criterion of *the right* is derived from the mentioned definition of *the good* in terms of happiness, that is, actions:

are to be estimated by their tendency to promote happiness. Whatever is expedient is right. It is utility of any moral rule alone which constitutes the obligation of it.

(Paley 1785, p. 61)

But it is God who carries out the calculus of happiness and our task is limited to discovering what his will is. The method for discovering such will:

> is to enquire into the tendency of the action to promote or diminish the general happiness. And this rule proceeds upon the presumption, that God Almighty wills and wishes the happiness of his creatures; and consequently, that those actions, which promote that will and wish, must be agreeable to him.
>
> (pp. 56–57)

God then enforces a system of moral government through the 'laws of nature' (p. 194, 203), that is, by enacting 'general laws', which in turn:

> are necessary to every moral government [...] any dispensation, whose object is to influence the conduct of reasonable creatures. For if, of two actions perfectly similar, one be punished, and the other be rewarded or forgiven, which is the consequence of rejecting general rules, the subjects [...] would no longer know, wither what to expect or how to act.
>
> (p. 65)

God finally provides a moral motivation through a system of punishments and rewards. Eternal life is required in order to round up the system, in so far as coincidence of virtue and happiness may be brought about only by compensating the righteous man's suffering in this world with eternal rewards.

Paley became the spokesman of the already mentioned Cambridge *via media*, a 'middle way' in religion between blind attachment to 'system' (whether Popish or Calvinist) and the contagion of infidelity, and in politics between radicalism and Toryism, yielding 'philosophic Whiggism', that is a defence of traditional Whig concerns such as innate rights and limits to government dropping traditional cant such as the *Magna Charta* and the pristine liberties of the Saxons and adopting instead philosophical argument (Waterman 1991b). The case for a third way in politics was defended in the *Principles* by a mix of consequentialism, natural law, and innate rights. Within this framework, conventional eighteenth-century pro-population policies were endorsed and mechanisms behind population growth were explored with a view at working out pro-population policies. The reasons – unlike most eighteenth-century political writers – are not dependent on considerations of national power but derive instead from Paley's normative criterion, the total sum of happiness. The assumption is that an increased population implies normally a growth in total, if not in average, happiness. He writes that the:

> final view of all rational politics is to produce the greatest quantity of happiness in a given tract of the country [...] it may be affirmed [...] with certainty, that the quantity of happiness produced in any given district, *so*

far depends upon the number of inhabitants, that [...] the collective happiness will be nearly in exact proportion of the numbers.

(Paley 1785, p. 587)

And yet, Paley was in a position to display different, and rather sophisticated, tools for defending such familiar claims. He introduces the idea of an optimal level of factors below or beyond which the output will not be optimal in relation to magnitudes (Waterman 1996). It is in this line that he establishes a link between population and luxury by adopting an intermediate position in the controversy on luxury, or better, going somewhat further than Smith in defending its usefulness. The argument is that it may be either useful or dangerous to the community, since it acts:

by two opposite effects; and it seems probable, that there exists a point in the scale, to which luxury may ascend, or, to which the wants of mankind may be multiplied, with advantage to the community, and beyond which the prejudicial effects begin to preponderate. The determination of this point, though it assumes the form of an arithmetical problem, depends upon circumstances too numerous, intricate, and undefined, to admit of a precise solution.

(Paley 1785, pp. 597–598)

It is worth reminding, however, that Paley, after defending the pro-population thesis by new arguments, was also ready to abandon it once Malthus had changed the terms of the question. In fact Malthus was proud of being able to count on Paley as one among his first converts.

Let us now re-examine Stephen's above mentioned statement according to which 'Malthus's references were to Paley'. What Malthus does in fact is, first, citing Paley once in *The Crisis* in order to criticize his views on population (Empson 1837, p. 483). Then he mentions him once in the first *Essay* with reference to his definition of morality as 'the will of God, as collected from general expediency' (Malthus 1798, p. 77). In the second *Essay* he quotes his *Principles* three times:

i   in Book 4, Chap. 2, fn. 14 again about the empirical way of 'coming at the will of God' by 'the light of nature' (Malthus 1803, vol. 2, p. 101), understood as a way alternative to Revelation;
ii in Book 4, Chap. 3, fn. 10 and Book 4, chap. 13 about the doctrine of population, and indeed in rather critical terms, since he qualifies Paley's proposal as 'criminal' (p. 107, 193);
iii in Book 4, Chap. 13 about idleness and luxury, and here again Malthus takes a rather critical attitude to Paley, this time concerning the latter's defence of luxury but just when enjoyed by the elite (p. 193).

Malthus also quotes Paley's *Natural Theology* twice:

i   in Book 4, Chap. 2, concerning human passions as either morally good or neutral (pp. 92–93);
ii   in Book 4, Chap. 13, fn. 26, where he notes Paley's conversion in matters of population as a result of his first *Essay* (p. 193).

Besides, he takes a clear stance against a few of Paley's claims. These are:

i   existence of a right of extreme necessity allowing the poor to appropriate the property of others;
ii   the claim that happiness is de facto equally distributed among different social classes;
iii   the claim that the necessities of life are *not* part of happiness.

Two more remarks should be added. First, the 'test of utility' as a way for discovering the contents of moral laws imposed by God is not the same thing as Bentham's principle of utility (Schofield 1987; Crimmins 1990; Cremaschi 2008, pp. 31–33), and besides it is not Paley's own discovery, but had been first formulated by John Gay while elaborating on Cumberland's suggestions and mentioned by Paley as something that was already commonplace. Second, the doctrine that the passions are either good or indifferent and provide the staple of virtue is an anti-Calvinist doctrine that Paley had learned from Gay, Butler and the Cambridge Platonists.

By way of conclusion, do we have enough evidence to prove Malthus's dependence on Paley in terms of a pupil–master relationship? As regards ethics, the answer is that Malthus's ethics lies along the line marked by Cumberland, Gay, Brown, making some room for authors such as Butler, who had a more complex doctrine, encompassing both consequentialist and rationalist views, and that the effort to single out points of convergence and divergence between Malthus and Paley may be pointless, since both belong to the same tradition and share a number of sources. Malthus's indebtedness with Paley's theodicy is another story. There is indeed an important connection between this work and the second *Essay*, but this has little to do with the conclusion of Stephen-historiography since in the *Natural Theology* Paley's alleged utilitarianism never shows up. This story will be told in some detail in Chapter 6, within the context of a discussion of Malthus's second theodicy.

Watts

Isaac Watts, a Dissenter, was the author of the *Logick* (1726) that was among Malthus's required readings at Cambridge. Another mark of his popularity is the wide circulation of another among his books, *The Improvement of the Mind* (1741), covering rather disparate topics in what is now called sometimes 'critical reasoning' or 'informal logic', which is also in Malthus's Library (Jesus College 1983, p. 180). Watts starts with a comparison of different methods of 'improving', namely observation, reading, instruction by lectures, conversation and study, Socratic disputation, Scholastic disputes, enquiring into causes and effects. Another is 'general rules for the improvement of knowledge', including such considerations as: consider the weakness of human nature; presume not too much 'upon a bright genius'; be humble and courageous enough as to retract any mistake; watch against 'the pride of your own reason'. Other more usual topics are induction, causality and multi-causality (Cremaschi 2010, pp. 14–17). Watts claims that the same general rules for formulating judgements on other subjects hold also in morality and religion, assumed to be two strictly related subjects, as well as in prudence, understood as a field separate from morality. Locke is Watts's authority in every field and, not surprisingly, also in ethics, yielding a kind of theological voluntarism combined with eudemonism. In fact Watts distinguishes 'moral good' from 'natural good' as what is conforming to the rule of our duty when opposed to what 'gives us pleasure or satisfaction' (Watts 1726, p. 140). Perfect happiness is defined as the attainment of the highest and most lasting natural good, and perfect misery as the highest and most lasting natural evil, but 'wheresoever pain overbalances pleasure, there is a degree of misery; and wheresoever pleasure overbalances pain, there is a degree of happiness' (pp. 140–141). The highest rule of duty is 'the will of our Creator' and conformity or nonconformity to it determines whether an action is 'morally good or evil' (p. 141). Our Creator 'has ordained that the highest natural good and evil should have a close connexion with moral good and evil' (p. 141).

Watts draws the current distinction, the one that may be found also in Hey's *Lectures*, between natural and revealed religion and insists too on the 'practical' character of both. He writes that natural religion may be divided into 'contemplative' and 'practical' and 'every branch of natural religion and of moral duty is contained and necessarily implied in all the revealed religions that ever God prescribed to the world' (Watts 1741, p. 434).

Non-official sources

Tucker

Abraham Tucker was a rather eccentric writer, who composed a bulky treatise including more or less orthodox speculations about rational evidence for religion, death and afterlife, and the rational justification of morality (Crimmins 1998, pp. 23–25). Leslie Stephen enlisted him among 'eighteenth-century utilitarians', assuming that, in so far as for him 'morality is merely the product of natural forces' (Stephen 1881, vol. 2, p. 117) he was too some kind of proto- or crypto-secularist, even though he assumed that the Creator had designed the mechanism moved by such 'natural forces'. Stephen's musings provided a source for further wild speculations by Bonar, indeed backed by no more evidence than Stephen's own chapter, about Tucker's role as a possible source for Malthus's ethics and epistemology. As mentioned, Stephen objected to Bonar that Malthus's references were to Paley, not to Tucker, but both agreed that they were all some sort of utilitarians.

Tucker's monumental work, *The Light of Nature Pursued* was post-humously published in 1768 in an expurgated edition, where the most un-orthodox digressions on body and soul were omitted, and published in 1805 (that is, *after* Malthus's own unorthodox considerations in the first *Essay*) in a new edition that included the less orthodox speculations and enjoyed some popularity in the nineteenth century, which in turn can account for Bonar's over-emphasis. Tucker's avowed purpose was exploring how much can be proved in matters of morality by Reason alone unassisted by Revela-tion. He departs from Lockean voluntarism as well as from Platonic ration-alism and tries to build a system of morality on a hedonist and associationist philosophy of mind. He follows roughly the line undertaken by Gay and tries to provide an alternative for moral sense by a doctrine of 'translation', the psychological doctrine according to which what was in the beginning a means becomes an end through association of ideas. This applies to moral precepts and virtue, for 'we often acquire a liking to things from their having fre-quently promoted our other desires' (Tucker 1805, vol. 1, p. 152). He adheres to eudemonism and construes morality as a system of prudential reasons with a vaguely Epicurean flavour, but he is far from being a revolutionary in nor-mative ethics and indeed he presents a rather conventional version of current morality. This Epicurean flavour is what led Stephen astray by making him believe that Tucker's system was 'naturalistic'. On the contrary, this system is strongly theistic and Tucker tries to prove its compatibility with the Christian Revelation. In fact his eudemonism is worlds apart from what will be Ben-tham's hedonism, and this is why the label 'utilitarian' is vacuous or trivial when applied to the former. In more detail, Tucker offers an argument to prove that 'satisfaction', that is the very 'complacency' generated in the mind by agreeable objects, is the proper end of action and does not need any fur-ther justification. To the question 'why is satisfaction good?' no further answer can be given and we can only rely on common sense (Tucker 1805, vol. 2, pp. 226–243). Happiness is not pleasure, being instead the aggregate of satisfactions, and the term properly denotes 'the surplus of successes a man has met with or may expect over and above his disappointments: if the sur-plus be any thing considerable, we pronounce him happy' (p. 234). The good man looks for happiness rather than pleasure, for he does aim to a greater sum of satisfactions rather than at a lesser one, but he also does not seek happiness in virtue, for virtue, even though it is the best tool for trying to attain happiness, is not the *Summum Bonum*, and it does not grant happiness (p. 256–285). Action is the main source of enjoyment, and the pleasures of life consist mostly in occasions to engage in our own pursuits. The theory of moral motivation is, as mentioned, eudemonistic and the 'moralist will begin with striving to inculcate this desire of happiness into himself and others as deeply as possible' (p. 43). The connection between happiness and virtue lies on prudential grounds, where prudence is understood as 'inferior prudence'. Tucker declares:

Life has been compared to a game, and we know the cards will beat anybody, but he that plays them carefully, will do more with the same cards than another who throws them out at random [...] Therefore virtue, taken in the largest sense, as including every right conduct, as well as upon small as great occasions, may well be styled the sole thing desirable as drawing all other good things in our power after it.

(pp. 279–280)

And prudence in fact is declared to be 'the principal virtue comprehending all the rest' (p. 355).

To sum up, Tucker is clearly a consequentialist, but not a utilitarian. His consequentialism consists in assigning 'expediency' the role of Archimedean point on whose basis it is possible to justify all moral rules (p. 246). And yet, rules may be 'expedient' either for maximizing some good or just in order to grant social life a smoother course; that is, many rules are adopted just for the sake of order and reliability, so that many actions, in themselves perfectly neutral, become right or wrong by the fact of conforming to a rule established 'by authority, custom or compact' (p. 232). This might, obviously enough, look like a 'forerunning' of John Stuart Mill, had not Mill been instead an unavowed follower of Tucker.

Tucker is bright enough to avow the existence of limits to morality once it is conceived as based on prudential reasons, since, if satisfaction is 'the ground work of all our motives [...] then are virtue and benevolence no more than means, and deserve our regard no longer than while they conduce towards their end' (p. 409). He admits that the objection is true that 'upon an opportunity offering wherein a man may gain some pleasure or advantage slily and safely without danger of after damage to himself, though with infinite detriment to all the world beside, and in breach of every moral obligation he will act wisely to embrace it' (p. 409), but then contends that 'such case can never happen in practice' and that since cheating is a dangerous habit, 'it had been more for his benefit to have adhered inviolably to his rule of honesty' (p. 410). He also admits that reasons for acting in a virtuous way are no more valid, when considered on merely prudential grounds, for somebody who is at the end of his life (p. 412), but he adds that even in this case one should admit at least some reasons for believing in another life (pp. 425–426), and would feel a need to act in a virtuous way simply because he has acquired the habit adopting the point of view of a citizen of the universe who takes the interest of his fellow-beings as a source of motivation and thus unconditionally adheres to moral rules in order to contribute to preserve their sanctity as a 'bulwark of order and happiness' (p. 502).

The work also includes speculations about the origin of evil and a handful of related questions, namely why is the distribution of rewards and punishments so unequal in this world, is there a future state, what is the duration of punishment in afterlife for the wicked. The most interesting item for Malthus scholars in such doctrines is the doctrine of the connection between mind and matter. Mind is supposed, by an 'hypothesis' accepted on the ground that 'nobody can disprove' it, to survive without the body but to lose its internal organization, which is in turn dependent on the body, so that it will not live a life of its own but will finally merge with *anima mundi*, the world's soul, and this after a transitional period during which it will be in 'vehicular state'. This means being carried around by a material 'vehicle' of small size and tiny consistence like the butterfly under whose shape the soul was supposed to fly away by the ancients. A claim somewhat familiar for the Malthus scholar is that life is to be seen as 'necessary preparation to qualify us for the employ-ments of another state' (Tucker 1768, vol. 3, p. 228) and that 'we work out our future fortunes by our present behaviour, and fit ourselves unknowingly for the several parts we are to act upon the next stage, by practising those assigned us in this' (p. 228). Tucker does not go as far as formulating the annihilationist hypothesis adopted by Malthus in 1798, and limits himself to speculation about survival of pure spirit devoid of inner organization and thus unable to have perceptions, as well as about a non-eternal character of pun-ishment after death. And yet, his ideas on the strict relationship between body and soul as well as on this life as preparation to afterlife may help in figuring out what Malthus may have had in mind when writing about the mind origi-nating from matter as a result of our exertions, and how he could later claim that, his annihilationist doctrine notwithstanding, he 'had always thought of' this life as a state of probation. Malthus's intention may have been to suggest that, as soon as 1798, he had already conceived this life as a state where we, so-to-say, unknowingly fit ourselves for the several characters we are to play in the next stage through the practice of those assigned to us in this life, which is a not too bad description of the first *Essay*'s doctrine while not bluntly contradicting the idea of a 'probation', or better, of something similar to it.

To make things more tricky for historians of ideas to come, the argument on the origin of evil is developed not in the main work, but instead 'in a gargantuan ten-pages footnote' (Waterman 1991a, p. 103) to the fragment *Freewill, Foreknowledge and Fate* (Tucker 1763, pp. 258–268). To make things even worse, the footnote was omitted, like other less orthodox passages, when the entire work was published in 1768 and, for some reason, forgotten in the unabridged 1805 edition. The argument runs as follows: (i) we may observe that in all the universe we find all spaces full of different beings, and these playing more than just one function in the context of the whole, and from this observation we may infer that 'also nature forms her productions by long preparation, and through several steps', like the seed develops into a full-grown plant through several stages; (ii) we may formulate, by analogy, the following conjecture: 'Why there may not be a like progression of the soul through her several forms of being; each being preparatory to the next [...] as our several ways of living upon this stage may fit us to perform different parts upon another?' (p. 264); (iii) as our strength, vigour and genius depend to a wide extent on what passed in our pre-existent state (as foetuses), so there is a 'probability that the same in our future birth will depend upon what has happened to us during our present state' (p. 264); (iv) the reason for such probability is that sensations pass though the mental organization in their way to the mind and this may happen only in so far as matter impresses 'variety of perceptions non otherwise than by being diversely modified [...] So that every man's understanding and imagination become diversely modelled according as he has been a soldier, a scholar, a mechanic, or a labourer' (p. 264), and we may conjecture that 'the professions we practiced in our life adapt us severally for some peculiar functions we are destined to perform in our next form of being' (p. 263); (v) we may also conjecture that 'future punishments may be derived through the same channel; human nature being so ordered, that the practice of vicious courses, by working improper mixtures into the organization, may render it disturbed and distempered, for since nature is the work of God, whatever misery shall follow by natural consequences is the effect of divine vengeance' (p. 265); (vi) the existence of evil being repugnant to the idea of God's infinite Goodness, confining it to the embodied and unorganized states 'reduces the quantity of it within a very narrow compass' (p. 265) for, as we learned from Newton, the quantity of matter compared to that of void in the universe is rather limited; (vii) Locke taught us that the mind never moves to action 'unless for avoidance of some uneasiness or upon the prospect of some satisfaction that would be lost without her endeavours to procure it: therefore a being possessed of happiness, and in full security that nothing could disturb or abate it, would remain in perpetual indolence, having no inducement to exert its activity' (p. 266); on this basis, we should assume that 'in order to be shaken from its own indolence the mind needs some apprehension of evil, and we cannot conceive this to happen without some actual suffering somewhere' (p. 266); this 'may be necessary to keep activity alive in the spiritual substance for avoiding the sources of it' (p. 266), and this is 'the best account that can be given for the origin of evil' (p. 266); (viii) even though embodied beings are present in some parts of the universe while wide empty spaces are devoted to host 'disembodied organizations' (that is, purely spiritual beings belonging to the Soul of the World, a community of Spirits closely merged together), as all parts in the whole of Nature are reciprocally connected, 'samples of actual suffering' are present in any part of the universe in so far as the purely spiritual beings have 'concern with the embodied, as exhibiting specimens of evil necessary to preserve them in happiness' (p. 266).

Tucker's work had a remarkable echo and went through several editions in Malthus's lifetime. Malthus was somehow familiar with this work and may even had met the author before the latter's death in 1774, since Tucker lived in a mansion a few miles away from the Malthus family. Yet, in the Malthus Library there is just the *Fragment* (Jesus College 1983, p. 174), and no explicit reference to the main work may be found in Malthus's writings. As regards Tucker's moral theory, there are no reasons to think that he provided a source for any specific idea, even though such ideas as an overarching role for happiness, the primacy of prudence, a room for benevolence, and a need for general rules do play an important role in Malthus's own ethics. The fact is, however, that they may be found in Butler, Gay, Brown and Paley. As regards Tucker's doctrines of the material nature of the soul, the vehicular state, and non-eternity of Hell, some of these meet with an echo in the last two chapters of Malthus's first *Essay*, but Malthus cannot be said to owe him any specific doctrine, since annihilationism is not expressly formulated by Tucker himself and the idea of the production of mind out of matter is somehow foreshadowed but not in so clear terms as in Malthus. On the other hand, it is simply false that in such views there was 'nothing inconsistent with his ecclesiastical orthodoxy' (Bonar 1885, p. 367), and the point is instead that Malthus's less orthodox conjectures were indeed unorthodox but also not particularly close to Tucker's own unorthodox ideas. Indeed opinions close to Malthus's conjectures had been expressed by respectable Cambridge divines. I have mentioned, for example, that serious resistance to the idea of eternity of punishment had been manifested by Paley, and that the idea that mind does not exist substantially and instead thought is just one among other attributes of the body was a conjecture taken seriously by Watson himself. Thus, Tucker's main work, far from providing the basis for Malthus's overall view, might as well have never been read by him, and in fact everything Malthus takes from Tucker comes from the 'gargantuan footnote' in the *Fragment*. And yet, what comes from the fragment on *Free Will* is one among Malthus's main ideas, namely that *evil exists in order to stimulate activity*, or that some amount of actual suffering is necessary for activity and accordingly for happiness. The rest, unorthodox as it is, is added by Malthus himself, elaborating on theological doubts concerning the nature of the soul and the duration of divine punishment. Annihilationism as a way of excluding the infinite duration of punishments does not show up in Tucker, and is clearly Malthus's own addition. Also the production of mind out of matter is Malthus's own, but it derives from Tucker's idea of an influence of the body on the mind transmitting the kind of organization the former has been able to acquire through activity. Tucker's conjecture of the existence of an *anima mundi* is absent from Malthus's *Essay*, where the rather different speculation is introduced of continuous creation of spirit out of matter, incompatible with Tucker's idea of pre-existence of the 'rational soul' to conception. Also the idea of eternal life for fully grown minds is incompatible with Tucker's vision of their final merging into the World Soul.

Hume

David Hume, even though still banned from Cambridge reading lists on alleged atheism, was rather obvious reading for Malthus. Needless to recall that Hume and Jean-Jacques Rousseau were the two extraordinary fairy godmothers who had come to his cradle when he was ten days old, while paying a visit at Malthus's home in Surrey (James 1979, p. 9). The Malthus Library includes the *Essays, A Treatise of Human Nature*, and the *History of*

England (Jesus College 1983, p. 81), and Malthus cites Hume several times (Cremaschi 2010, pp. 12–13). Hume is not among the sources of Malthus's moral doctrines, but his influence is important with reference to a related point, namely caution with regard to apparently 'scientific' treatment of moral and political phenomena and aversion to the opposite extreme of uncritically relying on 'practice'. Malthus quotes 'Of the Populousness of Ancient Nations' to the effect that 'of all sciences there is none where first appearances are more deceitful than in politics' (Malthus 1803, vol. 2, p. 185; Hume 1752, p. 392) drawing the implication that caution is necessary when dealing with social phenomena, and for this reason political economy is different from the strict sciences and belongs instead to the moral and political sciences. Malthus's firm conviction will always be that, in so 'complex and delicate' subjects as political and moral ones, 'partial and immediate effects' of any particular law, institution, or policy 'are often directly opposite to the general and permanent consequences' (Malthus 1807, pp. 7–8).

Adam Smith

Malthus had first encountered *The Wealth of Nations* in 1783 at Warrington Academy through the lecture course on Commerce offered there. He was clearly familiar with this work at the time of the first *Essay*, where he refers to its third edition of 1784, the one he had borrowed from Jesus College Library in 1788 shortly after it had been acquired (Waterman 1991a, p. 90). In Malthus's Library there is a copy of *The Wealth of Nations* in John Ramsey McCulloch's edition of 1828 (Jesus College 1983, p. 158), but he had been making precise references to the work on many occasions before, and it may be safely assumed that, after borrowing the work from Jesus College Library in 1789 (Waterman 1991a, p. 90) he had been in possession of another edition. In the Malthus Library there is also a copy of the eighth edition of *The Theory of Moral Sentiments* of 1797 (Jesus College 1983, p. 158), which he may also have read before 1798. Precise references to this work are absent from Malthus's writings, and it is accordingly impossible to decide when Malthus first read it and when he was referring to specific ideas from this work, but we should keep in mind that Malthus manifested the deepest esteem for the author and that the separation of Smith the economist from Smith the moralist had not yet been carried out. Indeed, Malthus would have been the strongest opponent to such an attempt, and in 1820 he was still fighting in defence of that project of a 'moral and political science' which he believed had been Smith's own project (Malthus 1820, vol. 1, pp. 1–2; Cremaschi 2010, pp. 48–49).

Malthus had it clear in mind from the very beginning of his career that the new science of political economy, exemplified at its best by *The Wealth of Nations*, was too a result of the 'new mode of philosophizing' (Malthus 1798, p. 7–8), and still many years after he played the trump of Adam Smith's authority against the 'New School', that is, the Ricardian school. For example, in *On Political Economy*, he repeats Dugald Stewart's description of

Smith as 'the Newton' of political economy (Malthus 1824, p. 257) and on other occasions is keen in referring to Smith as *his own* model and exemplar as contrasted with the 'New School' (Malthus 1820, vol. 1, p. 2–7), or cites approvingly McCulloch's declaration that Smith 'has done for political economy, what the Principia of Newton did for physics' (Malthus 1824, p. 257).

By way of conclusion, the sources of Malthus's ethics described here have been singled out on the basis of external evidence, such as their presence in Cambridge reading lists or in Malthus's library, as well as of internal evidence, such as direct reference or close similarity of arguments with those found in books we may assume – on independent reasons – he had read, and accordingly the conclusion is reasonable that when Malthus adopted one solution to some ethical issue he did so while keeping these sources in mind. Yet, the proviso is in order that sources matter, at least in a negative sense (for example, in order to rule out that when Malthus mentions 'utility' he is making a profession of Benthamite faith) but also that discovering sources is not a panache, for their effect on one author's train of thinking is systematically complicated by over-determination. In more detail, Malthus may have found an idea similar to one that can be found in Paley also in Butler, Hume and Adam Smith, or may have developed independently an argument similar to one of Paley's arguments while starting with a shared set of assumptions and a shared agenda, in turn dependent on Cumberland, Gay and Brown. Malthus may also have advanced claims similar to those of Scottish philosopher Dugald Stewart while drawing them, or their premises, from non-Scottish sources, for example Isaac Watts. Last of all, Malthus shared quite a lot with the 'experimental' English and Scottish tradition and instead had several points of disagreement with the other main eighteenth-century British tradition, the Hartley–Priestley–Belsham school, a tradition on which Bentham was heavily dependent, and this may help in making sense of disagreement with Bentham's followers in ethics and politics.

Bibliography

Bonar, J. (1885) *Malthus and his Work*. London: Macmillan.
Brain, Th. (1999) Watson, Richard. In *The Dictionary of Eighteenth-Century British Philosophers*. Volume 2 K–Z. Ed. by Yolton, J.W., Price, J.V., and Stephens, J. Bristol: Thoemmes Press.
Brown, Th. (1751 [1969]) On the Motives to Virtue. In *Essays on the Characteristics of the Earl of Shaftesbury*. Ed. by Eddy, E.D. Hildesheim: Olms.
Butler, J. (1726 [2006]) Fifteen Sermons Preached at the Rolls Chapel. In *The Works of Bishop Butler*. Ed. by White, D.E. Rochester, NY: University of Rochester Press.
Butler, J. (1736 [2006]) The Analogy of Religion, Natural and Revealed, in the Constitution and Course of Nature. In *The Works of Bishop Butler*. Ed. by White, D.E. Rochester, NY: University of Rochester Press.
Cremaschi, S. (2007) *L'etica moderna. Dalla Riforma a Nietzsche*. Rome: Carocci.
Cremaschi, S. (2008) 'Utilitarianism and its nineteenth-century critics'. *Notizie di Politeia* 24(90), pp. 31–49.

Cremaschi, S. (2010) 'Malthus's idea of a moral and political science'. *The Journal of Philosophical Economics* 3(2), pp. 5–57.

Crimmins, J. (1990) Religion, Utility and Politics: Bentham versus Paley. In *Religion, Secularization and Political Thought: Thomas Hobbes to J.S. Mill*. Ed. by Crimmins, J. Oxford: Routledge.

Crimmins, J. (1998) Introduction. Religious advocates of the Utility Principle. In *Utilitarianism and Religion*. Ed. by Crimmins, J. Bristol: Thoemmes.

Empson, W. (1837) 'Life, writings and character of Mr. Malthus'. *Edinburgh Review*, 64(80), p. 469–506.

Gascoigne, J. (1989) *Cambridge in the Age of the Enlightenment. Science, Religion and Politics from the Restoration to the French Revolution*. Cambridge: Cambridge University Press.

Gay, J. (1731 [1965]) Concerning the Fundamental Principles of Virtue or Morality. In *The British Moralists*. Volume 2. Ed. by Selby-Bigge, I.A. New York: Dover.

Hey, J. (1796–98) *Lectures in Divinity*. Cambridge: Burger.

Hey, J. (Unpublished) *Lectures on Morality*. Cambridge: Sidney Sussex College.

Hole, R. (2004a) Kipling, Thomas. In *Oxford Dictionary of National Biography*. Volume 31. Ed. by Matthew, H.C.G. and Harrison, B. Oxford: Oxford University Press.

Hole, R. (2004b) Watson, Richard. In *Oxford Dictionary of National Biography*. Volume 57. Ed. by Matthew, H.C.G. and Harrison, B. Oxford: Oxford University Press.

Hume, D. (1752 [1992]) Of the Populousness of Ancient Nations. In *The Philosophical Works*. Volume 3. Ed. by Green, Th.H. and Grose, Th.H. Aalen: Scientia Verlag.

James, P. (1979) *Population Malthus. His Life and Time*. London: Routledge.

Jesus College (ed.) (1983) *The Malthus Library Catalogue*. New York: Pergamon Press.

Kipling, Th. (1793) *Codex Theodori Bezæ Cantabrigiensis, Evangelia et Apostolorum Acta complectens*. Cantab.

Knight, F. (1971) *University Rebel: The Life of William Frend, 1757–1841*. London: Gollancz.

Malthus, Th.R. (1798 [1986]) An Essay on the Principle of Population. In *The Works of Thomas Robert Malthus*. Volume 1. Ed. by Wrigley, E.A. and Souden, D. London: Pickering.

Malthus, Th.R. (1803 [1989]) *An Essay on the Principle of Population. The Version Published in 1803, with the Variora of 1806, 1807, 1817 and 1826*. Ed. by James, P. Cambridge: Cambridge University Press.

Malthus, Th.R. (1807 [1986]) Letter to Samuel Whitbread Esq. M.P. on his proposed bill for the amendment of the poor laws. In *The Works of Thomas Robert Malthus*. Volume 4. Ed. by Wrigley, E.A. and Souden, D. London: Pickering.

Malthus, Th.R. (1820 [1989]) *Principles of Political Economy*. Ed. by Pullen, J. Cambridge: Cambridge University Press.

Malthus, Th.R. (1824 [1986]) Population. In *The Works of Thomas Robert Malthus*. Volume 4. Ed. by Wrigley, E.A. and Souden, D. London: Pickering.

Paley, W. (1785 [2002]) *The Principles of Moral and Political Philosophy*. Ed. by LeMahieu, D.L. Indianapolis, IN: Liberty Fund.

Paley, W. (1802 [1970]) *Natural Theology: or: Evidences of the Existence and Attributes of the Deity, Collected from the Appearances of Nature*. Westmead: Gregg.

Schneewind, J.B. (1998) *The Invention of Autonomy. A History of Modern Moral Philosophy*. Cambridge: Cambridge University Press.

Schofield, T.P. (1987) 'A comparison of the moral theories of William Paley and Jeremy Bentham'. *The Bentham Newsletter* (11), pp. 4–22.

Scott, E.L. (1981) Watson, Richard. In *Dictionary of Scientific Biography*. Volume 14. Ed. by Gillispie, Ch.C. New York: Scribner's.

Smith, A. (1759 [1976]) *The Theory of Moral Sentiments*. Ed. by Raphael, D.D. and Macfie, A.L. Oxford: Clarendon Press.

Smith, A. (1776 [1976]) *An Inquiry into the Nature and Causes of the Wealth of Nations*. Ed. by Campbell, R.H., Skinner, A.S. and Todd, W.B. Oxford: Clarendon Press.

Stephen, L. (1881) *A History of English Thought*. Second edn. London: Smith.

Thompson, D.M. (2008) *Cambridge Theology in the Nineteenth Century*. Aldershot: Ashgate.

Tucker, A. (1763) *Freewill, Foreknowledge and Fate. A Fragment by Edward Search*. London: Dodsley.

Tucker, A. (1768) *The Light of Nature Pursued*. London: Payne.

Tucker, A. (1805 [1977]) *The Light of Nature Pursued*. Second edn. New York: Garland.

Waterman, A.M.C. (1991a) *Revolution, Economics and Religion. Christian Political Economy, 1798–1833*. Cambridge: Cambridge University Press.

Waterman, A.M.C. (1991b [2004]) A Cambridge 'via media' in late Georgian Anglicanism. In *Political Economy and Christian Theology since the Enlightenment*. Houndsmills: Palgrave & MacMillan.

Waterman, A.M.C. (1996) 'Why William Paley was "the first of the Cambridge Economists".' *Cambridge Journal of Economics* 20(6), pp. 673–686.

Waterman, A.M.C. (2004) Hey, John. In *Oxford Dictionary of National Biography*, Volume 26 HAYCKOCK–HICHENS. Ed. by Matthew, H.C.G. and Harrison, B. Oxford: Oxford University Press.

Watson, R. (1772 [1815]) A letter from a Christian Whig. In *Miscellaneous Tracts on Religious, Political and Agricultural Subjects*. Volume 2. London: Cadell.

Watson, R. (1776a) *An Apology for Christianity*. Cambridge: Merrill.

Watson, R. (1776b) *The Principles of the Revolution Vindicated*. Cambridge: Merrill.

Watson, R. (1781 [1793]) *Chemical Essays*. London: Evans

Watson, R. (1785) *A Collection of Theological Tracts*. Cambridge: Merrill.

Watson, R. (1796 [1799]) *An Apology for the Bible*. London: Evans.

Watson, R. (1798) *An Address to the People of Great Britain*. London: Faulder.

Watson, R. (1818) *Anecdotes of the Life of R.W. Watson, Bishop of Llandaff*. Second edn. London: Cadell.

Watts, I. (1726 [1984]) *Logick*. New York: Garland.

Watts, I. (1741) The Improvement of the Mind. In *Selected Writings of Isaac Watts*. Volumes 7–8. Ed. by Pyle, A. and Stephens, J. Bristol: Thoemmes.

Whewell, W. (1846) *Lectures on Systematic Morality*. London: Parker.

Whitby, D. (1724) *Ethices compendium in usum juventutis academicae*. London: Innys.

Winstanley, D.A. (1935 [2009]) *Unreformed Cambridge*. Cambridge: Cambridge University Press.

3   Malthus's meta-ethics

Moral ontology

Happiness

In the first *Essay* Malthus declares: 'I do not mean *to enter into a philosophical discussion* of what constitutes the proper happiness of man; but shall merely consider two universally acknowledged ingredients, health, and the command of the necessaries and conveniences of life' (Malthus 1798, p. 107). The phrase '*to enter into a philosophical discussion*', which may sound rather innocent to our ears, conveyed a rather specific meaning to an eighteenth-century audience. A 'philosophical' discussion was not a discussion on the meaning of terms, logical entailments, justification of arguments etc., as contrasted with a discussion of positive issues, say, in economics or psychology or any other empirical science. A 'philosophical' discussion was instead a discussion of *causes* and *essences*, as contrasted with a purely 'mathematical' discussion of correlations between observed magnitudes or *phenomena*. This is the distinction Newton had in mind when he declared his intention to confine his own discussion by the famous statement '*hypotheses non fingo*'. Thus the term 'philosophical' refers to discussion of the essence of entities as contrasted with treatment of these entities as elements of a 'mathematical' theory. The latter is just a tool for predicting phenomena, not a possibly true description of the real world. That is, it is scientific theory understood in the same way as by twentieth-century instrumentalism, a philosophy of science according to which theories are neither true nor false, but just predictive tools, as vindicated by Andreas Osiander (1547) in his Preface to Nicolas Copernicus's *De Revolutionibus Orbium Coelestium*.

Here Malthus is declaring his intention to avoid commitments on the nature of happiness and to stick to a 'conventional' definition of the term, while suspending his judgement on its eventual nature being aware that there are several contrasting answers to the question. In fact in eighteenth-century Britain there were at least two competing doctrines circulating in moral discourse where the nature of happiness was concerned. One of them was Locke's combination of hedonism, the doctrine that the good is to be identified with pleasure, and associationism, the doctrine that the mental life consists of elementary impressions and thinking is no more than the combination of such impressions giving birth to complex ideas. This doctrine tended to make it coincide with a state where a greater amount of pleasure and a lesser amount of uneasiness are found, a doctrine further developed by David Hartley, John Gay, Thomas Brown, Joseph Priestley and William Paley. Another was the Platonic line of enquiry starting with Anthony Ashley Cooper the third Earl of Shaftesbury, and Locke's pupil, who argued that the 'chief Happiness' derives from the 'Mental Pleasures' (Shaftesbury 1711, p. 126) and the chief means of obtaining it are the 'natural affections' such as 'Love, Complacence, Good-Will' and 'Sympathy with the Kind or Species' (p. 99).

This line was further developed by Francis Hutcheson, who claimed that happiness lies in: (i) the exercise of the superior virtues 'especially that entire love and resignation to God, and of all the inferior virtues which do not interfere with the superior'; (ii) the enjoyment of 'such external prosperity as we can, consistently with virtue, obtain' (Hutcheson 1755, vol. 5, p. 222). A sceptical twist was given to this line by Adam Smith with his view of happiness as resulting primarily from imagination, justified by the consideration that the latter is able to amplify and reduce bodily pain and pleasure. Thus, for Smith, happiness is based on the hope of imaginary enjoyments such as those promised by love, or on faith in the existence of a benevolent Father who cares for all his creatures, or else on supposition of being the subject of sympathy and looked at with attention. But above all it depends on our *adaptability* to whatsoever permanent state, provided that it offers some occasion for tranquillity and enjoyment (Smith 1759, pp. 57, 235–237, 307, 149; Bruni 1987).

The hedonistic-associationist doctrine had also been twisted in a slightly sceptical direction by Paley who, in the *Principles*, had proved to be aware of troubles coming with the notion of happiness; for example he had written that 'pleasures differ in nothing but in continuance and intensity' (Paley 1785, p. 18) and that strictly 'any condition may be denominated happy, in which the amount or aggregate of pleasure exceeds that of pain' (p. 18). Thus happiness, as distinguished from pleasure, could mean only 'a certain state of the nervous system in that part of the human frame in which we feel joy and grief, passions and affection' (p. 13 fn.), and what we can do in order to decide whether one given condition is happy is: (i) to compute the continuance and intensity of pleasures; and (ii) to compare 'the apparent cheerfulness, tranquillity, and contentment of men of different tastes, tempers, stations, and pursuits' (p. 13 fn.). Thus happy is a 'relative term', which cannot be identified with either 'pleasure' or 'exemption from pain', nor 'greatness, rank, or elevated station', and 'there remains a presumption in favour of those conditions of life, in which men generally appear most cheerful and contented' (p. 19). All that, Paley concludes, suggests that happiness may probably lie in: (i) the exercise of social affections; (ii) the exercise of our faculties, either of body or of mind, the pursuit of some engaging end concerning whose attainment we may cultivate some 'hope'; (iii) health; and besides (iv) it depends on a 'prudent constitution of the habits' (p. 22).

After his own *'hypotheses non fingo'* on the ultimate nature of happiness, Malthus starts with one minimal assumption that he believes to be accepted by the two opposing parties. This is: whatever happiness is, it includes health – one out of Paley's four elements – and some amount of both basic and superfluous goods. It may be noted that he seems to share Paley's awareness of the problems related with the definition of happiness, but also that, unlike Paley, he does not even try to formulate a tentative definition. The second *Essay*, without dismissing the *'hypotheses non fingo'* clause, adds more detailed discussion of the nature of happiness. Malthus admits that sources of happiness do exist and specifies that these lie in the 'formation and steady pursuit of some particular plan of life' (Malthus 1803, vol. 2, p. 91), which may sound much like Paley's second element, as well as in a mix of material and emotive factors, such as the 'evening meal, the warm house, and the comfortable fireside' to which 'some object of affection' should be added 'with whom they are to be shared' (p. 91), which could be associated with Paley's first element. He also adds that passion between the sexes is 'one of the principal ingredients of human happiness' (p. 92). It is worth noting that Malthus's specifications go – on balance – in the opposite direction to Bentham's hedonism, since for the latter the assumption holds that, in order to be able to work out a felicific calculus, we have to assume that units of happiness are of an identical nature, and that nature should be such as to be able to be observed and measured. From this assumption Bentham derived the notorious claim that pleasure derived from pushpin counts as much as pleasure derived from poetry.

Besides, already in 1798 Malthus had introduced a distinction between 'exchangeable value' and 'real utility' (the very distinction that was described one century later by Pareto with the terms 'utility' and 'ofelimity') and the claim that only the latter contributes to 'the mass of happiness'. Note that, first, this distinction again goes in an anti-hedonistic direction, and was accepted by Adam Smith and rejected by Bentham. Second, such a distinction is precisely what Malthus had in mind some twenty years later when he was attacked by Ricardo who, in his *Notes on Malthus*, misunderstood him in so far as he attacked him on grounds of confusion, not realizing that he was merely adopting a claim widely shared among eighteenth-century writers on economic subjects, Adam Smith included (Cremaschi and Dascal 1998, pp. 39–40). Malthus writes:

> The fine silks [...] may contribute very considerably to augment the exchangeable value of its annual produce; yet they contribute but in a very small degree, to augment the mass of happiness in the society [...] with some view to the real utility of the produce [...] we ought to estimate the productiveness [...] of different sorts of labour.
>
> (Malthus 1798, pp. 115–116)

Third, Malthus has clearly in mind, already in 1798, that there is a reason for privileging happiness of the lower classes, and this reason lies in their numbers, which means that an increase in happiness of these classes carries a remarkable increase in the total sum of happiness in a given society. He had found this idea in book I, chapter 8 of Adam Smith's *Wealth of Nations*, a chapter that provides the starting-point for his own elaboration on population and where he asks:

> Is this improvement in the circumstances of the lower ranks of the people to be regarded as an advantage or as an inconveniency to the society? The answer seems at first sight abundantly plain. Servants, labourers and workmen of different kinds, make up the far greater part of every great political society. But what improves the circumstances of the greater part can never be regarded as inconveniency to the whole. No society can surely be flourishing and happy, of which the far greater part of the members are poor and miserable. It is but equity, besides, that they who feed, cloath and lodge the whole body of the people, should have such a share of the produce of their own labour as to be themselves tolerably well fed, cloathed and lodged.
>
> (Smith 1776, p. 96)

And an analogous idea was expressed by Paley – indeed in the same chapter on population that was targeted by Malthus in *The Crisis* – when pointing to the 'ease [...] and certainty, with which the means can be produced, not barely of subsistence, but of that mode of subsisting which custom has in each country established' (Paley 1785, p. 424) as the precondition for any increase in the 'greatest quantity of happiness in a given tract of country', which is the 'final view of all rational politics' on which the state and progress of population chiefly depend.

In fact, even though his argument against Godwin proves the impossibility of any decisive growth in the 'mass of happiness among the common people' (Malthus 1798, p. 35) or 'any very marked and striking change for the better, in the form and structure of general society; by which I mean, any grand and decided amelioration of the condition of the lower classes of mankind' (p. 98), he adds that these classes are '*the most numerous*, and, consequently, in a general view of the subject, *the most important* part of the human race' (p. 98). Malthus was apparently still true to this assumption twenty years later, when he proposed to evaluate policies 'with a view to the happiness of the great mass of society' (Malthus 1820, vol. 1, p. 522). This consideration was of a kind that was shared by the Utilitarians, and yet Malthus, at least from 1803 on, had a much more pro-Poor attitude than James Mill, Bentham and even Ricardo (the latter at least up to 1821, when he published the third edition of his *Principles*).

Fourth, Malthus sticks to a claim that is instead irreconcilable with any kind of utilitarianism, namely the assertion of an irreducible difference between misery and vice, as well as between virtue and happiness (obviously enough, they are different in a sense also for utilitarians, but virtue would have been for Bentham a typical 'fictitious entity', a shorthand for a tendency to felicific behaviour. For example, *'misery and vice'* are contrasted with *'happiness and innocence'* in the first *Essay* (Malthus 1798, p. 41); in the *Observations on the Effects of the Corn Laws* the goal of a wise and just policy is described as 'to improve, increase, and secure the mass of human virtue and happiness' (Malthus 1814, p. 101); in the *Principles* this goal is described as to make the poor 'respectable, virtuous, and happy' (Malthus 1820, vol. 1, p. 251). The remark is in order here that 'respectable' implies recognition to the 'common people' of their dignity as citizens, which is something more than utilitarians would admit of.

Another remark is that the distinction between 'virtuous' and 'happy' implies a *pluralistic* view of the good, distinct from the monistic view of Benthamite utilitarianism according to which, on principle, virtue is subservient to happiness and, in the long run, the quantity of happiness tends to coincide with the quantity of virtue. The question should also be explored in depth of the reasons why according to Malthus virtue could not be identified with happiness. The possible answers are: (i) for the same reasons for which it was not immediately identified by Bentham, i.e. because virtue is instrumental to the production of happiness; (ii) for the same reasons as for Gay, Brown and Paley, i.e. because the equation between quantities of virtue and happiness is brought about only in the afterlife; (iii) for further reasons, similar to Butler's, i.e. because virtue, besides being productive of happiness, is also valuable in itself. Malthus's reasons for keeping a neat distinction will emerge decades after, consistently with his views of 1798 and 1803, in his correspondence with Thomas Chalmers. The latter had insisted that the Church was a machinery contributing to a nation's wealth, in so far as it was instrumental in fostering 'moral and religious habits', adding that wealth 'should rather be made to comprise every thing that conduces to the enjoyment of man, whether that enjoyment comes to him or not through the medium of a tangible commodity' (Chalmers 1808, p. 202). One paradox into which the current distinction heads – Chalmers contends – is that a 'minister of religion, who impresses virtue and consolation upon his hearers, is an unproductive labourer. The same minister, if he concurs with a bookseller in the manufacture of a printed volume of sermons, is a productive labourer' (p. 209). The absurd implication of such distinction is that all that matters is the book as a material object that can be sold. 'The great point is the benefit he has done to the trade' (p. 210). Nothing else matters and it is a subordinate kind of consideration whether the effect of his sermons 'may be to call a wanderer from the delusions of intemperance, or to chace [sic] from a bosom the misery by which it is agitated' (p. 210). Malthus, in the *Principles* (1820), still defends the function of unproductive labour by the same considerations he had adopted before, but adds a warning on the importance of the distinction between virtue and wealth that seems to reflect his correspondence with Chalmers, and in a letter to Chalmers of January 1827 he writes that it is:

more correct in regard to common usage of language, and in accordance with all our common feelings to say that security, independence, moral and religious instruction, and moral and religious habits, are very superior in importance to what we usually mean by wealth, than to say that they ought to be included in the term [...] what will be the meaning of the language of our divines and moralists who dissuade men from the eager pursuit of riches, if riches are so defined, as to include every source of human happiness.

(Waterman 1991, pp. 242–243)

In another letter to Chalmers of March 1832 he repeats the same idea, insisting that:

It is paying morals a very bad compliment to put them in the same category with cottons [...] We have always been told, and most properly, to prefer virtue to wealth; but if morals be wealth, what a confusion is at once introduced into all the language of moral and religious instruction.

(pp. 242–243)

Finally, it is also to be noticed that Malthus had taken into account the possible alternative of reducing vice to misery (and by implication, virtue to happiness) and had explicitly rejected it in the second *Essay*. Here he admits that 'as the general consequence of vice is misery, and as this consequence is the precise reason why an action is termed vicious, it may appear that the term misery alone would be here sufficient, and it is superfluous to use both' (Malthus 1803, vol. 1, p. 19), but adds that 'the rejection of the term vice would introduce *a considerable confusion into our language and ideas*' (p. 19). In the 1817 Appendix he insists on the same point, arguing that 'vice' in matters of sexual morality would entail 'evils not different from evils arising from the excessive or irregular gratification of the human passions in general' (vol. 2, p. 250) and even, in case 'the advantages may greatly overbalance the evils' (p. 250), we should not establish what is good or evil on the basis of a balance of the overall situation in the individual case – as an act-utilitarian would do – since 'these evils do not lose their name or nature because they are overbalanced by good' and to cease 'to call them evils, would be as irrational as the objecting to call the irregular indulgences of passion vicious, and to affirm that they lead to misery, because our passions are the main sources of human virtue and happiness' (p. 250). The points at stake in the 1803 *Essay* and in the passage from the 1817 Appendix are two. One is language. A theory rather fashionable at Cambridge at the time Malthus was a student there was James Harris's Platonic theory of language. This was the target of Horne Tooke's alternative nominalist doctrine, which became popular among Unitarians and Benthamites. According to Harris's theory, ordinary language is a starting point to which we should stick as far as possible, and any artificial language based on conventional definitions tends to lead us astray; the reason is that language arises from a combination of *convention* and *nature*, and words are symbols of general ideas, and 'in nature, as well as in art, there are intelligible forms, which to the sensible are subsequent' (Harris 1751, p. 379). For a similar reason Watts' *Logick*, a textbook used by Malthus as a student, recommended not to alter the usual meaning of words (Watts 1726, p. 97; Cremaschi and Dascal 1996, p. 489). The other point at stake in the passage is one of ethical theory, namely the scope and function of consequentialism (that is, the twentieth-century distinctions between act and rule, agent or spectator, test or criterion). This point will be discussed in one of the next paragraphs.

Laws of nature

'Laws of nature', which are frequently invoked by Malthus, were one of the targets for Utilitarian attacks, and not by chance the use of this expression by Malthus was the subject of a discussion between Ricardo and Place, where the former was trying to give a charitable reading of Malthus's claims by translating the expression 'laws of nature' into the formula 'greatest happiness'. Ricardo writes in a letter to Place of 9 Sept 1821:

> Your remark on the word 'right' as used by Mr. Malthus is strictly correct perhaps [...] By 'right' and 'laws of nature' Mr. Malthus clearly means 'moral right', 'utility', 'the good of the whole'[...] I am not defending the accuracy of Mr. Malthus's language on this occasion. I know it is not strictly correct, I as well as you am a disciple of the Bentham and Mill school, but his meaning cannot be mistaken.
>
> (Ricardo 1821, p. 51–52)

Malthus was educated in the tradition of Anglican 'natural theology' and the presence of a number of commonplaces from such tradition may be easily detected in his writings. For example, in the first *Essay*, after having made an important concession to the hypothesis of the *immediate agency* of divine power in any causal connection in nature – an idea that may be found for example in Nicholas Malebranche, and that was admitted of, as a conjecture, by Newton himself – he writes that 'these operations of what we call nature have been conducted almost invariably according to *fixed laws*' (Malthus 1798, p. 48). Such 'laws of nature' (p. 48) or 'laws of our nature' (p. 35), or 'inevitable laws of our nature' (p. 74), are 'fixed' and 'constant' (p. 48). One could be tempted to conclude that they are not *prescriptive* or *moral* laws, and even less the 'metaphysical' kind of natural laws that have been the target of utilitarian and positivist scorn for two centuries but simply *descriptive* or *scientific* laws. But this conclusion would be rash. In fact, Malthus believes that the basic postulates of population theory express two of the 'fixed laws of our nature' (p. 8, 59), and that human nature is a part of Nature, created by God, who 'first arranged the system of the universe; and for the advantage of his creatures, still executes, according to fixed laws, all its various operation' (p. 8). Thus, in the 1817 Appendix, he feels entitled to say that 'the laws of nature [...] are the laws of God' (Malthus 1803, vol. 2, p. 216), repeating the same expression as had been used by Edmund Burke while identifying both kinds of laws with 'the laws of commerce' (Burke 1800, p. 32), and that the will of God is known to us through 'the repeated admonitions which he gives, by the general laws of nature, to every being capable of reason' (p. 107). It is in this light that we should read Malthus's expression 'the great law of necessity [...] a law so open to our view, so obvious and evident to our understandings' (Malthus 1798, p. 48).

One could say that for Malthus, too, the laws of nature keep a prescriptive as well as a descriptive aspect, once the distinction is made between an intrinsic or teleological normative dimension such as the one we could recognize in Aquinas's view and an extrinsic normative dimension of laws that in themselves are purely descriptive, which is assumed to hold once the order of the universe established for the advantage of God's creatures has been detected. In order to reconstruct what Malthus had in mind, let us give a retrospective look at the history of this idea that was the main element of the Stoic legacy to Scholasticism. The key idea in Stoicism was that of a divine reason immanent in the universe. While in the earlier *Stoa* this idea, placed in a necessitarian framework, left no room for a really normative code of ethics, since awareness of necessity was the only asset human beings were left with, in the second or first century of Ancient Age necessitarianism was softened enough as to allow some room for what Cicero translated into Latin with the word *officium*, roughly 'duty'. Within this new framework, the law of nature became *also* a prescriptive law, pointing to the right behaviour for human beings.

The distinction was exploited fully by Aquinas who formulated the idea of a *lex naturae* as distinguished from the *lex aeterna*, where the former is the eternal law *for us*, understood as prescribing the right behaviour. The sensitive issue which soon started to be discussed is whether such a law was the output of God's intellect or of God's will. Aquinas's most brilliant critic, William of Ockham, opted for the latter alternative, later named *voluntarism*, in order to save the postulate of God's omnipotence while not making room for any arbitrary or tyrannical character of his will. The solution was based on the assumption that God himself is bound by his own original decrees, those promulgated on the first day of Creation. The issue had been a hot one ever since the Reformation, since voluntarism was adopted by the Reformers in order to devaluate Nature while stressing the role of Grace. Within this framework, John Calvin, and more markedly his followers, implied a discontinuity between the (worthless) morality of 'pure nature' or worldly morality and revealed morality, declaring that only the latter really matters while the former is at most useful to preserve peace and order.

The Anglican reaction to Calvinism, starting with Richard Hooker's *Laws of Ecclesiastical Polity* (1593–1661), insisted on the claims that *Revelation* is not the sole source of norms to be obeyed and that there is another source, the *Law of Nature*, accessible to every human being in so far as he is endowed with the light of reason, and that such light is clearly visible notwithstanding the effects of the original sin. This reaction was tantamount to a U-turn, in so far as, while still claiming allegiance to Protestantism and execration for Popery, Hooker was as pro-Nature as any Scholastic ever dared to be. This reaction yielded among its developments in ethical theory both trends that have been illustrated, namely the Platonic and the empiricist or consequentialist. The idea of laws of nature became the latter trend's main asset since it allowed for a kind of third way going beyond the familiar alternative between intellectualism and voluntarism. This solution was adopted by Catholic, Lutheran and Anglican writers such as Nicholas Malebranche, Gottfried Wilhelm von Leibniz and Richard Cumberland. Its assumptions were that, on the one hand, what God does is *to impose* laws over the entities he has created (as contrasted with *acknowledging* the existence of such laws and then proclaiming them), but that, on the other hand, such laws are not the result of a tyrant's whimsical decisions, since God is benevolent and omniscient and accordingly establishes such laws as will produce the greatest quantity of happiness for his creatures. This implies that God acts through 'general laws' and that Reason and Revelation become parallel sources for moral law, since we may come to the same conclusions by an a-priori way going from God to his creatures or by an a-posteriori way going from the word as it is to the will of God as may be reconstructed from the world order. To sum up, Malthus adheres to the voluntarist view of the laws of nature which, even though it was the target of general scorn in the nineteenth and early twentieth century as a 'Medieval' doctrine, was the view shared by the proponents of the New Science, first among them Newton (Waterman 1991, p. 28–37; Zilsel 1942; Oakley 1961; Heimann 1978).

I come now to the main source of misunderstanding. It is a point where Malthus apparently comes closer to the Benthamite Utilitarians and actually does quote Paley approvingly. This point is the 'test of Utility', or the role utility plays in deciding the right or wrong character of a line of conduct. In the first *Essay* Malthus seems to admit of a consequentialist view of morality merely for the sake of the argument, since he seems to be arguing from his opponent's premises. He writes: 'Morality according to Mr. Godwin, is a calculation of consequences, or, as Archdeacon Paley very justly expresses it, the will of God, as collected from general expediency' (Malthus 1798, p. 77). In fact, he seems to adhere to the standard Anglican consequentialist-voluntarist view while de-emphasizing differences between the latter and Godwin's Atheistic consequentialism. Let us see what Paley's view of normative ethics was. Paley had declared that actions:

> are to be estimated by their tendency to promote happiness. Whatever is expedient is right. It is the utility of any moral rule alone which constitutes the obligation of it.
>
> (Paley 1785, p. 42)

And yet, even Paley's alleged 'Utilitarianism' – which, as argued in Chapter 2, would be more accurately classified under the description 'consequentialist voluntarism' – is basically different from Bentham's. Let me recall that the latter disregarded Paley's account as irrelevant or useless in so far as – he believed – it did not provide any solution different from those of other kinds of theological morality (Crimmins 1990). Let me recall also that, a few decades later, John Stuart Mill refused to defend Paley against William Whewell's criticism for the reason that the former, 'whatever principles of morals he professed, seems to have had no objects but to insert it as a foundation underneath the existing set of opinions, ethical and political' (Mill 1852, p. 173; Cremaschi 2006). Their arrogance notwithstanding, Bentham and Mill may have been right in so far as what Paley was vindicating was the familiar conflation of Christian morality and Ciceronian moral philosophy, not Bentham's and Mill's 'new morality'. The decisive point is that it is true that what matters for Paley are general consequences, but also that they matter only in so far as from an appraisal of consequences he comes back to a justification of natural law and innate rights, precisely those notions that for Bentham were the quintessence of obscurantism. The North-West passage leading from consequences and quantities of pleasure to natural laws and innate rights is God's will combined with his benevolence and omniscience. As a result, 'expediency' is merely the test of what should be accepted as a law imposed by God, not a criterion on which we may decide the right course of action. It is true that Paley's consequentialism and Bentham's utilitarianism might seem to be almost equivalent 'extensionally' in so far as they approve or condemn the same acts. This does happen to some extent, but the difference is that, when considered 'intensionally', that is, by listing the characteristics it needs to possess in order to qualify as such, Paley's right action is described in terms different from Bentham's, namely those of an act conforming to a law prescribed by God.

Another source of misunderstanding has been the relationship between *natural* laws and *economic* laws. In the *Principles*, within the context of that distinction between 'general laws' and usual 'propositions of political economy', 'laws of nature' are also mentioned in connection with the relationship between human society and its physical environment, and the focal point of that relationship for Malthus is rent (Malthus 1820, vol. 1, pp. 147, 229). He writes that in the production of food, as contrasted with other kinds of monopoly, 'the laws of nature are constantly at work to regulate their exchangeable value according to their value in use' (pp. 147–148). Thus rent has a special status. 'The separation of rents [...] is a *law* as invariable as the action of the principle of gravity', and rent 'is placed by the *laws of nature* on the land, by whomsoever possessed' (pp. 155, 229), while 'in the fertility of the soil [...] the great laws of nature have provided for the leisure [or personal services] of a certain portion of society' (p. 463), which implies a moral justification for the existence of the class of unproductive workers, that is producers of immaterial commodities, among them menial servants, as well as of landowners whose function is to provide an effective demand for services (Waterman 1991, p. 266–270).

Yet it should be kept in mind that in this case as well as in those of poverty and population, the laws of nature are believed to be 'good', and indeed *morally* good, but not in intellectualist terms, as an *inherent* quality of something, but in voluntarist terms, as a quality of the results produced by the action of such laws. In other words, such laws were justified in so far as they were such as to bring about a more favourable balance of happiness than other possible laws. This is well illustrated by one of the most infamous of Malthus's claims, the non-existence of a right to subsistence. He claims that relief from hunger could not be requested by the poor as a right, for no other reason than that it would have been physically impossible to grant subsistence to all the poor, due to the principle of population. Another not very popular claim, the defence of rent, is also justified on the basis of this framework, whereby the acquisition of rent was perceived as a right for anybody who happened to have property rights on the land, since rent is an 'addition' made by nature, and refusal to benefit from it would have supposedly benefited nobody else.

The general character of the laws through which God operates is also the key to Malthus's solution to the problem of evil. The effects of any general law always include, besides some desirable results, also some 'partial mischiefs' (Malthus 1803, vol. 1, p. 94) resulting from the combined effects of this and other general laws. This is what he calls 'partial evil', namely that the good character of general laws paradoxically derives also from the circumstance that their good effects are produced 'at the expense of a small comparative quantity of evil' (p. 94).

Moral epistemology

Religion, morality and the veil of ignorance

I have illustrated above how the tradition into which Malthus was educated tended to stress *natural* religion vis-à-vis revealed religion, as well as its *practical* character vis-à-vis speculative doctrines. This meant that the function of religion is to add one further motive for conforming to the self-evident laws of natural morality. This attitude resulted from the intention of defeating, on the one hand, extreme voluntarism and, on the other, irreligious hedonistic immoralism by their weapons, but the final outcome of such effort tended to get drawn into a familiar Scylla of moral theory. This was the one which Kant dubbed heteronomy, that is, acting in conformity with the moral law just because of fear of punishment or hope of reward, and thus on immoral motives.

In fact, the prevailing eighteenth-century Anglican natural morality became the target of much scorn by the proponents of the early nineteenth-century evangelical revival in Malthus's lifetime. Thomas Gisborne, who attacked Malthus and his population theory precisely for defending *natural* morality as opposed to Christian *revealed* morality, was one of such Evangelicals. It is fair to note that the Carybdis into which Evangelicals got drawn was, in turn, refusal of natural morality, or Augustinianism, which had already been labelled by Kant as just one more kind of heteronomy, the divine-command doctrine of morality. An available alternative to empirical natural morality was rationalistic natural morality, the one adopted by Clarke, the Cambridge Platonists, Price, and a few years after Malthus's death, Whewell. On the Continent the alternative was being adopted by Moses Mendelssohn and Kant. This alternative was never seriously envisaged by Malthus, probably because it was not considered to be a respectable one by the English Anglican establishment of the time (note that Price was a Dissenter) and would have been such up to 1845, when Whewell would have launched an Anglican version of Price's moral theory.

Paley, for example, declared that the end of Christian Revelation was 'to influence the conduct of human life, by establishing the proof of a future state of reward and punishment' (Paley 1794, p. 366); that it presupposes 'a knowledge of the principles of natural justice' and that it is meant 'not so much to teach new rules of morality, as to enforce the practice of it by new sanctions, and a greater certainty' (Paley 1785, p. 7). Such claims were the received opinion in his time and place, and were shared for example by Hey who used to teach that 'morality is nothing but a set of rules, adapted to promote happiness, social and private, established and recognized by the moral sense' (Hey 1796–1798, vol. 1, p. 316). We cannot establish how comfortable Malthus felt with this kind of argument. Apparently he had no problem with it at the time of the first *Essay*. We may conjecture that he grew more and more cautious about the somewhat Pelagian spirit it implied as he came closer to the Evangelicals.

In fact, in an undated sermon on Deut 29, 29 ('The secret things belong unto the Lord our God: But those things which are revealed belong unto us and to our children for ever, that we may do all the words of his Law'), he declares that the divine revelation is not meant to reveal us secret things, but only to teach us as much as is required in order to encourage us in doing God's will. He writes that the 'great end and scope of all religious information, whether by nature or revelation, – the purpose for which our reason was given us at first, or any particular manifestation of the divine will afterwards […] was *practice – the practice of solid and substantial virtue* – that we might do all the words of his Law' (Malthus 1997–2004, vol. 2, p. 20; words in italics crossed). And in the same sermon in the original draft he had repeated that '*the great end and design of all religion is practice: the practice of solid and substantial virtue – "that we might do all the words of his Law"*', which is deleted too and replaced by the following sentence: '*The great design of God in all his transaction with mankind, as far as themselves are concerned seems to be to make them happy; and to do this by such methods, as are suitable to their nature and capacities. Now as*', which is in turn deleted (p. 23). The sermon goes on to repeat the traditional eudemonist argument in the version provided by Gay, Brown and Paley, according to which 'there is no method by which a reasonable creature can attain his happiness but that of conforming himself to the will of his maker by a holy and virtuous conduct' (p. 23) but in the final version all this is introduced by the phrase: 'We learn from Scripture that' (p. 23) that is, shifting the claim's context from natural to revealed theology.

Deletions and additions have rather clear implications. On the one hand, the scope of revealed religion is enlarged vis-à-vis natural religion; on the other, Christian morality based on Revelation wins more weight vis-à-vis natural morality. All this is what one would expect from an Evangelical, but the core argument, that is, the eudemonist reason for adhering to God's will, remains unchanged albeit couched in a positive theological framework instead of a natural-religion framework.

Another related point is the duty to cultivate our intellect as a Christian duty, again not a strange idea in his time and place, but with the qualification that 'our abilities of every kind are greatly circumscribed' (p. 21). The proof thereof is that 'natural causes of every kind, and final causes for the most part, that is, the modes by which nature operates in every instance, and its destination in most, are utterly unknown to us' (p. 21), and the practical conclusion is that we should better 'pursue those truths that are within our reach: and cultivate the knowledge which we are capable of attaining to' (p. 21), and besides any intellectual excellence is of lesser worth than moral dispositions, that is, the Christian virtues of 'evangelical charity, meekness, piety' (Malthus 1798, p. 131), or 'sympathy and benevolence' (p. 130). It is worth noting that such teachings were comparatively commonplace, as proved by the circumstance that rather similar points were made by Unitarian Thomas Belsham (Cremaschi and Dascal 1996, p. 493).

But Malthus also believed – not surprisingly since this was one of Butler's main teachings – that not only consequences but also motives matter and that a really virtuous action cannot be that performed simply and solely 'from the dread of a very great punishment, or the expectation of a very great reward' (Malthus 1798, p. 135), but the quality of virtuous action depends primarily on intention. A need to preserve room for human freedom and accordingly for desert and guilt had motivated several seventeenth- and eighteenth-century authors in exploring possible implications of a traditional theological *topos*, the idea of a *Deus absconditus*, now translated into the idea of a veil-of-ignorance. Gottfried Wilhelm Leibniz, for example, had suggested that the beauty and justice of God's world government have been concealed from our view because such an arrangement was convenient with a view to a better exercise of virtue, in so far as 'rewards and punishments are kept still invisible from an external point of view and are apparent only to the eyes of reason or faith' (Leibniz 1702, p. 111), and that we should accordingly 'try to bring about the best outcome as far as future events are concerned, about which God did not yet reveal anything to us and left free room for our efforts' (Leibniz 1999, p. 2894). Adam Smith suggested that in our every-day mood, as active and healthy people, we tend to concentrate on what is near to us, with an increasingly decreasing attention for what is far from us in time and space (Smith 1759, p. 218–227), and since we would be distracted by such concern from contemplation of the court of divine justice – in a passage added in the second edition and then withdrawn in the third – he speculates that:

The great judge of the world has, for the wisest reasons, thought proper to interpose, between the weak eye of human reason, and the throne of his eternal justice, a degree of obscurity and darkness, which though it does not intirely cover that Great tribunal from the view of mankind, yet renders the impression of it faint and feeble in comparison of what might be expected from the grandeur and importance of so mighty an object.

(p. 128)

The result is that our moral sentiments are *less impartial* than they could be, were we not distracted by our tendency to concentrate on what is near in space and time, but also *more motivating* than they would be if we were contemplating all the time 'the great system of the universe' (p. 237), instead of taking care of the more humble department that was allotted to us, namely the care of our own happiness, of that of our family, friends and country. Kant, writing in 1788, suggested that, without the 'veil of ignorance', virtuous conduct would be as devoid of any moral value as the behaviour of marionettes, and in order to avoid this happening, the Governor of the world allows us only to conjecture his existence and his majesty, not to behold them or prove them clearly, and with all effort of our reason we have just a 'very obscure and doubtful view into the future':

and on the other hand, the moral law within us, without promising or threatening anything with certainty, demands of us disinterested respect; and only when this respect has become active and dominant, does it allow us by means of it a prospect into the world of the supersensible, and then only with weak glances.

(Kant 1788, p. 147)

For reasons not unlike those of Leibniz, Smith and Kant, that is, in order to leave some room for man's free choice and accordingly for human desert, Malthus also believes that a 'mist' hangs over metaphysical subjects and that 'doubts and difficulties' were left about 'the divine original' of the sacred writings (Malthus 1798, p. 134). The 'obscurity that involves all metaphysical subjects' (p. 133) is the effect of a providential dispensation, since it provides one more excitement arising from the thirst of knowledge aimed at invigorating the thinking faculty. Malthus adds that if 'a revelation from heaven [...] would dispel the mists that now hang over metaphysical subjects' (p. 134), namely about (i) the nature and structure of mind; (ii) affections and essences of all substances; (iii) 'the mode in which the supreme Being operates in the works of the creation, and the whole plan and scheme of the universe' (p. 134), this, 'instead of giving further vigour and activity to the human mind, would [...] tend to repress future exertion, and to damp the soaring wings of the intellect' (p. 134). Coming to the moral domain and to revealed religion, it is providential that 'the scriptural denunciations of eternal punishment' are not proved to be true by overwhelming evidence, since such a degree of certainty would mean that 'virtuous conduct would be no indication of virtuous disposition' (pp. 134–135), for 'how human beings could be formed to a detestation of moral evil and a love and admiration of God, and of moral excellence' (p. 135), and 'few would call an action really virtuous, which was performed simply and solely from the dread of a very great punishment, or the expectation of a very great reward' (p. 135). Wisdom is not fear of the Lord but 'love of the Lord, and the admiration of the moral good' (p. 135); a genuine Christian faith is 'an amiable and virtuous disposition, operated upon more by love than by pure unmixed fear' (p. 135).

In the aforementioned undated sermon on Deut 29, 29 he argues that, even though 'desire of knowledge is natural to the mind of man and was doubtless planted there by God for the most important purposes', yet there are 'secret' things, into which our eventual enquiry would be vain. The reason for such a conclusion is that we may observe that:

> our abilities of every kind are greatly circumscribed. The objects within our notice are, comparatively but few: and our apprehension of those few *imperfect*. Natural causes of every kind, and final causes for the most part, that is, the modes by which nature operates in every instance, and its destinations in most, are utterly unknown to us: and ignorant as we are of the *whole* designs of Providence, particular events in the course and conduct of things must necessarily confound and puzzle us.
>
> (Malthus 1997–2004, vol. 2, pp. 20–21)

And, with a phrase that recalls the concluding sentence in the first part of Kant's *Critique of Practical Reason*, according to which 'the inscrutable Wisdom thanks to which we exist is no less worth our veneration because of what it has kept unknown to us than because of what it has made known to us' (Kant 1788, p. 148). Malthus suggests that we should 'be thankful that our rational powers are as extensive as we find them to be, pursue those truths that are within our reach: and cultivate the knowledge which we are capable of attaining to' (Malthus 1997–2004, vol. 2, p. 21). And he concludes that the rule 'to be observed by us that we aim not at the knowledge of things which in their nature are beyond our comprehension' (p. 21).

Conscience

In what is perhaps his first sermon from 1789, while commenting on Job 27, 6 ('My righteousness I hold fast, and will not let it go: my heart shall not reproach me so long as I live'), Malthus defines conscience as 'a power or faculty, which furnishes us with such impressions of moral good and evil' or 'a sense of virtue and vice' (p. 8); more in detail, conscience firstly 'points out the distinctions of good and evil' (p. 9), and secondly 'exhibits to our view the law of our nature in plain and intelligible characters. It gives us a quick, immediate perception of our duty and of the rectitude or iniquity of our conduct; approves & prompts us to good actions, disapproves and dissuades us from others' (p. 9).

Both ideas are found in Butler, for whom conscience is the ultimate guide for action, since in many fields of life it is impossible to establish a system of exact rules, but we have to rely on our conscience's ability to single out the right decision. This ability is quite reliable, to the point that mistakes do not arise from erroneous conscience but instead from self-deceit, a perception of facts modified in such a way as to favour our interest which depends on some guilt on our side, as in the case of superstition and partiality (Butler 1726, pp. 103–109). Malthus also introduces the notion of 'moral pleasure', an idea he clearly had met in Butler. He remarks that 'nothing can be more pleasurable to the mind than to reflect that our conduct has been such as reason and conscience have approved' (Malthus 1997–2004, vol. 2, p. 10). The remark may be appropriate that these are classical ideas, rooted in the ancient Stoic and Middle-Platonic tradition, and then taken over by early Christian, Scholastic, and early Modern authors. As is well known, the idea of conscience is the main element in Kantian ethics, a system that was being elaborated in its final version precisely in the 1780s and the 1790s, and the issue of the existence of 'moral pleasure' is also discussed and given an affirmative answer in the *Critique of Practical Reason*, declaring that 'self-contentment' arises from freedom as well as from awareness thereof as a capacity to adhere to the moral law, which is 'the sole source' of 'unchanging contentment' (Kant 1788, p. 118).

The Golden Rule

The Golden Rule is mentioned in another sermon from 1789, on Matthew 7.12 ('Therefore all things whatsoever ye would that men should do to you, do ye even so to them'). Malthus – not unlike many other Christian authors – seems to believe that the rule had been first taught in the New Testament (Malthus 1997–2004, vol. 2, p. 7). In fact it is reported, besides other texts, in the book of *Tobit* (a text included in the Greek Bible commonly named *Septuaginta* as well as in the Biblical canon by the Catholic and Orthodox Churches), in the *Talmud*, where it is ascribed to Rabbi Hillel, the greatest rabbinical authority. But note that it is found also in texts from the Buddhist Canon as well as in Confucius's sayings. The Golden Rule had been rescued in modern times by Joseph Butler, according to whom it may be of help in many cases, particularly in those fields where exact rules cannot be formulated, but to this impossibility there is no general remedy apart from recourse to conscience (Butler 1726, p. 109). Curiously enough in those same years the rule had been treated with condescendence by Kant, writing that:

> the common saying *quod tibi non vis fieri* [...] could not play the role of a moral criterion since it does not exhibit the ground of duty and is at best a precept that may be derived (but with some exception) from the imperative of considering persons as ends.
>
> (Kant 1785, p. 430)

Actually, Kant's own normative ethics makes more room for Golden-Rule procedures than Butler's, but Kant was obsessed by the idea – which was indeed the main one he failed to spell out fully in print, with all the unavoidable misinterpretations that one could have expected – of judgement as the process through which the moral issue at stake in one context may be recognized, and was wary of mechanical applications of the popular rule that would simply understand will in terms of desires, not in terms of rational will.

The function of the Golden Rule is, according to Malthus, making self-love compatible with morality. The rule in fact submits 'inclinations and desires' to 'reason and equity' by checking 'that partiality which passions bring into our way of looking at things' (Malthus 1997–2004, vol. 2, p. 4). The reader should note here the commonplace opposition between two elements, reason and passion, and the identification of the former with 'equity', the innate principle of rational moral judgement that was traditionally assumed to be the basis of natural law. Malthus adds that the rule is recommended also by its 'utility', with an argument apparently taken from Butler that it is simple and easy to apply in dubious cases, that is, helps in avoiding self-deception, or the distortion in the way of seeing situations to which our conscience may be liable. Its adoption is recommended by Malthus also on the grounds of a consequentialist argument, similar to those of twentieth-century 'indirect utilitarianism'. In fact, we have a reason to adopt the rule 'if we desire to add to the common happiness of mankind in this world & to secure our own in the next' (p. 8), and if it were generally adopted:

> men by acting up to their respective obligations, & by maintaining a commerce of mutual good offices, would concur in fixing, & establishing the general happiness upon the most solid basis, that of publick virtue.
>
> (p. 7)

The test of utility

This point has been the main source of misunderstanding. In fact Malthus here apparently speaks the same language as Bentham and does quote Paley approvingly, which would be a proof of Malthus's utilitarianism, if only Paley himself could be correctly labelled as utilitarian. The point is the role utility plays in deciding the right or wrong character of a line of conduct. Paley had boldly declared that:

> actions are to be estimated by their tendency to promote happiness. Whatever is expedient is right. It is the utility of any moral rule alone which constitutes the obligation of it.
>
> (Paley 1785, p. 42)

And yet, the bold formulation notwithstanding, Paley's normative ethics is something incompatible with Bentham's utilitarianism. Bentham was aware of that, more than Bonar, Stephen and Hollander, and he disregarded Paley's account of morality as irrelevant or useless in so far as – he believed – it did not provide any solution different from those of other kinds of theological morality. John Stuart Mill, too, refused to defend Paley against William Whewell for the alleged reason that he had nothing different to say from Whewell and other 'priests'. I suggest that Bentham and the younger Mill, despite their sectarian attitude, were actually right, and Paley's *normative ethics* was after all – Paley's own meta-ethical hedonism and consequentialism notwithstanding – a familiar mixture of Christian precepts and ancient moral philosophy as summarized by Cicero, basically the same as in Joseph Butler or Thomas Reid, not Bentham's 'new morality'. Paley, starting with a consequentialist and hedonist starting point, tries to justify general laws, and on their bases justifies natural laws and innate rights, precisely those notions that were for Bentham the quintessence of obscurantism. The North-West passage leading from consequences and quantities of pleasure to natural laws and rights is for Paley God's will, on the basis of the premises of his benevolence and omniscience. As a result, 'expediency' is merely the test of what may count as a law imposed by God, not itself a criterion by which we may judge what is the right course of action. I have suggested that Paley's consequentialism and Bentham's utilitarianism may be seen as not too different 'extensionally', in so far as they, to some extent, approve or condemn the same acts, but also that when considered 'intensionally', that is, listing the characteristics an act needs to possess in order to qualify as right, Paley's description is quite different from Bentham's, that is, not that of a felicific act, but that of an act conforming to a law prescribed by God.

In 1798 Malthus seems to admit of a consequentialist view of morality merely for the sake of the argument, since he seems to be arguing from his opponent's premises. He writes:

> Morality according to Mr. Godwin, is a calculation of consequences, or, as Archdeacon Paley very justly expresses it, the will of God, as collected from general expediency.
>
> (Malthus 1798, p. 77)

In 1803 this argumentative move is made more complex. In fact he writes:

> And yet, what is morality, individual or political, according to Mr. Godwin's own definition of it, but a calculation of consequences? Is the physician the patron of pain, who advises his patient to bear a present evil, rather than betake himself a remedy which, though it might give momentary relief, would afterwards greatly aggravate all the symptoms? Is the moralist to be called an enemy to pleasure, because he recommends to a young man just entering into life, not to ruin

his health and patrimony in a few years, by an excess of present gratifications?

(Malthus 1803, vol. 1, p. 328)

Such elaboration on the previous rather simple formulation of the argument is perfectly at home in the context of a modified overall argument, where morality plays a more decisive function. In fact morality wins more importance, indeed it becomes the ground on which the question of theodicy is answered, in connection with the more detailed distinctions between different kinds of *actually existent* preventive checks, that is, a) misery, b) vice, c) checks of a mixed nature, or vice that brings about misery, and with the introduction of an *ideal* preventive check, that is, moral restraint. It is true that Malthus gives no great weight to moral restraint in terms of explanation of past phenomena (and here Hollander is right), but it is also true that moral restraint becomes the pivot around which his whole modified system now turns (and in this respect Hollander is wrong) in so far as (i) it allows for a satisfying theodicy and (ii) it allows for drawing a programme for a more happy, virtuous and less unequal society.

Let us see the contents of Malthus's normative ethics of 1803. The main normative claim in the second *Essay* is the following:

our principal duty is:

a   a strict attention to the consequences carried by the satisfaction of our passions;
b   the regulation of our conduct conformably to such consequences.

This formulation implies a central role for prudence, to be discussed in a following paragraph, and it also implies a central role for consequences in moral argument, indeed the role of standard of virtue. A critic may be tempted to say that virtue as such disappears in Malthus's account, since it is reduced to conduct such as would minimize undesirable consequences. It is true that this amounts to prudence, one of the traditional 'cardinal virtues', but the sore point is that it is what in eighteenth-century jargon was labelled 'inferior prudence', or instrumentally rational care for one's own interest, not superior prudence or *phronesis*, the intellectual excellence in matters of wise deliberation. This is an objection that Malthus did consider. After discussing the various kinds of checks to population, he defends his choice to stick to the couple 'misery and vice', avoiding reduction of the latter to the former even though misery is the general consequence of vice, and it is 'the precise reason why an action is termed vicious', namely avoiding introduction of 'confusion in our language and ideas' (Malthus 1803, vol. 1, p. 19 fn. 6).

We should not dismiss this as bourgeois hypocrisy or clerical conformism, as any supporter of the view of Malthus as a 'real Utilitarian' would be tempted to do. Instead, the reader should notice that two distinct issues are at stake here. The first is the issue of order in language and ideas, which is not a matter of external cosmetics, since the view of language Malthus had learned was the anti-conventionalist semi-Platonic view worked out by James Harris (while Ricardo had learned from Thomas Belsham the conventionalist view of language formulated by Horne Tooke). According to this view language arises out of convention combined with nature, and words are not proper nouns, but symbols of 'something within' (Harris 1751, p. 341) or of 'general ideas' (p. 343) since 'in nature, as well as in art there are intelligible forms, which to the sensible are subsequent' (p. 379). For this reason 'definitions are not arbitrary' since words refer to our own ideas as well as 'to the ideas in the minds of other men' and we have to investigate the meaning of a word 'according to the common use of speech' (Duncan 1748, p. 11), while ideas in some way regard 'things themselves', since 'whatever is true in Idea, is unavoidably so also in the Reality of things, where things exist answerable to these ideas' (p. 340). Accordingly, in communicating our notions we should 'use every word as near as possible in the same Sense in which Mankind commonly uses it' and 'the received Definitions of Names should be changed as little as possible' (Watts 1726, p. 97).

The second is the issue of the goodness of passions and of their connection with the agent's happiness. How to reconcile the agent's partial and temporary happiness with his long-term happiness as well as with humankind's general happiness were central issues in eighteenth-century Anglican ethics. Malthus starts with shared assumptions, namely that passions are good in themselves, the rationale for the distinction between right and wrong actions lies in its consequences, and such consequences regard happiness, albeit not individual short-term happiness, but collective happiness in the long run. One further problem was whether to call the possibility of an afterlife into question. Malthus's concern is avowedly:

> To distinguish *that class of actions, the general tendency of which is to produce misery*, but which, in their immediate or individual effects, may produce perhaps exactly the contrary. The gratification of all our passions in its immediate effect is happiness, not misery; and in individual instances even the remote consequences (at least *in this life*) come under the same denomination [...]. These individual actions therefore cannot come under the head of misery. But they are still evidently vicious, because an action is so denominated, the general tendency of which is to produced misery, whatever may be its individual effects; and no person can doubt the general tendency of an illicit intercourse between the sexes to injure the happiness of society.
>
> (Malthus 1803, vol. 1, p. 19; italics added)

It would not be too unfair to conclude that Malthus is claiming that the test of utility is not a *criterion* for *deciding* what is right and wrong, but instead a *clue* for *detecting* the will of God, who in turn has established in his full right (in so far as he is benevolent and omniscient) what is right and wrong, or that it is a test for establishing whether a maxim is a law of nature.

For example, to our limited knowledge an irregular union between a man and a woman might be productive of more happiness than misery and to rule it out by recourse to a preference for general rules (as a rule-utilitarian might do) would be attacked by an act-utilitarian as being a cruel and dogmatic example of rule-idolatry. Malthus's argument is on balance more strong, facing such attacks, than rule-utilitarianism in general is, since he argues for rule-consequentialism on the basis of the assumption of the existence of a God who has promulgated (non-arbitrary) laws for his own creation and has communicated such laws through the order of nature.

In Chapter 5 I will discuss how Malthus reacted to attacks from his Evangelical fellow-travellers by stressing the voluntarist element in his own theoretical building, adding more words, stressing and emphasizing, but basically building on foundations that had always been there. The main point had always been that motives are provided by passions, including hunger, sexual instinct, and so on, including even benevolence itself, but not by self-love alone, for Malthus had clearly in mind Butler's *reductio ad absurdum* of the claim that self-love is a universal motive, a refutation that Bentham apparently was ignorant of (and which he would have probably ignored had he been familiar with it), which marks a decisive difference between Malthus and Bentham. Utility is a test or a criterion, and 'all the moral codes which have inculcated the subjection of the passions to reason have been [...] really built upon this foundation, whether the promulgators of them were aware of it or not' (p. 158). Utility may be detected even at the roots of New Testament revealed morality, since the prescription found in Luke's Gospel to rescue innocent victims of aggression is to conform to the 'touchstone of utility' (p. 162) while it does not contradict the prescription found in the Epistle to Thessalonians to earn one's living by work (p. 158). Such a touchstone is the standard by which we should select our impulses and follow them only in so far as their consequences are apparently good, which here means: conducive to the greatest sum of happiness in the world. Malthus writes:

> As animals, or till we know their consequences, our only business is to follow these dictates of nature; but as reasonable beings, we are under the strongest obligations to attend to their consequences; and if they be evil to ourselves or others, we may justly consider it as an indication, that such a mode of indulging these passions is not suited to our state or conformable to the will of God. As moral agents, therefore, it is clearly our duty to restrain their indulgence in these particular directions; and by thus carefully examining the consequences of our natural passions, and frequently bringing them to the test of utility, gradually to acquire a habit of gratifying them only in that way, which, being unattended with evil, will clearly add to the sum of human happiness and fulfil the apparent purpose of the Creator.

Though utility, therefore, can never be the immediate excitement to the gratification of any passion, it is the test by which alone we can know, independently of the revealed will of God, whether it ought or ought not to be indulged.

(p. 157)

The function of general rules

General rules play a main role in Malthus's ethics no less than utility does, but this does not imply that Malthus's ethics is some version of rule-utilitarianism. This would be anachronistic for reasons that by now should be clear enough to the reader, namely that Malthus's ethics did make room for utility but it was not, for important aspects, a utilitarian ethic. For example, for any real utilitarian, including rule-utilitarians, Malthus's treatment of the virtue of marital faithfulness – as I will illustrate in detail in what follows – would carry serious problems. His request that a potential adulterer should sacrifice what would be, in the individual case, harmless prospective happiness in the name of regard to general happiness in the long run would sound as rule-idolatry. In fact Malthus, far from being an inconsistent utilitarian, is simply no utilitarian at all, and his request for an absolute respect of rules may sound strange to the utilitarian while arguing on his own premises, but would sound convincing to the utilitarian who would be prepared to argue, for the sake of the argument, on Malthus's premises.

Let us see now in some detail why Malthus believes he has to justify a general rule before formulating any normative judgement. Paley had ruled out the possibility of any act-consequentialism by a quasi-transcendental argument, that is, by the argument that 'general rules are necessary to every moral government [because otherwise] the subjects [...] would no longer know, either what to expect or how to act' (Paley 1785, p. 65), and that the 'want of this distinction between particular and general consequences [...] is the cause of that perplexity we meet with in ancient moralists' (p. 65). He adds that the distinction between *utile* and *honestum* was introduced by these moralists as a counterbalance to the most absurd consequences that could derive from their own premises, but it was ineffective for want of the idea of general rules (p. 65).

Malthus believes that the *laws of nature* 'in all cases are *similar and uniform*' (Malthus 1803, vol. 2, p. 88) and that in several cases partial evil may result from the interaction between two or more different universal laws. This gives birth to the problem of theodicy, in the generalized form of 1798 or in the qualified form of 1803, a problem to be discussed in the following chapters. The problem to be discussed here is a more limited one, or better one part of the general problem of theodicy, namely the reasons for the origin of evil, not from interaction between more general laws, but from man's infringement of one or more laws of nature. Malthus's answer is that:

natural and moral evil seem to be the instrument employed by the Deity in admonishing us to avoid any mode of conduct which is not suited to our being, and will consequently injure our happiness.

(p. 88)

Misery, in the form of diseases, famines and other calamities, results from having followed some of our impulses 'too far', so that, even though we have followed one law of nature as manifested by one particular impulse, yet we have come 'to trench upon some other law which equally demands attention' (p. 88). It could hardly be said that such 'penalty of our disobedience' is for the greater good of the agent, but the existence of evil in this case is accounted for by its function as an 'admonition' in so far as 'our sufferings operate as a warning to others' (p. 88). For example:

as dirt, squalid poverty, and indolence are in the highest degree unfavourable to happiness and virtue, it seems a *benevolent* dispensation that such a state should, by the laws of nature, produce disease and death, as a beacon to others.

(p. 89; italics added)

Yet, an embarrassing problem arises here for Malthus as it had arisen for previous proponents of theological voluntarism, namely, how can God enact laws for his own creatures on the basis of their general tendency to increase the 'happiness of society', irrespective of the fact that in individual cases these laws may cause suffering to the parties involved? Dirt and squalid poverty caused by imprudent behaviour are bad in themselves for the agent, but disease and death are even worse. How can we call a God benevolent who adds more evil to some of his own creatures in order to spare some amount of evil to other such creatures? And things are even worse when we shift from the case of the improvident poor to that of the addicted to promiscuous intercourse. Here the problem is why should God condemn an irregular connection between a man and a woman when such a connection adds to the happiness of both parties involved while not damaging anybody else? In Diderot's words, why should the Deity mingle with the rubbing of two mucosa membranes, provided that the parts involved would be careful enough as to take care of the consequences of such rubbing? I would say that the issue was never directly faced by Malthus, and even less was it faced by any of his opponents, none of whom liked to be suspected of attacking the sanctity of marriage. On the contrary, Bentham, James Mill and their most faithful followers, who would not have minded undermining the sanctity of marriage, were not Malthus's opponents but his most dogmatic followers as far as the principle of population is concerned (no matter how deep their disagreement on other accounts may have been), and accordingly not particularly keen on detecting missing links in his argument.

To sum up: Malthus's answer to the question about the reasons for the existence of evil in the form of punishment for transgressing some general laws is based on an idea that is now currently designated, following Alan Donagan's felicitous expression, the 'principle of Chaipha', that is, the principle 'that it was expedient that one man should die for the people'. This seems to bring us back to at least half of the problem of theodicy, namely, how can a God still be named benevolent who establishes arbitrary precepts and condemns those who fail to comply with them? The fact that such precepts for Malthus are not completely arbitrary – since they have been promulgated with a view to the greater happiness of the whole – is scant consolation for the individual involved, who still has to suffer in order that others may enjoy.

Moral psychology

Mind, inertia and the need for stimuli

For Malthus the need to overcome sluggishness seems to be the basic trait of human nature. This has something to do with the eighteenth-century British discussion of the mind–body relationship. A current of English thinkers, which included Joseph Priestley, David Hartley and Richard Price, starting with criticism of Descartes' and Locke's theories of the mind, had worked out a kind of philosophical materialism supposedly compatible with Christian doctrines. Abraham Tucker, as I have illustrated before, had gone a couple of steps forward, arguing that the mind as such is completely devoid of determinations and incapable of awareness and memory, that each individual mind wins its own individuality by the fact of being connected with the body, and that all our earthly existence is a condition where challenges have to be faced in such a way as to awake matter out of its sluggishness and foster development of mind. I have already suggested that this idea is what comes closer to a justification of Malthus's claim of consistence between his previous idea of generation of birth of mind from matter and that of earthly existence as a state of trial.

Perhaps, either following Tucker's suggestions or elaborating on opinions shared by Cambridge divines – I have mentioned Watson's considerations on mind and body – Malthus, also, in the first *Essay* declares that the distinction between mind and matter is 'a question merely of words' (Malthus 1798, p. 127). His speculations in the last two chapters on salvation and damnation also make sense only against the background of such speculations on the relationship between mind and body. According to such speculations, the world is the theatre of an ongoing process of creation of mind out of matter due to the constant stimulus of need, which compels human beings to action, and only those minds which will go successfully through such process will reach a state of immortality while the results of unsuccessful attempts will naturally revert to matter whence they came. These are the rather heterodox views that young Malthus advanced in 1798 and gradually withdrew, suppressing the two final chapters in the 1803 essay but still claiming in a footnote that their contents were useless within the framework of the *Essay* albeit still valuable per se. He took one more step back in 1817 when he withdrew the latter claim and declared instead that he found Sumner's elaboration quite satisfactory. Sumner's idea was that the principle of population may carry out a precise function within a view of our life as 'a state of probation' (Malthus 1803, vol. 2, p. 250). Malthus also adds that 'he had always thought' such a view to be right, which is not so easy to make compatible with the contents of the last two chapters of the 1798 essay, unless – following a suggestion that may be found in Tucker and has been discussed above – one should read 'probation' as another name for 'creation of mind out of matter'. Then, in the second *Essay* he still mentions the need for stimuli to make us overcome our 'natural indolence' (p. 93), but this too calls for charitable reading, since here Malthus conveys, cloaked under similar terminology, a doctrine that seems to be a different one, namely not *creation* of mind but just *developing habits* of activity.

The main point of Malthus's first theodicy indeed is preserved in the modified theodicy-cum-ethics of the second *Essay*. This is the idea that evil does not originate from Augustinian *natura lapsa,* i.e. nature corrupted by Original Sin, or from 'any original depravity of man' (Malthus 1798, p. 75), but from interaction between several general laws, and that 'Evil exists in the world, not to create despair, but activity' (p. 137). In the second *Essay*, as I discuss in detail in Chapter 5, this is mirrored by the central role granted to prudence, since that part of evil which arises out of the principle of population may now be checked if individual agents exercise the art of foreknowledge and wise choice.

In Chapter IV of the *Principles*, 'Of profits as affected by the causes practically in operation', he mentions 'activity' as a moral precondition for civilization and the progress of wealth. He writes that 'the society proceeds from the indolence of the savage to the activity of the civilized state' (Malthus 1820, vol. 1, p. 229) and that 'indolence or love of ease' is 'so general and important a principle in human nature' (p. 257) as to make the existence of 'effective demand' for commodities far from granted; Ricardo on the contrary was mistaken in taking for granted 'that luxuries are always preferred to indolence' (p. 258). This point is also mentioned more than once in the correspondence with Ricardo, and is among the reasons for Malthus's notorious claim that political economy is more similar to 'the science of morals and politics than to that of mathematics' (p. 2), since in political economy we need 'to refer not only to the physical qualities of the materials which are acted upon, but also to the moral as well as to the physical qualities of the agents' (p. 381; cf. Cremaschi 2010, pp. 46–48).

On this point Malthus also seems to disagree, at least partially, with Paley's argument in favour of inertia as a principle which is required to keep order in the moral as well as in the physical world. Paley had written in his *Natural Theology* that it is not true that idleness or aversion to labour is – as Hume for example had claimed – simply bad, for it is impossible to distinguish once and for ever between idleness and 'love of ease' and the latter is beneficial as a remedy to evils deriving from incessant and misdirected activity, adding that if it were possible:

> in every instance, to give a right determination to industry, we could never have too much of it. But this is not possible, if men are to be free. And without this, nothing would be so dangerous, as an incessant, universal, indefatigable activity. In the civil world as well as in the material, it is the *vis inertiae* which keeps things in their order.
>
> (Paley 1802, p. 548)

What Malthus shares with Paley's argument is the idea that the leisure of one part of society, made possible by the laws of nature in the form of rents, contributes to increasing the effective demand for goods as well as to establishing the preconditions for civil liberties, even though he is careful in sticking – unlike Paley – to a sharp distinction between leisure and idleness, which is always undesirable. The remark is in order that the 'macroeconomics' of Paley's Principles, presented in Part IV, Chapter 11, around the idea that consumption is logically even though not chronologically prior to production and that standards of living are culturally determined (Paley 1785, pp. 419–456), is one main source for Malthus's *Principles of Political Economy* where effective demand is one main factor (Malthus 1820, vol. 1, pp. 348, 377–381, 389–392). This idea is what makes for a difference between *The Essay*, where supply of labour seems to be the overarching factor in any economy, and the *Principles*, where demand rules (Waterman 1996).

An implication of this change is that in the *Principles* the working classes are also expected to enjoy some minimal amount of luxury, and this is good for the economy as a whole. Malthus believes by now that unproductive consumption by the working classes may be both possible and useful, and that a taste for luxury commodities such as tea and sugar is an alternative to indolence for the working classes, and developing such tastes is necessary for a balanced growth. For example, in an often-quoted letter of 26 Jan 1817 to Ricardo, he writes:

> You seem to think that the wants and tastes of mankind are always ready for the supply; while I am most decidedly of opinion that few things are more difficult, than to inspire new tastes and wants, particularly out of old materials; that one of the great elements of demand is the value that people set upon commodities, and that the more completely the supply is suited to the demand the higher will this value be, and the more day's labour will it exchange for, or give the power of commanding.
>
> (Malthus 1817, p. 122)

In the *Principles* he also enquires into the causes of different effects that a growth in national wealth may produce – either a growing population and more poverty or almost constant population and rising standards of living –

and among such causes he introduces 'the different habits existing among the people of different countries, and at different times', arguing that the causes of such different results may be traced to:

> all the circumstances which contribute to depress the lower classes of the people, which make them unable or unwilling to reason from the past to the future, and ready to acquiesce, for the sake of present gratification, in a very low standard of comfort and respectability; and those which produce the second result, to all the circumstances which tend to elevate the character of the lower classes of society.
>
> (Malthus 1820, vol. 1, p. 251)

Passions and self-love

Malthus had absorbed what had been the commonplace theory of human nature in British seventeenth- and eighteenth-century thought, a theory based on a dichotomy between passion and reason. It was a dualistic anthropology, more Stoic than Aristotelian or Platonic, to a wide extent shared by all authors, the respectable ones such as Butler as well as the execrated Hobbes and Hume, who just went a little further than others in stressing the weight of the dichotomy by claiming that reason is only instrumental, unable to contrast the passions as well as to provide any reason for actions that be independent of some pre-existing passion. This view of human nature still seems to be reflected in one of Malthus's first sermons from 1798, where he mentions two distinct faculties, namely: first, 'a power in common with the inferior creation of complying with the solicitations of passions or appetite' (Malthus 1997–2004, vol. 2, p. 9); second, 'a superior faculty or power, not possessed by other creatures, that of suppressing the inclinations of a hurtful appetite, of appeasing the impulses of a wrong passion, and of forming and regulating his whole conduct by certain laws' (p. 9).

The qualification of reason as merely instrumental also seems to be shared by Malthus at this stage, in so far as reason is described as 'that faculty which enables us to calculate consequences, is the proper corrective and guide in the pursuit of every enjoyment' (Malthus 1798, p. 77), but is not up to the task of turning an immoral man into a moral one. That one should not brutally indulge in the pursuit of one's own immediate pleasure 'is a truth absolutely incapable of demonstration' (p. 92), and in this field 'reasoning and argument are not instruments from which success can be expected' (p. 93); 'the superiority of the pleasures of intellect to those of sense' is a truth 'of a nature that perhaps never can be adequately communicated from one man to another' (p. 92) and 'is not an affair of reasoning, but of experience' (p. 93). It is true that 'every voluntary act is preceded by a decision of the mind', but 'the corporeal propensities of man do act very powerfully, as disturbing forces, in these decisions' (p. 90).

In order to make full sense of these claims, it is worth recalling something of the previous philosophical and theological discussion. The passions were, for neo-Augustinians such as the Calvinists and the Jansenists, the mark of human depravity and the consequence of original sin. Their main claim was that self-love is vicious without qualification, and indeed is the essence of vice in itself. As a reaction the Cambridge Platonists, Shaftesbury and Hutcheson had tried to rescue the passions by placing them at the bottom of a ladder whose top stair was love of God, and Nicholas Malebranche in France and the empiricists Cumberland, Gay, Hartley, Brown and Paley in England had argued that, even conceding that human nature were ruled by self-love, this would not imply that it is corrupt, since self-love is not unavoidably vicious and may be made compatible with moral righteousness since enlightened self-love rationally prefers a bigger good to a lesser one, and thus prompts the practice of virtue because it is on average productive of bigger advantages in the long run in life, and besides is a way of complying with the will of God, who alone is able to make us eternally happy in another life. In other words, this line of argument as fully developed by Gay and Brown was meant to prove that, even though the sceptics and materialists were right, self-love provided reasons not for immoralism but instead for adhering to Christian morality. The well-known passages about self-love in Adam Smith, traditionally misquoted as proofs of his wholehearted or qualified adhesion to Mandevillian immoralist claims, are on the contrary proofs of a semi-sceptical and semi-Stoical rescue of self-love within the boundaries of prudence in so far as it may be shown to be beneficial via the unintended results mechanism and to be compatible with justice and beneficence via the sympathetic mechanisms.

Malthus's argument for making self-love compatible with morality echoes Butler, Gay and Brown. He writes that self-love is 'the general occasion of injustice, fraud, oppression & iniquity' (Malthus 1997–2004, vol. 2, p. 4). Note that Pullen's comment (p. 4 fn.) on this point is particularly off track in so far as this is not meant to be disparagement of the principle of self-love but, on the contrary, endorsement of Butler's claim that self-love *may* be made compatible with virtue. In fact, it may be made the source of motivation for acting morally through the Golden Rule, through which it is made 'the means of pointing out & prompting us to acts of honesty, humanity & justice' (p. 4). Self-love, taking man as he is, cannot – *pace* Godwin – be eradicated since the general good is not practicable as a motive for action (Malthus 1798, p. 104), but it may be made compatible with a decent human community by morality and be made useful to human society simply through the unintended results mechanisms by which human beings cooperate in producing public good even without any awareness or intention of doing so. The passions in general are unavoidable and may also prove useful in allowing for the survival and improvement of mankind; they 'are so necessary to our being' that 'they could not be generally weakened or diminished, without injuring our happiness' (Malthus 1803, vol. 2, p. 89), or 'few or none of them would admit of being greatly diminished without narrowing the sources of good more powerfully than the sources of evil [...]. They are in fact the materials of all pleasures, as well as of all our pains; of all our happiness, as well as of all our misery; of all our virtues, as well as of all our vices' (p. 92). And Malthus approvingly quotes (pp. 92–93) Paley's claim that passions:

> are either necessary to human welfare, or capable of being made, and in a great majority of instances in fact made, conducive to its happiness. These passions are strong and general [...] From [...] excess and misdirection the vices of mankind (the cause of no doubt much misery) appear to spring.
>
> (Paley 1802, p. 547)

Even though 'obedience to the impulses of our natural passions would lead us into the wildest and most fatal extravagancies' (Malthus 1803, vol. 2, p. 89), Malthus adds in a footnote that will become the subject of controversy, that the 'gratification of all our passions in its immediate effect is happiness, not misery' (vol. 1, p. 19 fn. 6). The modified version of this footnote in the 1817 edition will be examined in detail in Chapter 6.

The problem the Creator of nature had to solve was how to admonish us for offending against his laws when we have unreasonably indulged our passions, but without diminishing their force, since weaker passions would be less effective in serving nature's design. He apparently solved the problem by establishing an unavoidable punishment meted out as a consequence by the general laws according to which the universe functions to discourage any excess in gratifying the passions. It follows that our:

> *virtue* therefore, as reasonable beings, evidently consists in educing, from the general materials which the Creator has placed under our guidance, the greatest sum of human happiness; and as ['all our', added in 1806] natural impulses are abstractedly considered good, and only to be distinguished by their consequences, a strict attention to these consequences, and the regulation of our conduct conformably to them, must be considered as our principal duty.
>
> (vol. 2, p. 93)

Our first passion is hunger, our second sexual drive. In the first case – that of the 'desire of food, and of those things, such as clothing, houses, & c. which are immediately necessary to relieve us from pains of hunger and cold', or, in other words, 'self-love' – desire carries out the function of putting in motion 'the greatest part of that activity from which spring the multiplied *improvements* and advantages of civilized life' (p. 89–90), which either make up the bulk of human happiness or at least are indispensable to it; thus this basic passion both yields 'inestimable benefits' and risks causing 'evils' (p. 90). Self-love – Malthus adds in the 1896 Appendix – has been made by the Great Author of nature much stronger a passion than benevolence because this was indispensable to the preservation of the human race, and this goal was so important that it could not be left to 'the cold and speculative consideration of general consequences' (p. 213).

Thus, for example, society felt in need of defending property, since, if people were not prevented from satisfying hunger with loaves of bread belonging to others, 'the number of loaves would universally diminish. This experience is the foundation of the laws relating to property' (p. 90), that is, the foundation of a 'distinction of virtue and vice' in matters that would be otherwise morally indifferent (p. 90). Violations of property could have been more easily avoided if the pleasure arising from satisfaction of this desire were 'diminished in vividness', but 'this advantage would be greatly overbalanced by the narrowness of the sources of enjoyments. The diminution in the quantity of all that contributes to human gratification would be much greater in proportion than the diminution in thefts; and the loss of general happiness on the one side would be beyond comparison greater than the gain to happiness on the other' (p. 90). From such a need for an artificial regulation of a passion that would be in itself innocent, arose one of the two basic 'artificial virtues' (the term is Hume's), that is, respect for property, the other being respect for the conjugal tie. It may be noted that the emergence of this virtue was one example of the spontaneous emergence of order as reconstructed by Adam Smith in both his works. Malthus was familiar with Smith from a rather early date and the *Theory of Moral Sentiments* may have been a source for this idea.

The second passion is the 'passion between the sexes'. This is, after desire for food, the 'most powerful and general' of our desires. Granted that 'virtuous love, exalted by friendship', is such a 'mixture of sensual and intellectual enjoyment' as to be the one most likely to suit human nature, to the point of overcoming 'great intellectual pleasures' (p. 90–91); an identical point was made in 1798 (p. 76), it is 'one of the principal ingredients of human happiness' (Malthus 1803, vol. 2, p. 92). It has a tendency to soften the human character and to encourage the emotions of benevolence and pity (p. 91). And although its irregular gratification is a source of 'not inconsiderable' evil, we cannot wish to avoid such evil through 'the extinction or diminution of the passion which causes it; a change which would probably convert human life either into a cold and cheerless blank, or a scene of savage and merciless ferocity' (p. 92).

To sum up, body and mind act upon each other, and the distinction between the bodily and the mental is, to a certain point, a matter of terminology, but basically, even though we may always assume that man is responsible for his deeds, and reason may to some degree control the drive of bodily cravings and the passions, the body influences the mind more strongly than the mind influences the body, and the passions are the basic motor of our activity and the basis of our happiness. Unlike Godwin, Malthus believes that man is not just a rational being (Malthus 1798, p. 90), for 'both theory and experience' contribute in proving that:

> even in voluntary acts, the corporeal propensities of man act very powerfully, as disturbing forces, in these decisions [...] A truth may be brought home to his conviction as a rational being, though he may determine to act contrary to it, as a compound being. The cravings of

hunger, the love of liquor, the desire of possessing a beautiful woman, will urge men to actions, of the fatal consequences of which, to the general interests of society, they are perfectly well convinced.

(p. 90)

Winch aptly comments:

Malthus treated all universal passions, impulses and wants, when considered abstractly or generally, as being natural or good; the satisfaction of such passions brought happiness. The desire to satisfy our material wants was also the impulse which underlay the process of civilization itself, and the passion between the sexes was the foundation on which the pleasures associated with conjugal affection, a prime softening agency, was based. The danger to happiness lay not in these impulses but in the 'fatal extravagancies' to which they gave rise. Since it was impossible to weaken the force of our basic impulses without injuring our happiness, regulation and redirection, rather than Calvinistic suppression or diminution, was the correct response.

(Winch 1987, p. 39)

And yet we may wonder whether, among other things, even Malthus's view of the mind–body relationship was changing two decades after, following his personal change of spiritual attitude and changes in the climate of ideas, with some concessions being made to both reason and sentiment, both contrasted with 'passion'. On balance, the decisive role of reason, and of prudence as an expression of the latter, is there all the time but sentiments win a role unknown in 1798 and 1803. In the *Principles*, for example, he mentions the dictates of 'nature and reason' (Malthus 1820, vol. 1, p. 88), suggesting that, 'however powerful may be the impulses of passion, they are generally in some degree modified by reason' (p. 106). Yet, in a sermon from 1827, he makes important concessions to Evangelical views about the role of sentiment in religion. He writes:

Taking man as he is, and it is of no use to take him as he is not, we find from experience that the cool decisions of reason have *a much more feeble* effect upon human conduct than the impulses of feeling. Nothing great and arduous in action, nothing amiable and delightful in conduct, was ever accomplished without the aid of the passions and affections.

And this is eminently true in regard to religion. It must necessarily be more a matter of feeling than of mere reasoning.

(Malthus 1997–2004, vol. 2, p. 16)

Moral sentiments

Notwithstanding the basic dichotomy between passion and reason, from the very beginning Malthus follows Butler, Shaftesbury, Hutcheson and Adam

Smith in making room for moral sentiments. Albeit not breaking through – at least in principle – the reason–passion dichotomy, these still bring in some kind of third factor. Malthus mentions sentiments that are violated by such barbarous practices as that of espousing children: 'benevolence and pity' (Malthus 1803, vol. 2, p. 91), 'the first feelings of nature' (Malthus 1798, p. 19), and 'the most natural principles of the human heart' (p. 25). He also mentions attachment to our 'families, connections, friends, and native land' (p. 13), 'love of independence, a sentiment that surely none would wish to be erased from the breast of man' (p. 27), the 'spirit of independence' (p. 33) that still remains among the English peasantry or the 'spirit of liberty and independence' (Malthus 1820, vol. 1, p. 81) which reigns among the Kyrgizians.

Even though Malthus may have found a few similar ideas in Shaftesbury and Butler, for the reasons I have discussed above Adam Smith may have been an important source also concerning this point, while the sketchy functionalist account of the origins and modification of moral sentiments which may be found in the *Essay* may also be a part of the Smithian legacy. A few remarks of this kind concern chastity in female and male individuals and others refer to the social stigma that accompanies poverty, to be discussed in some detail in what follows. They are both cases of tension between requirements of equal and impartial consideration and those of society's self-preservation, precisely like those discussed by Adam Smith when considering the unavoidable influence of 'fortune' in our consideration of merit and demerit and the final cause of this 'irregularity of sentiments' (Smith 1759, pp. 92–108).

The proto-functionalist account of moral sentiments here referred to is strictly related with the unintended-consequences principle that is in turn the foundation stone of the Scottish tradition in social theory, as developed by David Hume, Adam Smith, Adam Ferguson and John Millar. For Adam Smith, even the emergence and establishment of moral sentiments was not the effect of any human design, but instead the combined result of spontaneous tendencies of human imagination, adequacy of some of these reactions in terms of survival of human societies, and the tendency to forget the origins of customs and institutions once they are established. Yet he also believes that certain laws and customs are less inadequate than others, given the challenges faced by human societies and the spontaneous reactions of human nature as it faces changing conditions. The lesson Malthus may have learned from him is that subjective intentions are no guarantee concerning actual consequences of given courses of action, and their tendency to produce some kind of consequences may only be ascertained through experience. In many cases, every attempt 'however benevolent its apparent intention, will always defeat its own purpose' (Malthus 1798, p. 33). Malthus's paramount instance of this phenomenon is provided by the Poor Laws which, he claims, have contributed to lowering the real price of labour and generating a lack of prudence and loss of dignity.

Bibliography

Bruni, F. (1987) 'La nozione di lavoro in Adam Smith'. *Rivista di filosofia neoscolastica* 79(1), pp. 67–95.

Burke, E. (1800) *Thoughts and Details on Scarcity*. London: Rivington.

Butler, J. (1726 [2006]) Fifteen Sermons Preached at the Rolls Chapel. In *The Works of Bishop Butler*. Ed. by White, D.E. Rochester, NY: University of Rochester Press.

Chalmers, Th. (1808) *An Enquiry into the Nature and Stability of National Resources*. Edinburgh: Moir.

Cremaschi, S. (2006) The Mill-Whewell Controversy on Ethics and its Bequest to Analytic Philosophy. In *Rationality in Belief and Action*. Ed. by Baccarini, E. and Prijić Samaržja, S. Rijeka: University of Rijeka, Faculty of Arts and Sciences and Croatian Society for Analytic Philosophy.

Cremaschi, S. (2010) 'Malthus's idea of a moral and political science'. *The Journal of Philosophical Economics* 3(2), pp. 5–57.

Cremaschi, S., and Dascal, M. (1996) 'Malthus and Ricardo on economic methodology'. *History of Political Economy* 28(3), pp. 475–511.

Cremaschi, S., and Dascal, M. (1998) Persuasion and Argument in the Malthus-Ricardo Correspondence. In *Research in the History of Economic Thought and Methodology*. Volume 16. Ed. by Samuels, W.J. and Biddle, J.E. Stamford, Conn.: JAI Press.

Crimmins, J. (1990) Religion, Utility and Politics: Bentham versus Paley. In *Religion, Secularization and Political Thought: Thomas Hobbes to J.S. Mill*. Ed. by Crimmins, J. Oxford: Routledge.

Duncan, W. (1748 [1970]) *The Elements of Logick*. Menston: The Scholar Press.

Harris, J. (1751 [1993]) *Hermes or a Philosophical Inquiry concerning Universal Grammar*. London: Routledge – Thoemmes.

Heimann, P.M. (1978) 'Voluntarism and immanence: conceptions of nature in eighteenth century social thought'. *Journal of the History of Ideas* 39(2), pp. 271–284.

Hey, J. (1796–1798) *Lectures in Divinity*. Cambridge: Burger.

Hooker, R. (1593–1661 [1977]) *Of the Laws of Ecclesiastical Polity*. Cambridge, MA: Harvard University Press.

Hutcheson, F. (1755) A System of Moral Philosophy. In *Collected Works*. Volumes 5–6. Ed. by Fabian, B. Hildesheim: Olms.

Kant, I. (1785 [1911]) Grundlegung der Metaphysik der Sitten. In *Kant's gesammelte Schriften*. Volume 4. Ed. by the Königlich Preussischen Akademie der Wissenschaften. Berlin: Reimer.

Kant, I. (1788 [1913]) Kritik der praktischen Vernunft. In *Kant's gesammelte Schriften*. Volume 5. Ed. by the Königlich Preussischen Akademie der Wissenschaften. Berlin: Reimer.

Leibniz, G.W. (1702 [1994]) Meditation sur la notion de justice. In *Le droit de la raison*. Ed. by Sève, R. Paris: Vrin.

Leibniz, G.W. (1999) De iustitia ac amore voluntateque Dei. In *Sämtliche Schriften und Briefe, Sechste Reihe*. Volume 4/C. Ed. by Schepers, H. *et al.* Berlin: Akademie-Verlag.

Malthus, Th.R. (1798 [1986]) An Essay on the Principle of Population. In *The Works of Thomas Robert Malthus*. Volume 1. Ed. by Wrigley, E.A. and Souden, D. London: Pickering.

Malthus, Th.R. (1803 [1989]) *An Essay on the Principle of Population. The Version Published in 1803, with the Variora of 1806, 1807, 1817 and 1826*. Ed. by James, P. Cambridge: Cambridge University Press.

Malthus, Th.R. (1814 [1986]) Observations on the Effects of the Corn Laws, and of a Rise or Fall in the Price of Corn on the Agricultural and General Wealth of the Country. In *The Works of Thomas Robert Malthus.* Volume 3. Ed. by Wrigley, E.A. and Souden, D. London: Pickering.

Malthus, Th.R. (1817 [1951]). Malthus to Ricardo 26 Jan 1817. In *The Works and Correspondence of David Ricardo.* Volume 7. Ed. by Sraffa, P. with the collaboration of Dobb, M.H. Cambridge: Cambridge University Press.

Malthus, Th.R. (1820 [1989]) *Principles of Political Economy.* Ed. by Pullen, J. Cambridge: Cambridge University Press.

Malthus, Th.R. (1997–2004) *The Unpublished Papers in the Collection of Kanto Gakuen University.* Ed. by Pullen, J. Cambridge: Cambridge University Press.

Mill, J.S. (1852 [1981]) Whewell on Moral Philosophy. In *The Collected Works of John Stuart Mill.* Volume 10. Ed. by Robson, J.M. London: University of Toronto Press.

Oakley, F. (1961) 'Christian theology and the Newtonian science: the rise of the concept of the laws of nature'. *Church History* 30(4), pp. 433–457.

Osiander, A. (1547 [1947]). Preface. In Copernicus, N., *De Revolutionibus: preface and book I.* Ed. by Dobson, J.F. assisted by Brodetsky, S. London: The Astronomical Society.

Paley, W. (1785 [2002]) *The Principles of Moral and Political Philosophy.* Ed. by LeMahieu, D.L. Indianapolis, IN: Liberty Fund.

Paley, W. (1794 [1970]) *A View of the Evidences of Christianity.* Westmead: Gregg.

Paley, W. (1802 [1970]) *Natural Theology: or: Evidences of the Existence and Attributes of the Deity, Collected from the Appearances of Nature.* Westmead: Gregg.

Ricardo, D. (1821 [1951]) Ricardo to Malthus 10 Sept 1821. In *The Works and Correspondence of David Ricardo.* Volume 9. Ed. by Sraffa, P. with the collaboration of Dobb, M.H. Cambridge: Cambridge University Press.

Shaftesbury, Earl of (Cooper, A.A.) (1711 [1999]) An Inquiry concerning Virtue. In *Characteristics of Men, Manners, Opinions, Times.* Ed. by Klein, L.E. Cambridge: Cambridge University Press.

Smith, A. (1759 [1976]) *The Theory of Moral Sentiments.* Ed. by Raphael, D.D. and Macfie, A.L. Oxford: Clarendon Press.

Smith, A. (1776 [1976]) *An Inquiry into the Nature and Causes of the Wealth of Nations.* Ed. by Campbell, R.H., Skinner, A.S. and Todd, W.B. Oxford: Clarendon.

Waterman, A.M.C. (1991) *Revolution, Economics and Religion. Christian Political Economy, 1798–1833.* Cambridge: Cambridge University Press.

Waterman, A.M.C. (1996) 'Why William Paley was "the first of the Cambridge Economists".' *Cambridge Journal of Economics* 20(6), pp. 673–686.

Watts, I. (1726 [1984]) *Logick.* New York: Garland.

Winch, D. (1987) *Malthus.* Oxford: Oxford University Press.

Zilsel, E. (1942 [2002]) The Genesis of the Concept of Physical Law. In *The Social Origins of Modern Science.* Ed. by Raven, D., Krohn, W. , and Cohen, R.S. Dordrecht: Kluwer.

4   Malthus's early normative ethics
A morality of liberty

Malthus's Whiggism

Malthus's first *Essay* is famous first for the fact that it contains the first for-mulation of the principle of population, and second for its vehement attack on the Poor Laws. Even though criticism of the Poor Laws implied an attack on the paternalistic outlook by which established institutions and current legislation were inspired, and was accordingly criticism 'from the left', Mal-thus's primary polemical target was provided by such 'systems of equality' as those formulated by Godwin and Condorcet. This was an unavoidable effect of circumstances. In fact, the years when Malthus wrote first *The Crisis*, the unpublished tract of 1796, and then the first *Essay*, were those of French wars and ruthless repression of British Jacobinism.

Malthus's discourse may be easily misinterpreted – and indeed has been the subject of drastic misunderstanding – when read out of such context. When read in context, it turns out to be instead one more contribution to Whig discourse, and indeed an attempt to renew Whig language and theoretical weaponry. In terms of 'party labels, Malthus was firmly placed in the Whig camp' (Winch 1987, p. 49). More precisely, he was a Foxite Whig, a supporter of opposition to the Pitt government and an opponent to traditionalist Whiggism in the name of a new kind of 'scientific' Whiggism (Nakazawa 2012). Within the fragmented Whig camp, Malthus's target in *The Crisis* was provided by the faction led by Lord Portland, the most traditionalist sect in the alignment, still fond of mythology about the country gentleman, 'that old and noble character, the jealous guardian of British freedom' (Empson 1837, p. 479). Malthus manifests the opinion that in 'the Portland party, it is in vain to look for a revival, fettered with blue ribbands, secretaryship and military commands: freedom of action may be as soon expected from prisoners in chains' (p. 479). His programme focuses on an attempt to include wider social groups in the British political society, with the hope that such enlarged participation may lessen the weight of opposing factions and provide a pow-erful enough counterweight to both the Monarchy and the Government. He concludes:

It appears to me that nothing can save the Constitution but the revival of the true old Whig principles in a body of the community sufficiently numerous and powerful to snatch the object of contention from the opposing factions [...] The only hope that Great Britain has, is in the returning sense and reason of the country gentleman, and middle classes of society, which may influence the legislature to adopt the safe and enlightened policy of removing the weight of objections to our constitution by diminishing the truth of them.

(p. 479)

That is, in 1798 Malthus was attacking enemies on the left but keeping an eye on the defence of liberty against tyranny, be it monarchical absolutism or republican despotism, and with the intention to fight 'tyrannical laws' inconsistent with the 'genuine spirit of the constitution', contradictory to all 'ideas of freedom', and carrying a 'disgusting tyranny' (Malthus 1798, p. 36). One among his concerns was in fact that Jacobinism would have been the dupe of Reaction by spreading fear of violent revolution among those middling ranks which were the possible stronghold of Whiggism. Instead, knowledge of the true causes of poverty, with all its unpalatable implications, would have helped nonetheless in enlightening the lowers classes and turning them away from unviable and dangerous revolutionary programmes, in convincing the higher and middle classes to support attempts to gradually improve existing institutions while dispelling that fear of 'revolutionary excesses' which was threatening 'to deprive Europe even of that degree of liberty which she had before experienced to be practicable' (Malthus 1803, vol. 2, p. 202).

Chapter 10 of the first *Essay* illustrates how existing social arrangements are endowed with the kind of 'dynamic stability' that has been described by Waterman (1988, p. 89). The chapter mounts a mental experiment by which a state of society similar to the one actually existing is derived – through the action of 'laws inherent in the nature of man, and absolutely independent of all human regulations' (Malthus 1798, p. 70) – from an hypothetical starting point assumed to be a state of equality, virtue and plenty as the one hypothesized by Godwin. Malthus's claim is that this would derive from the *inevitable laws of our nature*, neither from any *original depravity of man* nor from any *opposition between public and private good* created by deficient human regulations. In other words, no Augustinian theology is required, either in the original version or in some secularized disguise, in order to account for the origins of social evil. Indeed, Malthus has it clear in mind that, the foundation of natural law that had been worked out in the Cumberland–Gay–Brown tradition, afforded also an account for the origin of partial evil as a result of conflict between different general laws as well as a way of reconciling partial evil with the general good without any need of introducing the Original Sin and corrupted human nature.

Malthus's starting point allows for a Godwinian society with neither private property nor marriage, with perfect equality, widespread virtue and benevolence as the ruling motive for action. It then goes on to prove that, under such conditions, the population would double in at most 25 years (p. 68). After that, it illustrates how, even though it is true that 'the equalization of property, added to the circumstance of the labour of the whole community being directed chiefly to agriculture, would tend greatly to augment the produce of the country' (p. 68), yet, taking a number of empirical factors into account such as the different degrees of fertility of the soil and the fact that if all the grazing country would be ploughed up manure would no longer be produced, this increase could at most double the average produce in 25 years. He then goes on to prove that, in the next 25-year time-span, the doubled population would double itself again while it would be impossible for the produce to grow any further; but also conceding that it would be possible to increase it to the same (absolute) extent, that is, to make it three times as big as it was in the beginning, it would not keep up with a four times bigger population. The consequence would be a return to a condition of scarcity, with all the side-effects carried by diminishing benevolence and growing poverty, namely, ill-health, injustice and fraud. As a remedy to these evils, 'some of the laws which at present govern civilized society, would be successively dictated by the most imperious necessity' (p. 71), that is, security of property would be introduced and the institution of marriage established. This would in turn introduce inequality of conditions, and Malthus's *quod demonstrandum erat* would be proved, that is, it would be proved that an equalitarian and communist society is self-defeating in so far as such kinds of society:

> from the inevitable laws of nature, and not from any original depravity of man, in a very short period, degenerate into a society [...] divided into a class of proprietors, and a class of labourers, and with self-love for the main spring of the great machine.

> (p. 75)

Bonar's idea that the great economist 'went beyond his province' starts to sound frankly absurd after reading La Vergata's reconstruction of eighteenth-century endless discourse about mathematics, population and Divine Providence, where population appears to be the divine's province, and theodicy the introductory chapter to demography (La Vergata 1990, pp. 20–40). Johann Peter Süssmilch, the most influential among Malthus's predecessors, understands demographic theory as a kind of demographic theology based in Revelation. This is 'one among the main fruits of the typical eighteenth-century combination of natural theology and demography, and of the strict link between the topic of fecundity and that of the providential economy of nature' (p. 41).

It is as well to keep in mind that fighting only enemies on the left was a compelled choice, resulting from the historical context, and that Malthus believed that the dividends paid at last by a war on poverty would have been cashed by the poor no less than by all citizens, since in a society where dependent social relations prevail any system of civil liberties would lack its social preconditions, and:

> we probably should not now enjoy our present degree of civil liberty, if the poor, by the introduction of manufactures, had not been enabled to give something in exchange for the provisions of the great lords, instead of being dependent upon their bounty.
>
> (p. 103)

The comment is in order here that Malthus is obviously echoing Montesquieu and Adam Smith, and the quote seems indeed a summary from the latter's account for the end of feudalism. Smith had written that feudal lords lost their political power as soon as they gave up the source of personal dependence by which they used to keep people under control, that is, as soon as they started to spend surplus produce from their possession in those 'trinkets of frivolous utility' of which wealth consists, following the 'vile maxim' of the masters of mankind: 'All for ourselves and nothing for other people'. In fact:

> as they could find a method of consuming the whole value of their rents themselves, they had no disposition to share them with any other persons. For a pair of diamond buckles, perhaps, or for something as frivolous and useless, they exchanged the maintenance, or what is the same thing, the price of the maintenance of a thousand men for a year, and with it the whole weight and authority which it could give them. The buckles, however, were to be all their own, and no other human creature was to have any share of them [...] and thus, for the gratification of the most childish, the meanest, and the most sordid of all vanities, they gradually bartered their whole power and authority.
>
> (Smith 1776, p. 418)

Malthus's main reason for opposing paternalism was allegiance to 'the true principles of liberty and equality' (Malthus 1798, p. 57). In fact, he believed that the Poor Laws tended to lessen the poor's spirit of independence, discourage their industry, lessen their sense of dignity, and give local authority unlimited power over their lives. Besides, such regulations were unjust and tyrannical also to rate-payers, that is, to a mass of people who were just slightly better off than the poor themselves. As an result, 'the whole class of the common people of England' is subject to 'tyrannical laws' incompatible with 'all ideas of freedom' and yielding 'disgusting tyranny' (p. 36). Thus, in name of one value, benevolence or charity, the English institutions had forfeited another no less important one, 'the valuable blessing of liberty' (p. 38). But – he argues – there is one effective and humane alternative to evils carried by the Poor Laws, namely, giving the poor more independence by offering them a chance to earn their own living by honest means. We should admit that hard labour is an evil too, but it is 'a lesser evil, and less calculated to debase the human mind, than dependence' (p. 103).

Malthus's first theodicy

In the last two chapters of the first *Essay* Malthus avowedly engaged in theodicy, which was still a hot topic since it had been brought to the forefront by Pierre Bayle, who had proposed to settle the post-Reformation controversy about God's foreknowledge, grace and predestination by declaring that God cannot be at once all-powerful, omniscient and benevolent. What Leibniz's rejoinder in his *Essai de Teodicée* yielded was, first, a new name for an old subject and, second, a restyling of old – and rather weak – arguments. The new name, deriving from *dyke* (justice) and *theòs* (God), means a defence of God's justice vis-à-vis evil in the world. The subject had been discussed under a different name, at least from Augustine's times on, in many treatises bearing the title *De Malo*. After Leibniz, a novel development was that the subject tended to expand, annexing gradually the whole of natural theology (Lorenz 1998; Brogi 2006, pp. 59–119). As illustrated in Chapter 2, theodicy was a central item also for Anglican natural theology, and in the Cumberland–Gay–Brown–Paley tradition it had become strictly intertwined with the foundations of ethics. Evil was strategically reduced to partial evil, connected by a cause–effect relationship with general good, and moral laws in turn were justified by their means end relationship to general good. Malthus's further step – in a sense a necessary one after the possibility of ascribing the origins of social evil to some original depravity of man had been ruled out – was establishing a link not just between theodicy and ethics, but also between theodicy and politics.

In fact Malthus declares, following Gay and Brown, that physical and moral evil derives from 'the inevitable laws of our nature and not from any *original depravity of man*' (p. 75; italics added). This seems to rule out the doctrine of original sin, and surely does rule out that neo-Augustinian and Calvinist view of human nature as *natura lapsa*, or corrupted nature, which had been a polemical target for Anglican divines. Malthus's own theodicy follows Cumberland in so far as the key idea is that partial evil caused by general laws can be *mitigated*, but neither eliminated nor *explained away* by such arguments as that Nature has a divine origin or that evil has a purely negative character, consisting in the privation of good. Thus, Malthus's 1798 theodicy, unlike Leibniz and the Cambridge Platonists, is not of a neo-Platonic kind but follows instead Cumberland's more modest attempt not to explain evil away but to argue instead that *partial* evil always contributes to produce *general* good. In somewhat dismal terms, it offers the scant consolation that one's evil may turn out to be another's good. Malthus declares accordingly that the general laws of nature are causes of partial evil and that, even though their effects can be corrected by other laws of nature, evil cannot be completely eliminated (p. 104). This in turn depends on two reasons: (i) laws of nature must be *general* and cannot admit of exceptions; (ii) impulses in human nature corresponding to such laws cannot be made *weaker* unless the Creator's aims be at risk of not being achieved, and thus 'it is the lot of man, that he will frequently have to choose between two evils' (p. 92).

As Waterman (1991, pp. 58–64) argues, the *Essay*'s second part was meant to be one more attack on Godwin, arguing on his own premises in order to prove that inequality is required in order to stimulate activity and spiritual growth. I would suggest, unlike Waterman, that the amount of unorthodox admissions made in this part may have looked less damaging to Malthus's eyes by the fact of being part of an argument aimed at dismantling Godwin's conclusions on his own assumptions, and by the fact of being a discussion confined to *natural*, as opposed to *revealed*, theology, the only ground available for a discussion with somebody who did not profess himself a Christian. This does not detract from the validity of Waterman's conclusions that Malthus's natural theology and theodicy were seriously defective, at some point inconsistent, and on balance incompatible with Christian positive theology (pp. 110–112). Malthus's 'solution' to the problem of evil argues that physical evil is necessary in order to stimulate activity, and that such stimulation amounts to gradually eliciting mind form matter or, in other words, that the creation of mind is a process taking place in time and the 'original sin' consists of the sluggishness of matter. This solution goes with the idea that eternal life is the final point to which the best products of such process – namely, fully intellectually and morally developed human minds – are destined, while faulty pieces are set aside for reconversion into inert matter. Such rather odd developments make sense again only when read as quasi *ad hominem* arguments, that is, if we assume that Malthus chose to fight Godwin by his own weapons, in this case the latter's theory of mind. Given Godwin's idea of creation of mind, required as a prerequisite to his own doctrine of unlimited progress, Malthus needed to prove that, in order to stimulate exertion of human faculties, not just inequality but even moral evil is required (pp. 97–101). Godwin, in the revised version of Book 8, Chapter 3 (Chapter 7 in the second and third editions) was prepared to admit that 'inequalities of property perhaps constituted a state [...] which constituted, the true original excitement to the unfolding the powers of the human mind' (Godwin 1993, vol. 4, pp. 326–327), but immediately hedged the concession made by adding that, even though this was 'necessary as the prelude to civilisation, it is not necessary to its support. We may throw down the scaffolding when the edifice is complete' (p. 327). Malthus's counter-argument, as shown by Waterman (1991, pp. 97–101), consisted of an attempt to prove that man never can 'throw down the ladder by which he has risen to this eminence' (Malthus 1798, p. 101) and that inequality of property will always be a required stimulus for human exertions. Besides, he believed he had found a secret weapon for completing his own refutation while still arguing on Godwin's premises in Tucker's mentioned footnote, where an alternative doctrine of the production of mind out of matter was presented, and he believed that this doctrine may contribute to prove that no unlimited improvement of human nature in this life could take place that would spiritualize man to the point of extinguishing the force of sexual drive in favour of intellectual delights, no less than the force of self-love in favour of concern with the public good (pp. 76–77 and 100–106).

The place for morality in a dismal world

Malthus admits that misery and vice are 'two bitter ingredients in the cup of human life' (p. 17) and he argues, against Godwin, that they depend on causes deeper than human institutions. The latter indeed are:

> causes of much mischief to mankind; yet, in reality, they are light and superficial, they are mere feathers that float on the surface, in comparison with those deeper-seated causes of impurity that corrupt the springs, and render turbid the whole stream of human life.
>
> (p. 65; cf. Malthus 1803, vol. 1, p. 317)

Evil, including moral evil, does not derive 'from any original depravity of man' (Malthus 1798, p. 75) but instead from 'inevitable laws of our nature' (p. 75). In fact, besides passions, which may be sources of temptations, 'the greater part of mankind' is subject to 'the evil temptations arising from want' (p. 95), and it is a matter of probability and experience that the majority of mankind, given the impressions to which they have been exposed and which have contributed to shape their character, will not be virtuous, and that even 'the influence of the most virtuous character will rarely prevail against very strong temptations of evil' (p. 96).

What morality is seems not to be a matter for dispute, and Malthus assumes he can argue with Godwin on the basis of shared criteria and definition of morality. Godwin defines morality as 'a calculation of consequences', and such definition may be assumed – Malthus believes – to be basically the same as Paley's, who defined morality as 'the will of God, as collected from general expediency' (p. 77). Malthus assumes that there are 'natural' virtues and moral sentiments. For example he writes that 'the dictate of nature and virtue' (p. 11) suggests an early attachment to one woman; 'the first feelings of nature' (p. 19) recommend compassion for aged and helpless parents, and 'the most natural principles of the human heart' (p. 25) enjoin care for children. Benevolence too is a virtue, and Godwin's wish for 'substitution of benevolence as the master-spring and moving principle of society, instead of self-love' (p. 64) is in itself laudable even though impossible to implement. It is true that benevolence is a valuable corrective of self-love (p. 104), but we cannot dream that concern with the general good may become sometimes a viable motive for human action in general (p. 105). Even the Poor Laws were instituted for the 'most benevolent purpose' and they do occasionally mitigate some cases of 'very severe distress' (p. 35), a result that would be in itself valuable in case it did not bring along negative side-effects. Also freedom is a basic value, and Godwin is right in claiming 'unlimited exercise of private judgement' (p. 64). The same holds true for the 'spirit of independence that still remains among the peasantry' (p. 33) and for 'love of independence, a sentiment that surely none would wish to be erased from the breast of man' (p. 27). Last but not least, activity and industry are basic virtues, strictly connected with love of freedom and dignity; indeed 'hard labour' is 'less evil, and less calculated to debase the human mind than dependence' (p. 103) for 'evil exists in the world, not to create despair, but activity' (p. 137), and 'sobriety and industry' seem to be conditions for happiness (p. 34). On balance, virtue seems to go with happiness; for example 'virtuous love' is 'a delightful passion whose gratification sometimes more than counterbalances all its attendant evils' (p. 27) and obstacles in the way of marriage are 'a species of unhappiness' (p. 35); vices connected with the preventive check to the growth of population 'involve both sexes in inextricable unhappiness' (p. 28), and removal of one among the greatest checks to idleness and dissipation resulting from the Poor Laws tends to diminish the mass of happiness among the common people (p. 35).

The Poor Laws were instituted – as already mentioned – 'for the most benevolent purpose' and they do mitigate 'some cases of very severe distress' (p. 35). The problem, yet, is that: (i) they yield a doubtful blessing to the poor who are supported by parishes; (ii) they yield such a mass of unhappiness for the whole of the population that it would outweigh the blessing they carry for a few, even in case it were pure blessing with no side-effects, in so far as they carry with them 'disgusting tyranny' incompatible with 'all ideas of freedom' (p. 36). Malthus's criterion for value-judgement is a neatly consequentialist one, namely 'the aggregate mass of happiness' (p. 36); this implies that partial evils are to be balanced with those partial goods with which they are intertwined, but also that such partial goods as mitigation of distress in individual cases should be balanced with those partial evils they are tied up with. The conclusion is that:

> if the Poor Laws had never existed, though there might have been a few more instances of very severe distress, yet that aggregate mass of happiness […] would have been much greater.
>
> (p. 36)

Note that the 'partial evil general good' principle, the overarching principle in the Cumberland–Paley tradition, does not hold true just for theodicy but is also the basis for moral judgement; in fact one action's, institution's, or law's goodness is to be judged on the basis not only of the balance of good and evil it yields in the individual case, but also of the total amount of good and evil carried as unintended consequences.

A check upon the growth of human population is provided by reason; the latter in fact discourages many from pursuing the dictates of nature in an early attachment to one woman, and this restraint 'almost necessarily, *though not absolutely so*, produces vice' (p. 14; italics added). Note that the possibility of non-vicious restraint is already there in 1798, albeit as a rather remote possibility. The difference between the first and the second *Essay* is that non-vicious restraint is believed in 1798 to have been irrelevant *in the past*, and the prospect of its practice *by the majority* in the future is believed to be implausible. Thus, the dilemma in 1798 is that the degree of 'happiness and innocence of a people', are measured by the rapidity of its growth in numbers, since prosperity and virtue tend to make 'virtuous love' a viable option for greater numbers, and this yields population growth, which in turn carries misery and vice. As a consequence, comparative ease and a degree of virtue are accessible to the mass of people only intermittently. This is the reason why the problem of evil, or theodicy, heavily influences any discussion of moral issues. The problem is that not only physical but also moral evil cannot be totally eliminated, and this is the reason why Godwin's dream of a harmonious society is self-defeating. In other words, evil includes not only misery but also vice and 'it may be safely asserted, that the vices and moral weakness of mankind, taken in the mass, are invincible' (p. 96). The reason for this is that the passions out of which such moral weaknesses originate could not be diminished without drying up sources of good to a greater extent than sources of evil. Perhaps there is:

> no one general law of nature that will not appear, to us at least, to pro-
> duce partial evil; and we frequently observe at the same time, some
> bountiful provision, which acting as another general law, corrects the
> inequalities of the first.
>
> (p. 104)

Another reason is that both physical and moral evil provide an occasion for some good or, in other words, the highest achievements of civilization are made possible by evil, and besides moral evil is one more incentive to virtue. In more detail: (i) the 'noblest exertion of human genius' and the 'finer and more delicate emotions of the soul' are made possible 'by the established administration of property, and by the apparently narrow principle of self-love' (p. 103); (ii) such Christian virtues as 'evangelical charity, meekness, piety' are worth more than mere acuteness of intellect, an 'ardent love and admiration of virtue seems to imply the existence of something opposite to it' and any perfection of character requires to be generated by 'the impression of disapprobation which arises from the spectacle of moral evil' (p. 131), and accordingly 'it seems highly probable that moral evil is absolutely necessary to the production of moral excellence' (p. 131).

On balance, the picture is pessimistic, and the eventual reason for this lies in the strategy adopted of refuting Godwin by boldly arguing on the latter's premises. Virtue does keep some room in the picture but it is in a sense appreciable but powerless. In other words, it does contribute to make indivi-dual lives happier, it does correspond to man's destination as planned by his Creator, and it is also – at least to some extent – required for a nation's prosperity, but the fact is that the history of mankind is under the sway of more tangible and brutal factors. In principle, the lowers classes are 'the most numerous, and, consequently, in a general view of the subject, the most important part of the human race' (p. 98), which implies that an improvement in their condition is from every point of view the most desirable object. And yet, if 'the laws of nature' are 'to remain the same', it is as well not to dream of '*unlimited* improvement' (p. 96) for all we can envisage is at most 'an improvement *the limit of which cannot be ascertained*' (p. 97; italics added); in fact, prosperity and innocence of a population only bring a phase of increased happiness but, since they bring growth of population as well, they also pave the way for increasing vice and misery in a later phase. This is not necessary or unavoidable for each individual, and yet it is what happens almost unavoidably for society as a whole. The scant consolation left seems to be a hope that some spirit of independence and dignity may be preserved even among peasants, at the price of *less* mitigation of cases of severe distress, and that the better educated and more affluent part of the population may keep a sense of dignity, freedom and humanity, and accordingly take evil affecting the lower classes as an opportunity for their own progress in the path of virtue. The consolation offered – I would dare to add – is after not so dazzling as to make the overall picture any brighter.

Malthus's first theodicy under fire

The first *Essay*'s theodicy was – to say the least – not too warmly received. On the one hand it was hardly noticed by secular Whig reviewers, who were not too keen on defending theological orthodoxy, on the other it occasioned a rather chilly comment by the *British Critic*, the watchdog of Anglican orthodoxy, and a couple of suggestions for improvement, which proved to be highly influential indeed, by adepts to the newly born current of Anglican Evangelicalism. The harshest reaction yet was the romantic and traditionalist one, whose contribution, while amounting to nothing in matters of theory, was decisive in establishing the myth of Malthus the ogre; for example, as Pullen reminds:

> Samuel Taylor Coleridge referred to 'the stupid ignorance of the Man' (MS note in Coleridge's copy of the Essay, BL, 6). Robert Southey described him as a 'mischievous booby' (New Letters of Robert Southey, ed. Kenneth Curry, 1.357) and a 'precious philosophicide' (*ibid.*, 1.551), and William Cobbett wrote of 'the barbarous and impious Malthus' (*Rural rides*, ed. G.D.H. Cole and Malthus Cole, 1930, 1.26).
>
> (Pullen 2004, p. 367)

The comment is in order here that these were reactions by romantics and traditionalists of a religious or less religious kind, and that their fury was raised by what they felt to be scorn towards a traditional set of values, the communal ties of the 'country' world – the alleged hotbed of traditional virtues, with pride of place to paternalistic compassion – and intolerable trespass by what was vaguely perceived as crude Enlightenment philosophy into the *sancta sanctorum* of such virtues, namely marriage and the family.

Malthus tolerated patiently abuse by such critics, but never took their arguments seriously and never deigned to respond them (James 1979, pp. 117–121; Gilbert 1998). What he did care for, were reactions by his Whig fellow-travellers and even more, and increasingly so, by his evangelical friends and allies. It has been well known for a long time how in the second *Essay* he 'withdrew' the two final chapters, avowedly following advice by friends (Otter 1836, p. liii; Rashid 1984, p. 137), and it is also possible now to answer the question who these friends were or, at least, we can say that among them were a few of his Cambridge colleagues. We have now documents of reactions by Edward Daniel Clarke, a Jesus College Fellow, and by Bewick Bridge, a Peterhouse Fellow bound to become later a colleague at the East India College. Clarke's letter of 20 August 1798 (Malthus 1997–2004, vol. 1, pp. 73–77) reports Bridge's opinion on the last two chapters, which he feels Malthus would have better omitted 'not from an Objection to the Sentiments contained in them, but because the Subject of them has not been sufficiently discussed' (p. 75), as well as more detailed objections on apparent support of materialism or denial of existence of mind as distinguished from matter, and apparent adhesion to annihilationism or denial of the soul's eternity. The letter concludes that the two chapters:

> have more the air of a Syllabus than a finished Essay; & this View of them strikes more forcibly after reading the very excellent Composition which precedes them, & to which they do not seem a necessary Appendage. That the Author entertained a similar Opinion I am convinced from the Tenour of his Prefaces, & a Note which he has added. But a Man of his Understanding knows very well that the Public will admit of no Apology, for sending forth Arguments on doctrinal Points, which have not been digested.
>
> (p. 75)

One more observation by Bridge is that:

> A casual Reader, would swear he is a Materialist; & yet I can gather sufficient Evidence from his own Writings, to prove that he rejects the Doctrine of Materialism. The same Person might also think he admitted the Doctrine of Annihilation – and yet I firmly believe he has no Intention to excite such an Opinion.
>
> (p. 75)

Clarke goes on to report the following discussion in which he had himself defended the compatibility of annihilationism and Scriptural doctrines, on the claim that annihilation may be understood as a state of misery, while Bridge had denied the equivalence as well as the compatibility between annihilationism and Scriptural doctrine (p. 76–77).

Criticism was not confined to private discussions. The *Analytical Review* (1799, pp. 119–125) which expressed the voice of lay intellectuals, albeit not particularly keen in noting possible divergences from religious orthodoxy, was not too soft about possible Hobbesian implications. For example they wrote that we seem:

> according to his system, to be doomed to make his choice between prostitution and infanticide; and the philosophy of Hobbes thus appears to be established, which states the natural state of man to be a state of warfare. We cannot doubt that this essay will receive much of the public attention.
>
> (p. 125)

The British Critic (1801), the voice of the High Church, tartly remarked that Malthus denies perfectibility to the human species, 'but liberally confers it upon every particle of matter' (p. 278). And Malthus had already announced in a Letter of 1799 to the *Monthly Magazine* his intention, 'in deference to the opinion of some friends whose judgment he respected', to omit, in a future enlarged edition of the *Essay*'s 'principal part', the discussion of the last two chapters as their subject 'is not necessarily connected with it' (Rashid 1984, p. 137). Otter describes what happens in words closely following Malthus's own words. He writes: 'He expunged two whole chapters from his first work, in deference to the opinion of some distinguished persons in our church' (Otter 1836, p. liii). This does not rule out the possibility that he might have remained convinced of the goodness of such a doctrine as annihilationism even though he had convinced himself that it was not worthwhile discussing it in print. In fact, in the same letter, he asks his critic to reflect:

> whether it is more derogatory to the Deity, to suppose that an immortal spirit may require some time or process for its formation; or to suppose that man might be placed at once in the most exalted state of happiness, exactly in the same manner formed to, or confirmed in virtue, as if he had passed with approbation through this life; but that the Supreme Being saw with satisfaction the toil, the tears, the pains, the continual failure of numbers, in this world, and was pleased with the spectacle of unnecessary evil?
>
> (Rashid 1984, p. 137)

Thus, in the second *Essay* Malthus, so to say, 'withdrew' the two final chapters, or better, he provided a new version of these chapters, where any reference to *creation* of mind out of matter and annihilationism was omitted while offering a new complex theoretical answer to the question on evil in the world.

Unlike Rashid, I would suggest that 'withdrawal' of these chapters did not depend on Sidgwick-like utilitarian calculus of a belief's utility. Malthus, after all, repeatedly professed faith in the beneficial character of truth itself. He wrote for example that the 'most baleful mischiefs may be expected from the unmanly conduct of not daring to face the truth' (Malthus 1798, p. 346). Thus I would suggest, with the help of a modest dose of charity, that Malthus did not act on such calculus, but instead in perfect good faith, and this is supported by the undeniable circumstance that he did not *withdraw* the theological chapters, but wrote instead a *new version* of those chapters that included an alternative theodicy. The question may still be left open whether he was just clumsily trying to pave attacks from orthodox quarters or instead believed that *production of spirit from matter* was a description in a more philosophical language of what in popular language is described as *probation, judgement*, and *salvation*. A sentence in the 1803 Preface, which may prompt option for the second answer, reads as follows:

> I should hope that there are some parts of it not reprinted in this, which may still have their use; as they were rejected, not because I thought them all of less value than what has been inserted, but because they did not suit the different plan of treating the subject which I have adopted.
>
> (Malthus 1803, vol. 1, p. 2)

Granted that the sentence (in turn withdrawn in 1806) refers to the two final chapters, it may suggest that Malthus believed that his own theological speculations were still *valuable*, but also that they had become *useless* precisely because he had now an alternative answer to the questions tackled in the two chapters. This was the doctrine justifying 'moral restraint', presented in the two new theological chapters. What made them a different thing from the 1798 chapters was the role of morality as a *practical* answer to the question of evil. The problem with the first *Essay*'s theodicy is that it contained highly problematic claims, for example, that moral evil is necessary in order to inspire abhorrence for vice, that some creatures are predestined to destruction in so far as they will not reach a sufficient degree of moral perfection, that virtue consists in acting out of altruistic love even though human beings normally act out of self-love, and that moral conduct consists in acting out of fear and hope (Waterman 1991, pp. 110–111). The greatest contradiction, yet, seems to arise from the claim that virtuous action, or action conforming to the moral law, seems to be just a *result* of the process of creation of mind out of matter, not an *element* of the same process, or, in other words, that there is no moral preventive check to evils caused by the principle of population since the preventive check is only vice. The problem is that this claim contradicts the more general claim that partial evil caused by one general law may be mitigated by the effects of others.

Malthus apparently realized rather soon that not just his sketchy second part was a failure, but also that the whole doctrine had serious problems, and set out to work out a revised version. In the meanwhile Paley's new theodicy appeared, and it seemed to offer what was required in order to fill the gap in Malthus's system; as a consequence, it was quickly incorporated into the new version of the theory with so decisive a function that what in 1798 was an appendix became in 1803 the core of the work. His statements to the point that the last two chapters might be dropped because they were unnecessary are to be taken seriously. What Malthus tried to do after 1798 was working out a more empirical and analytically more sophisticated theory of population deeply embedded in his overall political economy – which in turn was, more than a clumsy sketch of a pure economic theory, a kind of self-aware 'moral and political science' – and even more inextricably connected with theodicy via an articulated moral theory that came at this stage to play a central role.

Bibliography

Analytical Review (1799) 'An Essay on the Principle of Population'. 28 (July–December), pp. 119–125.

British Critic (1801) 'An Essay on the Principle of Population'. 17 (March), pp. 278–282.

Brogi, S. (2006) *I filosofi e il male: storia della teodicea da Platone ad Auschwitz*. Milano: Franco Angeli.

Cobbet, W. (1822–26 [1930]) *Rural rides*. 3 vols. Ed. by Cole, G.D.H. and Cole, M. London: Davis.

Coleridge, S. (1803) MS note. In Malthus, Th.R. *An Essay on the Principle of Population*. London: J. Johnson (British Library, British printed collection, 1801–1914: Coleridge).

Empson, W. (1837) 'Life, writings and character of Mr. Malthus'. *Edinburgh Review*, 64(80), pp. 469–506.

Gilbert, G. (1998) Introduction. In *T.R. Malthus. Critical Responses*. Volume 1. Edited by Gilbert, G. London: Routledge.

Godwin, W. (1793 [1993]) Enquiry Concerning Political Justice. In: *Political and Philosophical Writings of William Godwin*. Volume 3. Ed. by Philp, M. London: Pickering.

James, P. (1979) *Population Malthus. His Life and Time*. London: Routledge.

La Vergata, A. (1990) *Nonostante Malthus*. Torino: Bollati Boringhieri.

Lorenz, S. (1998) Theodizee. In *Historisches Wörterbuch der Philosophie*. Volume 10 ST–T. Ed. by Ritter, J. and Gründer, K. Basel: Schwabe.

Malthus, Th.R. (1798 [1986]) An Essay on the Principle of Population. In *The Works of Thomas Robert Malthus*. Volume 1. Ed. by Wrigley, E.A. and Souden, D. London: Pickering.

Malthus, Th.R. (1803 [1989]) *An Essay on the Principle of Population. The Version Published in 1803, with the Variora of 1806, 1807, 1817 and 1826*. Ed. by James, P. Cambridge: Cambridge University Press.

Malthus, Th.R. (1997–2004) *The Unpublished Papers in the Collection of Kanto Gakuen University*. Ed. by Pullen, J. Cambridge: Cambridge University Press.

Nakazawa, N. (2012) 'Malthus's political views in 1798: a "Foxite" Whig?'. *History of Economics Review* 56(3), pp. 14–28.

Otter, W. (1836 [1986]). Memoir of Robert Malthus. In *The Works of Thomas Robert Malthus*. Volume 5. Ed. by Wrigley, E.A. and Souden, D. London: Pickering.

Pullen, J.M. (2004) Malthus, (Thomas) Robert. In *Oxford Dictionary of National Biography*, Volume 36. Ed. by Matthew, H.C.G. and Harrison, B. Oxford: Oxford University Press.

Rashid, S. (1984) 'Malthus' theology; an overlooked letter and some comments'. *History of Political Economy* 16(1), pp. 135–138.

Smith, A. (1776 [1976]) *An Inquiry into the Nature and Causes of the Wealth of Nations*. Ed. by Campbell, R.H., Skinner, A.S. and Todd, W.B. Oxford: Clarendon Press.

Southey, R. (1965) *New Letters of Robert Southey.* 2 vols. Ed. by Curry, K. New York: Columbia University Press.

Waterman, A.M.C. (1988) 'Hume, Malthus and the stability of equilibrium'. *History of Political Economy* 20(1), pp. 85–94.

Waterman, A.M.C. (1991) *Revolution, Economics and Religion. Christian Political Economy, 1798–1833*. Cambridge: Cambridge University Press.

Winch, D. (1987) *Malthus*. Oxford: Oxford University Press.

5 Malthus's intermediate normative ethics
A morality of prudence

Paley's 'limited' theodicy and the function of morality

Paley's theodicy

Malthus's second *Essay* is no nineteenth-century *scientific* treatise, to be contrasted with the still *speculative* eighteenth-century first *Essay*. This was the impression the two essays used to make, but it is a mistaken one. After all, the second *Essay* was written not so much in another century as just five years after the first. Admittedly, it is no coincidence that the new work is four times longer, for it contains much more empirical material including statistics, but it is also true that the nature of the argument in the second *Essay* is by no means altered in such a way as to be transformed into a *scientific* – as opposed to *speculative* – kind. To put it more bluntly, the second *Essay* is not *less, but more* philosophical than the first, and its core is provided by something largely absent in the first: not one additional scientific or empirical element but an ethical theory. This change in the structure of the argument, giving a more decisive role to morality, is a side-effect of the adoption by Malthus of Paley's theodicy, which is based on the traditional doctrine of earthly life as a state of 'probation' and clearly a more orthodox view than the idea of creation of mind out of matter. This is connected with the oft-quoted fact that at this point the effects of the principle of population could be contrasted not only by preventive checks falling under the category of 'misery and vice', but also by another kind of preventive check that Malthus calls 'moral restraint'.

Theodicy was a major concern for Paley from the very beginning of his career. The thesis he had intended to submit for his final *disputatio* at Cambridge had originally been entitled: '*Aeternitas paenarum contradicit divinis attributis*', that is, 'Eternal punishment contradicts God's attributes', a claim that sounded subversive (and is somehow echoed in Malthus's theological concerns in the first *Essay*). Paley's moderator, Richard Watson, had amended the title by inserting a '*non*', thus turning it into an orthodox thesis (Watson 1818, p. 19). The subject was to become the key topic in Paley's *Natural Theology* (1802), where his solution is based on a calculus of pain and pleasure throughout the universe (including all sentient beings). Such calculus was meant to prove that the aggregate sum of pleasure in the world – if we consider the quantity of pleasure enjoyed by animals, including that of insects sucking flowers, to be greater than that enjoyed by human beings – outweighed that of pain. The pain suffered by human beings is compensated, on the other hand, by the eternal happiness they are meant to prepare themselves for, since earthly life may be understood as a state where human beings undergo trials in order to expiate their faults so as finally to deserve happiness in eternal life (Thompson 2008, p. 28–30).

In Paley's account, the existence of a Creator is proved by the fact that *certain parts* of his creation appear to have been designed with an in-built teleology. The example with which he opens the work is the celebrated one of a clock one may happen to find on the floor. He argues that the reason why it happened to be in that place cannot be – unlike for a stone – that 'it had lain there for ever' (Paley 1802, p. 1). He adds the further hypothesis that the clock is so designed as to be able to produce another clock. He goes on arguing that such further hypothesis adds even more probability to the conclusion (which the first hypothesis would be enough to corroborate) that it 'must have had, for the cause and author of that construction, an artificer, who understood its mechanism, and designed its use' (p. 18). Paley's aim is to prove that there is, besides evidence to the fact that the world has been ordered by a planner, also evidence to the fact that he is wise and benevolent and has happiness for his creatures in mind. In other words: God's attributes such as goodness and wisdom are proved by two considerations: the first is that 'in a vast plurality of instances in which contrivance is perceived, the design of the contrivance is beneficial' (p. 491); the second is that 'the Deity has superadded pleasure to animal sensations, beyond what was necessary for any other purpose, or when the purpose [...] might have been effected by the operation of pain' (p. 491).

The above considerations may be supported by phenomena observed in the natural world, primarily in the biological domain. It is a telling circumstance that, just as Samuel Clarke's physico-theological argument appeared right after Newton, so Paley's biologico-theological argument appeared shortly after Linnaeus's work. In fact the *Natural Theology* turns around one part of *natural* science, namely the life sciences, taken as the new basis for *natural* – as opposed to *revealed* – religion. The phenomena mentioned are meant to prove that there is a large amount of pleasure among animals, when compared with human beings, and this is the final proof that in the world the quantity of pleasure is greater than the quantity of pain. For example:

> Plants are covered with aphides, greedily sucking their juices, and constantly, as it should seem, in the act of sucking. It cannot be doubted that this is a state of intense gratification. What else should fix them so close to their operation, and so long?
>
> (p. 491)

Or again, Paley invites the reader to observe young shrimps jumping over the sea surface and to suppose that all such activity manifests 'a state of positive enjoyment' for each individual shrimp, and then asks: 'what a sum, collectively, of gratification and pleasure have we before our view?' (p. 492). More sophisticated considerations are the one that weakness and fecundity in a species are in due proportion, or the one – echoing the 'principle of plenitude' – that nature is filled with life to the point that no room is left empty, and when there is 'a vacancy fitted to receive the species', the fecundity of some species 'operates with its whole effect' (p. 511). Starting with these biological examples, we are invited to reason by analogy and consider human life so as to try to 'resolve all appearances into benevolence and design' (p. 499). Paley assumes that we will safely conclude that throughout the whole of life 'looking to the average of sensations, the plurality and the preponderancy is in favour of happiness by vast excess [...] happiness is the rule, misery the exception' (p. 497). He warns that we should correct our prima facie impressions by the consideration that we may fail to appreciate those benefits which are quite widespread, that we should regard those effects alone which are accompanied with proofs of intention, and that we should consider just prevailing tendencies or the lot reserved to greater numbers.

Apart from the involuntary comic effect that may arise from the choice of sucking as a source of pleasure as a proof of the Deity's goodness, the point is that it is the stimulus of pleasure that has been chosen by the designer of the animal kingdom for achieving the end of preservation, it is apparent that Paley's argument is in a sense still the old Argument from Design attacked by Philo in Hume's *Dialogues*, and the prevailing wisdom among commentators has been that Paley 'just ignored Hume's criticism' (McLean 2003, p. 169). In fact it was the same argument made more prudent, as if Paley had Hume's objections in mind and was careful to avoid unnecessary assumptions to which cheap objections could be made, such as that the universe *as a whole* is ordered as a machine, and limited himself to more circumscribed claims, such as that the eye, no less than the clock, is an example of an organized entity with an in-built teleology. In other words, 'Paley's argument is elaborated in such a way that it sidesteps or addresses' (p. 171) many points from Hume's criticism.

Theodicy is in one sense the culmination of Paley's natural theology. The whole doctrine proves that the universe is endowed with some kind of teleological order and the author of such order has been constantly keeping his creatures' happiness in mind. With this conclusion, the issue of theodicy is supposedly settled. But we could still ask: why do we experience evil? To Paley's honour, we have to admit that he does not believe he has explained evil away by the argument that one's evil is another's good. What he actually does is to admit that for the problem of 'the origin of evil no universal solution has been discovered' (Paley 1802, p. 523). Besides, it is true that he advances once more the same arguments as had been formulated by Cumberland, Gay and Brown, but he does so in a less arrogant tone, and while combining them with two more arguments, closer to the Platonic tradition. On the first account, he suggests that the most comprehensive solution is 'that which arises from the consideration of *general rules*' (p. 527). The considerations we should keep in mind are: (i) 'that important advantages may accrue to the universe from the order of nature proceeding according to general laws' (p. 527); (ii) that the latter 'often thwart and cross one another' (p. 527); (iii) 'that from these thwartings and crossings frequent particular inconveniences will arise' (p. 527); (iv) that it agrees with our observation 'to suppose, that some degree of these inconveniences takes place in the works of nature' (p. 527). One additional argument Paley has recourse to is 'the doctrine of imperfections' that heavily relies on the principle of plenitude as well as on the idea of the Great Chain of Being. This additional argument suggests that it 'is probable that creation may be better replenished by sensitive beings of different sorts, than by sensitive beings all of one sort [...] that it may be better replenished by different orders of beings rising one above another in gradation, than by beings possessed of equal degrees of perfection' (p. 529). The alternative line of argument is – as suggested – the Plotinian, Augustinian and Leibnitian thesis according to which evil does not exist, in so far as it consists in '*finiteness*' (p. 530). Both answers, that is, the doctrine of imperfections and the doctrine of finiteness, 'are of a nature too wide to be brought under our survey, and it is often difficult to apply them in detail' (p. 531). Thus, instead of such 'metaphysical arguments', we should stick to considerations 'of a more limited, but more determinate kind' (p. 531). These are that bodily pain, death and other 'external evils' contribute in making for a world furnished with advantages on one side, and beset with difficulties, wants and inconveniencies on the other, but, since 'the great principle of human satisfaction is engagement' (p. 538), a world so contrived, 'is the proper abode of free, rational, and active natures, being the fittest to stimulate and exercise their faculties' (p. 539), and Paley mentions at this point Tucker's distinction between 'active' and 'passive' pleasures, a distinction that corresponds to, and better, overturns, the ancient Epicurean distinction between two kinds of pleasure.

The doctrine of earthly life as a state of *probation* is presented by Paley as 'the most reasonable' of all views under which human life has ever been considered, for 'many things in it fit with this hypothesis, which suit no other' (p. 562). In this view, human life is seen as:

> a condition calculated for the production, exercise, and improvement, of moral qualities, with a view to a future state, in which, these qualities, after being so produced, exercised, and improved, may, by a new and more favoring constitution of things, receive their reward or become their own.
>
> (pp. 562–563)

This view – Paley adds – seems to be at one with the view of the world as a well-ordered whole, for 'a future state' is required in order to rectify those disorders which are left in the world, and accordingly the belief in providence and that in a future state 'must stand or fall together' (p. 563).

A remarkable claim by Paley concerns the role of passions. There are two main reasons why moral, not just physical, evil cannot and should not be eliminated. The first is that mischief, of which human beings are occasion to one another, has as its first cause the character of man as a free agent, and, were God to deprive man of his free agency, he would put an end to his moral character. The second is that:

> passions are either necessary to human welfare, or capable of being made, and, in a great majority of instances, in fact made, conducive to his happiness. These passions are strong and general; and, perhaps, would not answer their purpose unless they were so. But strength and generality [...] become, if left to themselves, excess and misdirection. From which excess and misdirection the vices of mankind (the causes, no doubt, of much misery) appear to spring.
>
> (p. 547)

Another remarkable fact about the *Natural Theology* is that in this work Paley turns his own claims about population upside down, accepting Malthus's principle and the idea that population growth is a cause of 'civil evil', that is, 'poverty, which, necessarily, imposes labour, servitude, restraint' (p. 540). He admits that mankind:

> will in every country breed up to a certain point of distress. That point may be different in different countries or ages according to the established usages of life in each [...] But there must always be such a point, and the species will always breed up to it. The order of generation proceeds by something like a geometrical progression, The increase of provision, under circumstances even the most advantageous, can only assume the form of an arithmetic series, Whence it follows, that the population will always overtake the provision, will pass beyond the line of plenty, and will continue to increase till checked by the difficulty of procuring subsistence.
>
> (pp. 539–540)

Malthus returned the favour by adopting Paley's theodicy as a substitute for his own early theodicy, and this change carried several important implications, all going in the direction of a less pessimistic view of life and a less drastic trade-off between equality and liberty.

Malthus's second theodicy

A die-hard myth in Malthus scholarship is that he 'dropped' his theodicy in the second *Essay*. I have suggested instead that the second *Essay* – far from being a 'positive' treatise of demography sharply different from the metaphysical and theological first *Essay* – was mainly an essay in applied ethics. In other words, the 1803 *Essay* includes a theodicy no less than the 1798 *Essay* and the difference between them depends on a different solution given to the same problem. Since the solution in 1803 is that not only misery and vice can counterbalance the action of the population principle but also the moral restraint can do so, and accordingly morality wins pride of place. To state it more boldly, the two ethical chapters are at the centre of the work, not at the end like the first *Essay*'s two theological chapters and, far from being an intrusion, are the new pivot around which the whole argument turns (Waterman 1991, pp. 144–150).

What allowed for this modification was adoption of one important idea from Paley. This idea, that had become popular in the years following the French Revolution and could be found in quite different writers, was that Christianity is 'the religion best adapted to restrain men's passions and control their appetites' (Pretyman 1789, p. 16; Hole 1989, pp. 132–137). Edmund Burke argued that government:

> is a contrivance of human wisdom to provide for human wants [...] Among these wants is to be reckoned the want, out of civil society, of a sufficient restraint upon their passions. Society requires not only that the passions of individuals should be subjected, but that even in the mass and body as well as in the individuals, the inclinations of men should frequently be thwarted, their will controlled, and their passions brought into subjection.
>
> (Burke 1790, pp. 110–111)

He added that 'religion is the basis of civil society' (p. 141) and, more in detail, only Christianity provides such a degree of internal constraint as to make political liberty possible. An evangelical writer such as Thomas Gisborne intended to fight a view of morality as based on the principles of honour or on that of expediency, that is Paleyite morality, since only morality conceived as the will of God can provide real motivation (Gisborne 1789), and a sense of religion, combined with the dictates of reason, is a necessary item for the shaping of the British elites (Gisborne 1794). Another Evangelical, William Wilberforce declared that our task as Christians is 'the work of rectifying the disorders of the passions, and of implanting and cultivating the virtues of the moral character' (Wilberforce 1797, pp. 53–54).

In *A View of the Evidences of Christianity* Paley contends that the great effect of Christianity is bringing order into the moral world, that the truth of the existence of a future state 'rectifies every thing [...] gives order to confusion: makes the moral world of a piece with the natural' (Paley 1794, p. 410), and in the *Natural Theology* he specifies that human passions are necessary for human welfare, and they are 'strong and general; and perhaps would not answer their purpose unless they were so' (Paley 1802, p. 547), but, if left to themselves, strength and generality become 'excess and misdirection', and this is the spring of human vices. Paley believes that this account shows how religion may provide support to 'reason and self-government' without having recourse 'to any native gratuitous malignity in the human constitution' (p. 548).

Adopting this idea, Malthus's argument was restructured by singling out excess and misdirection of the passions, which in themselves are good, as a cause of evil. Note that the passions now take the place previously occupied by the original sluggishness of matter, which in turn was a substitute for the original depravity of man, an idea that both Malthus and Paley always wanted to avoid. The restyled argument now sounds as follows:

i the Creator's goals:

a that the earth be replenished;
b the improvement of the human faculties;

ii obstacle: natural indolence and misdirected passions;
iii means:

a self-love or desire of means of subsistence;
b tendency to increase of population with greater rapidity than supplies;

iv problem to solve: how to keep a balance between both impulses;
v key to solution: prudence as a private and (unintentionally) public virtue;
vi stop-gap remedy for unavoidable partial evils: benevolence (rather marginal in 1803 and increasingly important in the following editions);
vii dilemma left: how is an omnipotent, benevolent and omniscient Creator compatible with all this?
viii dilemma settled:

a the structure of society cannot avoid including partial evil (inequality) but the latter may be reduced to an unknown extent;
b troubles for divine omnipotence, benevolence and omniscience derive mostly from moral evil, but most physical evil could be avoided by private virtue;
c a reformed society where most members would be encouraged in being virtuous would further reduce the quantity of evil;
d in such a society partial evil might be greatly reduced if moral restraint were widely practised.

Malthus always had it clear in mind that 'misery and vice' are 'too bitter ingredients in the cup of human life' (Malthus 1798, p. 17), but also that they depend on deeper causes than human institutions; the latter are indeed:

causes of much mischief to mankind; yet, in reality, they are light and superficial, they are mere feathers that float on the surface, in comparison with those deeper-seated causes of impurity that corrupt the springs, and render turbid the whole stream of human life.

(p. 65; cf. 1803, vol. 1, p. 317)

Malthus's belief in the existence of such 'deeper-seated causes' has little to share with neo-Augustinian pessimism. The difference is that, for Malthus no less than for Paley, physical and moral evil derives from 'the inevitable laws of our nature, and not from any original *depravity of man*' (Malthus 1798, p. 75). This seems to rule out the Augustinian doctrines of original sin and *natura lapsa*, or corrupted nature, which were the polemical target for both Cumberland and the Cambridge Platonists. The 'deeper-seated causes' are nothing else than general laws, as far as they, either alone or combined with others, may cause partial evil. This in turn may be mitigated by effects of other general laws, but the problem with the account adopted is that evil does not cease being evil, and cannot be explained away by either metaphysical arguments of the Leibnitian kind like those of the Cambridge Platonists summarized in Alexander Pope's verse 'whatever is, is right' (Pope 1734, verse 294). Malthus's strategy instead aims at proving that partial evil is compatible with general good, and this carries a peculiar problem, namely that something should be done for victims of partial evil, and this is the point on which Malthus's changes in the second *Essay*'s various editions concentrate. In the first *Essay* the high purpose of the creation was declared – much in a Cumberlandian spirit, easily mistaken for a Benthamite one – to be 'the greatest possible quantity of good' (Malthus 1798, p. 132). And also in a Sermon on Deut 29.29 the remark may be found that the 'design of God in his transactions with mankind, as far as men themselves are concerned seems to be to make them happy' (Malthus 1997–2004, vol. 2, p. 23). Note that the remark is an almost word-by-word paraphrase of John Gay's main claim. Does this still mirror Malthus's convictions after 1803? The passage was written perhaps in 1811 (the paper is watermarked 1811), a time when he was already an Evangelical, but is crossed in the manuscript. Despite all the uncertainty arising from dubious dates and deletions, perhaps it should not be overlooked as a Sunday-school edifying story but may be thought to express one central eighteenth-century natural theological doctrine implying rejection of the Calvinist view of God's inscrutable will and which may have been at least compatible with Evangelicalism, whose main idea was God's mercy.

Let us see in detail how Malthus's claim about the purpose of Creation settles the question of theodicy. The argument is that the general laws of nature are causes of partial evil; such evil may be corrected by the effects of other laws of nature (Malthus 1798, p. 104) but cannot be avoided completely for two reasons: (i) the laws of nature must remain general and cannot admit of exceptions; (ii) those impulses in human nature that instantiate such laws cannot be made weaker, unless the purposes of the Creator run the risk of being defeated, and thus, 'it is the lot of man, that he will frequently have to choose between two evils' (p. 92). Such evils as diseases, misery, famines 'indicate us that we have followed these impulses too far, as to trench upon some other law which equally demands attention [...] and we heed not to this admonition, we must incur the penalty of our disobedience, and our sufferings operate as a warning to others', even though this is learned through 'slow and late results of experience' (Malthus 1803, vol. 2, p. 88). Diseases, for example, are not an inevitable infliction of providence but 'an indication that we have offended against some of the laws of nature', and they are no proof of lack of goodness in our Creator, since 'as dirt, squalid poverty, and indolence are in the highest degree unfavourable to happiness and virtue, it seems a benevolent dispensation that such a state should, by the laws of nature, produce disease and death, as a beacon to others' (p. 89). The remark may be repeated here that for an unlucky individual whose destiny is that of providing a warning to others, musing on the necessary part he plays in the divine script for the cosmic drama may afford scant consolation. Problems arising from the principle of population should be construed in analogy with any other law of nature, for this principle too is, like any other general law 'a cause of evils, which in turn are incidental to these necessary qualities of strength and generality; and these evils are capable of being very greatly mitigated and rendered comparatively light by human energy and virtue' (p. 93). Evils include not only misery but also vice, and 'it may be safely asserted, that the vices and moral weakness of mankind, taken in the mass, are invincible' (Malthus 1798, p. 96). As Paley had suggested, the passions lying at the root of such moral weaknesses could not be diminished without narrowing more sources of good than sources of evil, and accordingly they require 'regulation and direction, not diminution or extinction' (Malthus 1803, vol. 2, p. 92). Besides, effects of moral evil are amplified by physical evil, at least for the majority of human beings, who, as a consequence of 'the *fixed and unalterable laws of nature*, must ever be subject to the evil temptations arising from *want*, besides other *passions*' (p. 95), for reasons 'independent of any political and social institutions whatever' (p. 95).

To sum up, a modified theodicy carries as a side-effect wider room for morality. In the first *Essay* a moral theory was already there, but its function was mainly that of providing a basis for a theodicy, that is, proving that the experience of evil in the world is compatible with God's justice. The problem with this function is that it left no room for a kind of conduct that could be both virtuous and able to contribute in reducing the quantity of evil in this world. Besides, it presented physical evil as just an occasion for stimulating activity so as to prepare a number of human beings for happiness *in an afterlife*. In fact, the only checks to the principle of population are *in practice* just misery and vice. In the second *Essay* ethical theory is treated at length in order to provide a basis for what has become by 1803 the main ammunition for fighting the battle against partial evil, namely *prudence* as a ruling virtue. The outcome is that the prudent man may both improve his own lot in this life and contribute to making human society more decent. The partial evil that is left is the suffering endured by victims of their own lack of prudence or of that of their parents.

In various respects this view is the opposite of Malthus's gloomy view of 1798. Is the new worldview an *optimistic* one? Malthus's traditionalist and romantic critics believed that it was. Robert Southey, the neo-conservative Romantic follower of Coleridge, wrote that Malthus demonstrates that:

> All checks to population, till the power of production can be pushed no farther, and actual room for farther increase be wanting, must be attributed to error and ignorance in man, not to unerring nature and omniscient goodness. When that point has been reached, it has been demonstrated the practice of one virtue will secure the happiness of mankind and render it permanent. Either chastity is possible, or it is not; in the one case his argument has been shown to be groundless, in the other inapplicable: one of the horns of this dilemma must wound him, and either wound be mortal. He has played off his positive check and his preventive check, but they have not saved him from this check-mate.
>
> By these miserable sophisms Mr. Malthus has obtained the high reputation which he at present enjoys; his book having become the political bible of the rich, the selfish, and the sensual [...] But to our astonishment we find that, though in this present edition the author has retained and enlarged all these arguments, and insisted upon their application; at the end of the volume he admits every thing which he has controverted in the beginning, and is clearly and confessedly a convert to the doctrine of the perfectibility of man! He draws a picture of Christian society, in which the well being of all is founded upon this very virtue of chastity, the non-existence of which was to destroy all the theories of Godwin and Condorcet.
>
> (Southey 1804, p. 298)

Southey perhaps was not completely off track, and yet he does not see a serious problem. The problem is that Malthus on the one hand does admit of a remarkable amount of perfectibility of man, which he had denied in 1798, but on the other still thinks of his decent society in terms of a compound where a remarkable amount of partial evil will still be there, just *outweighed* but not *mitigated* by a greater amount of general good. Things gradually changed in later editions where, as I illustrate in Chapter 6, the consequences are felt of the fact that Malthus's new Paleyite theodicy was further developed and corrected by John Bird Sumner and Thomas Chalmers with important changes resulting in the overall argument, yielding the implication that: a) partial evils were not only *compensated* by general good, as in 1798, but could also be systematically *mitigated*; b) they could be mitigated not only by *prudence*, as in 1803, but also by *benevolence*.

Natural virtues

Malthus believes that there are a number of duties recommended by the light of nature and further confirmed by Revelation (Malthus 1803, vol. 2, p. 96).

Such duties correspond to laws of nature but, as far as the individual is concerned, what is required is primarily cultivation of a number of virtues or attitudes, eventually consisting of some implanted instincts steered and regulated by prudence. His ethics – not unlike Hume's, Smith's and Butler's – may be legitimately classified as virtue ethics, since what it comes down to is more cultivation of dispositions than compliance with rules. Yet, what makes it different from various twentieth-century versions of virtue ethics is coexistence of virtues with laws and rights. I have illustrated in Chapter 3 how law plays a central role in Malthus's meta-ethics, namely, how the problem of justifying moral judgements is settled only when we can establish that some rule is a law of nature. In this chapter I will illustrate also how respect for rights is a basic virtue in the public sphere.

It is also worth noting that Malthus does not seem to make too much use of the traditional classification of virtues that had come to be accepted by Christian theologians after the fourth century into four cardinal virtues, namely prudence, fortitude, justice and temperance, and three theological virtues, namely faith, hope and charity. He does occasionally mention some of these, but he talks systematically of benevolence, not charity, and his main problem – not surprisingly since it had been one typical seventeenth- and eighteenth-century puzzle – is whether it is compatible with self-love; then he expatiates on chastity, which is clearly one kind of temperance; he makes prudence the overarching virtue; and he makes public morality turn around justice and interprets rights not as innate rights of man, but rather as respect of really existing rights, or giving everybody his due. A clear division of virtues into two categories, to which Malthus seems to refer systematically, is instead Hume's division into *natural* and *artificial* virtues. Note that there is no doubt that Malthus was familiar with Hume's work and the terminology is clearly Humean, and yet the distinction as such was not so controversial. In fact the underlying idea is older, as far as it mirrors the distinction between a pre-political social state and a political state in a stricter sense that was a Ciceronian (or even Aristotelian) idea widely accepted from Grotius's times on.

Benevolence

Before discussing benevolence in Malthus's ethics, let me clarify what he and his readers understood by the word. It is defined by Dr. Johnson (1755) as 'disposition to Good; kindness; charity; good will'. The Latin term *benevolentia* was a translation of the Greek *eunoia*, which describes a good-willing disposition to somebody. It is mentioned in Plato's *Gorgias* as one of the attitudes appropriate to the wise (G 486e 6–487a 3) and in Aristotle's *Nichomachean Ethics* it is defined as a desire for other people's good, which may be the beginning of friendship 'but it is not the same thing as friendship, for it can be felt towards strangers, and it can be unknown to the object' (EN ix 5, 1166 b 30). In Cicero *benevolentia* is mentioned more than once in connection with friendship with a meaning not unlike Aristotle's *eunoia* (O 20, 77, 80;

LAE 2006, 343). In Marcus Aurelius's *Ad se ipsum* has a more universal scope (SI vɪɪɪ, 26). The Greek term appears in Hellenistic writers, both Jewish and Christian, such as Philo and Clemens of Alexandria, as one of God's attributes, echoing those of the Platonic sage. As a whole, yet, *benevolentia* had no precise meaning and played no specific function in medieval theology to the point that Aquinas, for example, just mentions it occasionally with reference to charity.

Benevolence as such was discovered in the sixteenth century, that is, after an opposition became fashionable – as a result of the joint exertions of neo-sceptics and neo-Augustinians – between self-centred and other-centred love. Since the very possibility of willing the other's good was questioned, *benevolence*, as something more basic than *charity,* became a key idea, or better, the name for a problem. Hobbes echoes the new sceptical and Augustinian mood when he claimed that society arises '*non a mutua hominum benevolentia, sed a mutuo metu*' (Hobbes 1646, p. 161), not from mutual benevolence between human beings, but instead from fear. After him, everybody's effort was to prove the very possibility of benevolence, and for example Cumberland contended that universal benevolence plays as all-encompassing a role as that played by prudence in Aquinas, since, like for the latter prudence provided the root of morality as such and was the *mater virtutum,* 'the mother of the virtues', for him benevolence toward God and all his creatures is the starting point from which all particular moral laws derive, to the point that in Chapter 1 of *De Legibus* he declares that it is the 'mother of all laws of nature' (Cumberland 1672, p. 4).

Butler's programme was drawing a third way between self-love and general benevolence, that is, between Hobbes and Mandeville on the one hand and Cumberland on the other. His argument is that human beings do not act only out of self-love, for human nature is complex and allows for a number of passions, including the two basic drives of self-love and benevolence, and besides a steering principle, namely conscience. The claim he wants to defend is that virtue and self-interest tend to coincide (Butler 1736, pp. 177, 180–183). Even when we act out of self-love we want to satisfy certain affects, and happiness or enjoyment bears no immediate relationship to self-love, but instead arises out of gratification of these affects. This implies that benevolence and desire for the public good, when considered as 'natural' affects, not as 'virtuous' ones, may be subservient to self-love no less than any other particular passion may be. Benevolence, however, albeit one of our Creator's qualities, is not the sole moral virtue, for 'we are so constituted as to condemn falsehood, unprovoked violence, injustice, and to approve of benevolence to some preferably to others abstracted from all consideration, which conduct is likeliest to produce an overbalance of happiness and misery' (p. 313) and thus benevolence, considered in itself, is 'in no sort the whole of virtue' (p. 312).

Hume contends that benevolence is an instinct originally implanted in our nature, consisting of extensive sympathy, and it is a calm passion, more known by its effects than by immediate feeling or sensation. Its eventual nature is an open question, and whether it consists ultimately of disguised self-love or it has its own foundation in the human nature is one of the several philosophical questions which are a matter of speculation but bear no consequences on practice. On the one hand, 'there is no such passion in human minds, as the love of mankind' (Hume 1739–40, vol. 1, p. 309) but, on the other, to 'the most careless observer, there appear to be such dispositions as benevolence and generosity' (Hume 1751, p. 268) and, in appendix 2 to the second *Enquiry*, he argues that there are a thousand instances proving the existence of 'a general benevolence in human nature, where no real interest binds us to the object' (p. 93–94). These sentiments:

> have their causes, effects, objects, and operations, marked by common language and observation, and plainly distinguished from those of the selfish passions. And as this is the obvious appearance of things, it must be admitted; till some hypothesis be discovered which, by penetrating deeper into human nature may prove the former affections to be nothing but modifications of the latter. All attempt of this kind have hitherto proved fruitless, and seem to have proceeded entirely, from that love of simplicity, which has been the source of much false reasoning in philosophy.
>
> (p. 92)

Paley declares that benevolence is one of the virtues taught by Scriptural morality, since in the Bible 'general rules are laid down, of piety, justice, and purity' (Paley 1785, p. 4). As far as natural morality is concerned, Paley believes that the question has not yet been settled among moralists whether benevolence should be classified as one out of four virtues, together with prudence, fortitude and temperance or as one of two basic virtues: prudence and benevolence (p. 25). Universal benevolence seems to be a presupposition as basic as it was for Cumberland, for the laws of nature have been chosen on the basis of their ability to bring about the maximum amount of happiness, and for this reason 'whatever is expedient is right' (p. 61). But this, more than recommending benevolence as a virtue for human beings, implies God's universal benevolence. Duty, more than benevolence, is the keyword in Paley's normative ethics, and even though some room is made for charity, the latter is understood not as universal benevolence, but as 'promoting the happiness of our inferiors' (p. 132). It is true yet that charity is 'the principal province of virtue and religion' (p. 132), for worldly prudence will direct our behaviour towards our superiors, and politeness towards our equals, and it is precisely towards our inferiors that behaviour needs to be directed by religion and virtue.

The above overview may help in making sense of Godwin's ethics as well as of Malthus's rejoinder. The former has been labelled in standard histories of utilitarianism as an early utilitarian one. The usual sense of puzzlement arises vis-à-vis such classifications, namely, if Malthus was a utilitarian and Godwin was one too, what precisely did they have to quarrel about? In fact Godwin's ethics includes a consequentialist dimension, but it is different from the doctrine that had been first presented by Bentham in 1789, in that it denies the possibility of calculating precisely consequences, underrates the possibility of reconciling self-interest with other-regarding interest, and stresses the role of benevolence as a motive for action. Is this utilitarianism? Giving an answer may be mainly a matter of words. Godwin is closer than Paley and Malthus to Bentham as far as his doctrine is a non-theological one but, on balance, it is more sentimentalist *vulgata* combined with some version of Epicurean hedonism plus elitist perfectionism than Benthamite utilitarianism. Godwin's most basic claim, similar to Hume's, is that we are capable of being influenced by disinterested considerations, and the second is that 'benevolent intention is essential to virtue' (Godwin 1793, pp. 186–194). More in detail: there is an agreeable sensation attached to beneficence no less than to self-love; then forgetfulness (precisely Nietzsche's grand idea, which he himself admittedly had drawn from the 'English psychologists') has the result of converting what at first were just means into ends (pp. 190–195); and then reflection confirms our choice, that is, we find by observation that we are surrounded by beings of the same nature as ourselves, and we are able in imagination to become impartial spectators of the system of which we are a part; the self-love doctrine is but a paradox, and it is not easy to conceive 'an hypothesis more singular than this', namely that we engage in acts of generosity wholly and exclusively influenced by considerations 'of the most selfish description', but this is in opposition to experience and introspection. The conclusion is that the 'direct motive' to virtuous action is purely disinterested and what we have in mind is the profit and advantage of our neighbour; and yet this does not contradict the idea that the 'indirect and original motive' is the love of 'agreeable sensations'. Godwin's programme for social reform or revolution implied abolition of private property, the family and government in order to implement perfect equality among human beings. Such a social order would be a viable one, granted that interaction between individuals can be regulated by benevolence alone. In an ideal society no scarcity of resources and no source of conflict would subsist, since material needs could be satisfied by half an hour's manual work by *every* member, and conflict arises solely from unjust social institutions.

Malthus, too, believes benevolence to be a basic virtue, and Godwin had pointed to an ideal that Malthus also felt was something 'devoutly to be wished', namely the 'substitution of benevolence as the master-spirit and moving principle of society, instead of self-love' (Malthus 1798, p. 64). But he qualifies his prima facie adhesion to Godwin's ideal by adding two considerations: first, that while benevolence is a master instinct and a basic virtue, so is self-love, dictated as it is by one of the laws of nature; second, that benevolence, as a natural instinct too, could, like every other natural drive, be followed to an excessive extent. In more detail, the 'principle of benevolence' is:

one of the noblest and most godlike qualities of the human heart, generated perhaps, slowly and gradually *from self-love*; and afterwards intended to act as a general law, whose kind office it should be, to soften the
partial deformities, to correct the asperities, and to smooth the wrinkles
of its parent; and this seems to be the analogy of all nature. Perhaps there
is no one general law of nature that will not appear, to us at least, to
produce partial evil; and we frequently observe at the same time, some
bountiful provision, which acting as another general law, corrects the
inequalities of the first.

(p. 104)

I have already mentioned, Malthus's opinion according to which the Golden
Rule shows how self-love may be made compatible with humanity and benevolence
and may also provide a motive for action that goes beyond self-regarding
motives. This line of argument seems to derive from Butler's refutation of the
'selfish theories'. The latter's argument was that self-love could prompt us to
satisfy our instincts, but happiness or pleasure originating from such a gratification would have no direct connection with self-love itself; that love for
one's neighbour may be considered to be either a virtuous principle or a natural affection; in the first case it is gratified by awareness of our effort in fostering other people's good, but in the second case, that is, when considered as
a *natural affection,* it finds its own gratification in the fact of successfully
promoting such good (Butler 1726, p. 111). Hume's idea of 'fellow-feeling' or
sympathy as the channel through which self-love may be generalizing into love
for others so that injustice, albeit 'so distant from us, as no way to affect our
interest, it still displeases us' (Hume 1739–40, vol. 1, p. 320) could have been
another source for his argument. Malthus could also have kept Adam Smith's
idea of sympathy in mind, should he have already been familiar with the
Theory of Moral Sentiments in 1798, a circumstance that is plausible enough
but not proved. It is true that some vague hints at Smith's impartial spectator
could be found in the Sermon on Job 27.6, preached several times before 1798
(Malthus 1997–2004, vol. 2, pp. 8–11) but they are not explicit and the source for
considerations about conscience appearing in this sermon could be Butler instead.

Malthus goes on to argue that for many purposes self-love may act as a
cheaper and more reliable substitute for benevolence, and he advances an
argument to prove his claim. He contends that steering our action while taking
the general good as its goal would carry high 'transaction costs' dependent on
the fact that the required information is hard to obtain. He writes:

If no man were to allow himself to act, till he had completely determined,
that the action he was about to perform, was more conducive than any
other to the general good, the most enlightened minds would hesitate in
perplexity and amazement; and the unenlightened, would be continually
committing the grossest mistakes.

(Malthus 1798, p. 104)

And the consequence he draws is that self-love is a more reliable guide to action than a desire for the general good, since knowledge is easier to obtain about what would benefit ourselves than about what would benefit everybody. Accordingly, if we may assume that in a state where everybody cared for his own interest, the general good would be better promoted than in a state where everybody was inactive because of uncertainty, then we should opt for the former.

This is a modified version of the claim advanced by Jansenist Pierre Nicole (1675) that the effects of self-love cannot be distinguished by the external observer from the effects of charity. Butler elaborated on the equivalence of self-love and charity as far as their observable effects are concerned (Butler 1736, pp. 180–183). Adam Smith argued that society could subsist on the basis of self-love alone, granted that the latter is limited by justice, and that benevolence could indeed contribute in making social life easier but never take self-love's place (Smith 1759, p. 86) and that a society may work smoothly without any awareness by its members of their contribution to its functioning, not unlike the wheels of the watch, which 'are admirably adjusted to the end for which it was made' and would not produce it any better 'if they were endowed with a desire and intention to produce it' (p. 87). Note that Malthus is echoing Adam Smith also when he argues, repeating the Stoic 'concentric circles' commonplace, that unlimited benevolence is a task appropriate to a perfect being, while to a limited creature like man only his relatives, friends, neighbours and at most fellow-countrymen had been recommended by Nature (p. 237). Malthus in fact adds in the 1806 Appendix that benevolence 'as the great and constant source of action, would require the most perfect knowledge of causes and effects, and therefore can only be an attribute of the Deity. In a being so short-sighted as a man, it would lead into the grossest errors' (Malthus 1803, vol. 2, p. 214). Note that the limits-to-knowledge thesis here referred to as a basis for limiting the scope of bene-volence was about to become one basic asset in the hands of critics of utili-tarianism such as William Whewell. In fact in the nineteenth-century controversy between utilitarians and intuitionists an important argument employed by the latter was the impracticability of utilitarian standards and procedures (Cremaschi 2006).

Benevolence is, no less than the sexual drive, one of the basic impulses of our nature; both are 'natural passions' and neither is good in an unqualified way or carries unfailingly good consequences. In so far as we are not only animals, but also reasonable beings, we must 'attend to their consequences; and if they be evil to ourselves or others, we may justly consider it as an indication that such a mode of indulging these passions is not suited to our state or con-formable to the will of God' (Malthus 1803, vol. 2, p. 157). Not unlike all other laws of nature, also the 'emotion which prompts us to relieve our fellow creatures in distress', whose 'apparent end' is 'to draw the whole human race together' (p. 157) while prompting human beings 'to mitigate some of the partial evils arising from general laws, and thus to increase the sum of human happiness' (p. 157) is '*general*, and in some degree *indiscriminate* and blind' (p. 156).

In 1798 Malthus had argued that 'the proper office of benevolence is to soften the partial evils arising from self-love, but it can never be substituted in its place' (Malthus 1798, p. 104). In 1803 he specifies that, 'as moral agents', we have a duty to bring the foreseeable consequences of our natural passions to the 'test of utility' and to gratify them only in that way which 'will clearly add to the sum of human happiness' (Malthus 1803, vol. 2, p. 157). In other words, there may be no less an excess of benevolence than of any other passion, and all virtues – including benevolence, that is, something that comes near to, or stands for, the Christian theological virtue of charity – should be, not unlike any other natural drive, moderated by the overarching virtue of temperance. Thus, this impulse to relieve our fellow-creatures in distress, 'like the impulses of love, of anger, of ambition, of eating and drinking, or any other of our natural propensities, must be regulated by experience, and frequently brought to the *test of utility*, or it will defeat its intended purpose' (p. 156). Benevolence, as a conclusion, is not the highest virtue, but is just one among other impulses or propensities. The prescription to follow such impulse is not, as such, a law of nature confirmed by Revelation; it is only so when the impulse is moderated and steered by reason, which is the only faculty that can teach us to what extent following it is conforming to general utility and to the will of our Creator. All this sounds more or less Aristotelian and Ciceronian but it certainly does not sound Benthamite, since it does not prescribe to maximize anything, but rather to find a golden mean. It is as well to add that all this did sound lacking in Christian charity to evangelical ears, and this will be the decisive reason for evangelical criticism and recantations by Malthus to be discussed in Chapter 6.

To sum up, it seems that Malthus always maintained, all recantations notwithstanding, that in human nature self-love had been made stronger by our Creator than benevolence, and this was done for the wisest reasons. The basic reason is that *benevolence cannot be an appropriate motive* for so limited and imperfect a being as a human being, first of all because our knowledge – unlike that of our Creator – is limited. This does not detract from the value of benevolence as a virtue and as an additional motive, but any effort to make society more humane has a chance of success only if fuelled by real-world – that is, self-interested – motives.

Chastity

The other basic virtue existing before social institutions is chastity. Before discussing Malthus's views concerning this virtue, let me clarify what Malthus and his readers meant by this word. Chastity is defined in Dr. Johnson's Dictionary as 'Purity of the body', adding as an illustration a quote from Jeremy Taylor, the father of Anglican Casuistry, declaring that it 'is either abstinence or continence: abstinence is that of virgins or widows; continence, of married persons: chaste marriages are honourable and pleasing to God' (Johnson 1755). The English word, no less than corresponding ones in neo-Latin languages, derive from the Latin *Castitas*, used by Cicero while arguing that the institution of a set of virgins in goddess Vesta's service, hence called *Vestales*, had been conceived in order that 'other women may perceive by their example that their sex is capable by nature of complete chastity' (Cicero L, p. 211). In Plato, Aristotle and other Greek and Hellenistic philosophers no exact match may be found, but *sophrosyne*, temperance, applying among other things also to venereal pleasures was one of the basic virtues. A couple of terms appear in the New Testament, more precisely in Paul's Epistles, later on both rendered in Latin translations by the mentioned Ciceronian word; they are *agneia*, purity, and *enkrateia*, self-restraint (Gal 5, 23; 1 Thess 4, 3; Rom 6, 19; 2 Cor 6, 6). One leading idea for Paul is the sanctity of the body, deriving from the fact that it belongs to the Lord; another is that passions such as lust are marks of the 'old man', to be transformed into such affections as pure and fraternal love, the mark of the 'new man'. Among the fourth-century Christian writers there was an upheaval of ascetic tendencies, both as a reaction to and an imitation of Gnostic currents. The monk Jerome wrote that marriage is a sinful condition and only absolute chastity is compatible with the Christian faith (Jerome AI, p. 130); Augustine's 'orthodox' rejoinder to such aberrations was that marriage is in itself good, and yet less than the widow's continence, which in turn is a lesser good when compared with the maiden's virginity. In more detail, the end of marriage is, strictly, procreation; in a looser sense, marriage has three distinct ends, namely procreation, communal life between spouses, providing a remedy to concupiscence, or, more prosaically, countering the male's temptation to indulge in promiscuous intercourse. Besides, marital sex is perhaps no sin when explicitly aimed at procreation, but clearly a sin, at least a 'venial' – as contrasted with 'mortal' – sin when not serving this purpose. And, last of all, not just continence – that is, a moral attitude – but virginity, which is after all just a gynaecological, not a moral condition – bears moral value, indeed a greater one than continence (Augustine BC, pp. 12–14).

The fact that lust is one of the seven capital vices notwithstanding Medieval catalogues of virtues make no room for chastity as such, considering it to be a part of temperance, which is, in turn, one of Plato's four virtues imported by Ambrose of Milan into Christianity, under the label 'cardinal virtues'. Aquinas typically lists four *cardinal* plus three *theological* virtues, yielding a sum of seven, which corresponds to the list of capital vices just in number, albeit with no one-to-one correspondence between individual vices and virtues. He also provides an alternative, basically Aristotelian, list of eleven virtues, where chastity is annexed to temperance. It may be added that, even though Thomas Aquinas is credited with having proposed more balanced views than Augustine, it is true on the one hand that the tone is more relaxed, but on the other it is also true that in matters of practical consequences he does not go very far. What is different is the theoretical basis, centred on nature, which confers at least a less dualistic and ascetic flavour to what are still roughly the same prescriptions; for example, he keeps Augustine's idea of two basic ends of marriage, namely procreation and the remedy for concupiscence. Indeed he does not make much of the third end Augustine had at least mentioned, that is, of the 'natural compact between the sexes' (Augustine BC, pp. 6–7), and in Book 3, Chapter 122 of the *Summa Contra Gentiles* declares marital sex acceptable in principle, but only in so far as its own end, namely procreation, is respected (Thomas Aquinas SCG, vol. 3, pp. 378–379). Aquinas's foundation of sexual morality in nature aims at finding intrinsic reasons – as contrasted with God's command – for declaring actions right; this task is performed by reconstructing a pattern of ends served by some kind of behaviour facing given characteristics of man: for example, in Chapters 122–124 he illustrates how the institution of marriage is good in so far as human beings, like birds but unlike other mammalians, are born still incapable of looking after themselves, and women are unable to provide alone for their children (and if a woman were so rich as to be able to do that, this would be an exception, not the rule, and prescriptions are to be founded upon the rule, not upon exceptions); besides, children need both firm supervision and education, and women *lack the required amount of both physical strength and reason* (Thomas Aquinas *SCG*, vol. 3, pp. 378–385).

Richard Cumberland, while breaking away from Aristotelian teleology, lays down the basis for a consequentialist voluntarist approach to sexual morality in terms of natural tendencies; these may be assumed to be good ones in so far as they are subservient to some overall good. He develops a discussion of chastity in terms of regulation of an instinct, 'the appetite of venereal enjoyments', that is indeed useful in so far as it serves 'the preservation of the species' and yet needs regulation; accordingly, there are rules on which this instinct may be declared acceptable, and yet 'chastity, from the same rules, fixes bounds' (Cumberland 1672, p. 368) to the satisfaction of this instinct. He adds that the rules regulating chastity 'both in a single and a married state, are not only to benefit the minds and bodies of the chaste person, but to found new families, to preserve old ones, and to extend friendships arising from affinities created by marriage' (p. 368).

Paley declares that, among the beneficial effects of marriage as an institution, besides comfort for individuals, particularly for women, and the peace of society, there is the 'production of the greatest number of healthy children, their better education, and the making of due provision for their settlement in life' (Paley 1785, p. 168) and he goes as far as to derive the prohibition of extra-marital sex from an appraisal of its consequences, more or less beneficial to society as a whole, and pointing to marriage as an institution most favourable to the growth of population and therefore morally approved. He writes that the necessity of confining the intercourse of the sexes to the marriage union is justified by the circumstance that it is only in the latter that this intercourse is sufficiently prolific and allows for sufficient child care (p. 422); thus, even leaving 'the injunctions of the Scripture' aside, 'it is immoral, because it is pernicious, that men and women should cohabit, without undertaking certain irrevocable obligations' (p. 173). Besides recommending marriage for its positive consequences for society, he insists on its positive consequences for individuals, particularly for women, and accordingly includes chastity among the virtues related to our duty to ourselves in so far as indulging in the opposite vice is likely to diminish one's own happiness (p. 26).

It is remarkable that Paley and Malthus argue following similar lines, that is, by proving that certain laws are 'laws of nature' since, given certain factual data, if generally complied with they would produce positive consequences. They also formulate the same recommendation, i.e. marriage with marital fidelity and pre-marital abstinence. This coincidence notwithstanding, Malthus argued in 1798 an opposite view about the general good, not maximum population growth but instead relief from population's pressure, and Paley in 1803 accepted Malthus's view while incorporating it into his own argument in a manner that appeared even to Malthus more convincing than his own previous formulation.

Godwin, the main target for Malthus's polemics in the first *Essay*, and still one important target in the second, had attacked marriage and the family as constituent parts of the set of oppressive institutions under which humankind had been living and, in the appendix to book 8, chapter 8, envisaged for his own ideal society comparatively stable unions between a woman and a man, based on friendship and sexual attraction, and lasting as long as both partners' agreement will persist (Godwin 1993, vol. 4, pp. 338–339). He had even ventured into speculation about the possibility that pleasures of intellectual intercourse would lessen desire for sexual intercourse. But he had also claimed – somewhat inconsistently – that such a stable kind of union would be highly favourable to population growth. At this stage he may have believed that this would be an asset for his doctrine, since before Malthus nobody had questioned population growth as a goal, but just five years later Malthus questioned this very point as a fatal weakness.

Let us come now to Malthus on chastity. He defines this virtue as the cultivation of an innate tendency to develop an attachment to one person of the other sex with faithfulness to such an attachment, and adds that such attachment is not a 'forced produce of artificial society', but has instead 'the most real and solid foundation in nature and reason; being apparently the only virtuous means of avoiding the vice and misery which result [1806: so often] from the principle of population' (Malthus 1803, vol. 2, p. 97). In more detail, in the first *Essay* he declares that a 'powerful instinct' exists leading to 'early attachment to one woman' (Malthus 1798, p. 14) and that the 'passion between the sexes' is one basic component of human nature, which is 'in algebraic language a given quantity' (p. 48) and whose apparent end 'is the continuation of the species, and the formation of such an intimate union of views and interests between two persons as will best promote their happiness, and at the same time secure the proper degree of attention to the helplessness of infancy and the education of the rising generation' (Malthus 1803, vol. 2,

p. 156). Malthus believes that it is for these reasons that the Author of Nature established that 'virtuous love' should be a delightful passion, whose gratification 'sometimes more than counterbalances all its attendant evils' (Malthus 1798, p. 27) and that 'the pleasures of pure love will bear the contemplation of the most improved *reason* and the most exalted *virtue*' (p. 76). An implication is that 'every obstacle in the way of marriage must be undoubtedly considered as a species of unhappiness' (p. 35), and a difficulty carried by this implication is that deferring marriage seems to fall prima facie into 'misery', the first of the two checks indicated in 1798 to population growth. Identifying the proposed remedy with one of the very ills denounced as effects of the principle of population was not the best way of making his theory convincing, and Malthus was forced to make a long detour in order to be able to prove that moral restraint, that is, postponement of marriage accompanied by premarital chastity, is *not* just some kind of 'misery'. This will be one of the themes of his changes in subsequent editions that will be analysed in the following.

Malthus's criticism of Condorcet's utopian plans for a society without marriage and family is that such plans seem to point, for the future of mankind, to 'a promiscuous concubinage, which would prevent breeding, or to something else as unnatural', and this would destroy 'that virtue, and purity of manners' (p. 57), which is apparently praised by Condorcet himself. He concedes to Godwin that abolition of marriage would not necessarily lead to promiscuous concubinage, since 'the love of variety is a vicious, corrupt, and unnatural taste, and could not prevail in any great degree in a simple and virtuous state of society' (p. 71), and that it would instead yield connections between partners of a different sex which would be stable as long as both should find it convenient. His main objection to such 'virtuous free love' is that, once implemented, it would provide the conditions most favourable to population growth, since some of the existing restraints to the decision of engaging in a stable partnership with a person of the other sex would be removed.

Artificial virtues

As a response to man's two basic passions 'two fundamental laws of society' have been agreed upon, namely 'the security of property, and the institution of marriage' (p. 73). Before the institution of society, stability of possession was unknown. Its introduction was soon dictated by natural laws, or by the law of necessity, as men learned from experience that it was the only means of granting greater production of necessaries and the survival of far greater numbers. Even in case a radical redistribution were carried out, so that an absolute equality of possession were established, a difference would re-establish itself in a short time among the parsimonious and prudent on the one hand and the imprudent and profligate on the other, as well as between the off-spring of prolific marriages and that of less prolific ones (Malthus 1803, vol. 1, p. 323).

Given that *this* is the kind of society we live in, there are kinds of behaviour that, albeit perfectly innocent in a state previous to the institution of marriage and the family, have become vicious by now, and there are other kinds of behaviour that are now required even though they were not so in a previous state. Before the introduction of stability of possessions, appropriating whatever thing it was in our power to do was in itself perfectly innocent. This ceased to be true after the institution of property. Such an institution, thus, is not 'natural' in a stricter sense, but, even though not an *original* one, it is at least *necessary* as far as it was required in order to provide individuals with a motivation to work, save and invest. For example, if:

> people were not prevented from gratifying their natural desires with the loaves in the possession of others, the number of loaves would universally diminish. This experience is the foundation of the laws relating to property, and of the distinction of virtue and vice, in the gratification of desires otherwise perfectly the same.
>
> (Malthus 1803, vol. 2, p. 90)

In an analogous way, before the institution of marriage, attachment to one person of the other sex was prompted by nature alone, and thus marriage, albeit an *artificial* institution no less than property is, has – unlike property – some *natural* basis. But from the point of view of human society the upbringing of new generations is too important a task to be left to individual goodwill, and thus, in order to make responsibility for the offspring fully reliable, some formal institution was required.

And yet, even though the shift from the state of nature to the social state carries a remarkable amount of benefits, it also carried some partial evil as a side-effect. Such partial evil is precisely inequality, not an unexpected idea – one is tempted to comment – by somebody who had been visited by Rousseau himself while in his cradle. Malthus writes that 'when these two fundamental laws of society, the security of property and the institution of marriage, were once established, inequality of conditions must necessarily follow' (vol. 1, p. 324) and from 'the inevitable laws of human nature, some human beings will be exposed to want' (p. 325). Since inequality is an unavoidable evil resulting from interaction between different general laws, there is a reason founded in the 'laws of nature' for non-existence of that 'right to subsistence' which Paley – following a claim constantly defended by natural-law thinking – had instead affirmed (Horne 1985). In fact, the Franciscan Scholastics had argued that property is an artificial institution, admissible just because of its positive effects but not justified by nature, and as such implying some permanent duty of compensation for those who, by the fact of being born in a world where land had already been appropriated, are excluded from common ownership. The other Scholastic current, that is, the Dominicans, to which Aquinas himself belonged, argued from an opposite premise, namely that the institution of property is to a point an artificial, albeit not an arbitrary, one, since it is – not unlike marriage for Malthus – rooted in one basic characteristic of human nature and required in order to allow for flourishing of some basic human potentialities. But, even on such a premise, the conclusions reached by the Dominicans concerning the right to subsistence and the priority of right to life on right to property were basically the same. Arguing on these premises, the Scholastic philosophers and early-modern natural-law thinkers claimed that a state of necessity suspends existing property rights and makes it fully legitimate for the poor, when this is required in order to secure survival, to help themselves to the rich man's property. This idea did not disappear even in authors like Locke who adopted a more 'individualistic' starting point than the late Schoolmen. In fact Locke himself admits in the first *Essay on Government* that charity 'gives every Man a Title to so much out of another's Plenty, as will keep him from extream want, where he has no means to subsist otherwise' (Locke 1690, p. 170).

Malthus's background was distant enough from the Dominican or Thomist view and closer to the Franciscan view of natural law as *lex imposita*. This is the doctrine according to which there are *physical laws* established at the time of Creation and moral laws established at the same time and we may reconstruct starting with the world order we may observe. The assumption that makes this possible is that we may learn to adapt ourselves to such order, and by doing so we also find out what is most expedient for the preservation of mankind, but discovering this – given God's benevolence – we also discover what is conforming to God's will. This was the Anglican natural-law tradition whose founder was Richard Cumberland, a tradition that I have proposed to call 'consequentialist voluntarism'. This doctrine was favourable to an empirical approach to nature, in so far as the latter was understood as something different from both an Aristotelian teleological order and a Platonic order of essences to be detected by intuition like that illustrated by the Cambridge Platonists. Nature was assumed instead – following Galileo's and Newton's lesson – to amount to a network of causal connections detected by observation without going beyond the phenomena in order to enquire into some underlying essential order (Cremaschi 2002; 2010, pp. 9–13).

On such a basis, in order to justify the Scholastic argument for the existence of a right by the poor to some of the property of the rich, one should prove that recognition of such a right had been taught to us by our Creator as *the most expedient* way for preserving mankind; by implication one should prove also that such a right *could* effectively be enforced in the real world. But this is precisely what seems to be refuted by Malthus's most innovative achievement in political economy, that is, the law of diminishing returns. This was an idea foreshadowed by James Steuart (1767, vol. 1, pp. 34–37), Anne-Robert-Jacques Turgot (Turgot 1767) and James Anderson (1777), but it was first developed into a systematic account by Malthus, or at least he 'assembled from a few well-known but imperfectly understood bits and pieces of Political Arithmetick a neat and well-rounded theory' (Waterman 1988, p. 92). The idea is basically that scarcity is not a vector of exogenously determined resources, but rather a functional relation between resources and variable human inputs. When so understood, the output, even if positively related to human input, yet tends to grow in an increasingly slower way. In other words, Malthus works out a circular-causation model whose purpose is 'to show that the two interdependent variables of the system in question would gravitate towards an equilibrium configuration' (p. 93). It is from this discovery that the principle of population derives, for the degree of scarcity is related to population size, and there is one given level of population at which there will not be enough food, at least for somebody. Malthus's answer to the proponents of the right to subsistence is that man neither does nor can possess 'a right to subsistence when his labour will not fairly purchase it' (Malthus 1798, p. 127) or that 'by the laws of nature [...] no person has any claim of right on society for subsistence' (p. 128). In the 1807 Appendix he repeats that 'nothing like a claim of right to support can possibly be maintained' (Malthus 1803, vol. 2, p. 212) till we deny the premise that population growth is a consequence of a growth in the means of subsistence and the parallel one that the latter is a consequence of a growth in population, with the proviso that the former must be slower than the latter because of the effects of diminishing returns, which are the basis for that circular-causation model of food and population which provides an account of society as a system in a state of equilibrium. To sum up, Malthus's denial is based on an 'impossibility theorem', namely the argument that a right whose enforcement implied its own self-defeat would be no right at all.

Let us examine discussion of the other institution, marriage. Malthus assumes that this, 'or at least the institution of some express or implied obligation on every man to support his own children' (vol. 1, p. 324) was the other decisive step, besides private property, towards civilized life at early times in the history of humankind. It was necessary to establish regulations concerning the commerce of the sexes, since 'while every man felt secure that all his children would be well provided for by general benevolence, the powers of the earth would be absolutely [word withdrawn in 1806] inadequate to produce food for the population which would inevitably ensue' (p. 323), and 'the most natural and obvious check seemed to be to make every man provide for his own children' (p. 323). Marriage is a desirable state (vol. 2, p. 94), and – he adds in 1806 – 'a state peculiarly suited to the nature of man, and calculated greatly to advance his happiness and remove the temptations to vice' (p. 151). It seems reasonable that such a desirable state should be some kind of prize, as an encouragement to probity and industry; instead, prevailing opinion represents marriage and procreation as *duties*, irrespective of one's ability to provide for children. Besides, both the Poor Laws and private benevolence tend to facilitate the rearing of families among the lower classes, thus 'removing from each individual that heavy responsibility which he would incur by the laws of nature' (p. 120) and also contribute in creating 'an encouragement to marriage by the respect and honour which await the married dame, and the neglect and inconveniencies attendant on the single woman' (vol. 1, p. 50). These opinions should be modified by educating the lower classes to the virtue of prudence. If we could combine the motive of interest with that of duty in trying to persuade people to abstain from marriage before one is able to rear a family, 'it does not seem absolutely hopeless that some partial improvement in society should result from it' (p. 332).

Rights

Even though in twentieth-century terms Malthus's ethics might be classified as virtue ethics, not rights-based ethics, in his view the rights of man do exist. Note that such a belief would be strange enough for an alleged Utilitarian, but I will discuss the point at some length in the following. Note also that, as already discussed, Malthus acknowledges the existence of innate rights, while declaring that he has good reasons for not going into the matter, for this issue was not his 'business at present' (vol. 2, p. 197; Malthus 1798, p. 128). Note that this proviso is again a kind of *hypotheses non fingo* clause, parallel to the one he had invoked concerning happiness. In both cases, Malthus seems to have in mind the kind of 'experimental' moral philosophy that had been inaugurated by Cumberland, where conclusions are reached starting with plausible hypotheses and trying to prove that such hypotheses may account for the given phenomena. His belief in the real existence of rights is confessed for example in the context of his criticism of Thomas Paine's doctrine. He makes it clear that this doctrine is mistaken, 'but not because man is without rights, or that these rights ought not to be known' (p. 126); the point is just that *one* of these alleged rights does not exist, namely the right to subsistence.

As regards other rights, his attitude differs widely from Bentham's, whereby the rights of man were 'nonsense upon stilts'. On the contrary, he seems to agree with Godwin as to the desirability *in principle* of a society where equality is the rule, while disagreeing with him on the viability of such a dream, and he does agree on the desirability in practice, not just in principle, of a society in which the 'unlimited exercise of private judgement' (p. 64) would be established, as opposed to one where the individual is made the slave of the public. One of the weak points in Godwin's plan – he notes in his Letter to Godwin – is the impossibility, in practice and in principle, that the working poor could make combinations in order to raise wages, for any of them will be tempted to – and, note, will 'have an inviolable right to' – offer to work more hours for more money, for 'no man can be prevented from working as many hours as he liked without the interference of Government, which I know you would reprobate as well as myself' (Paul 1876, vol. 1, p. 325; James 1979, p. 68).

Love of equality

Even though it flies in the face of the Malthus-the-reactionary mythology, it is a fact that more than once he manifested commitment to the equality of human beings as an ideal, one not fully implementable but nonetheless a normative standard on which assessment of policies and institutions should be based. This was no reluctant concession by a not-too-convinced Anglican priest to the spirit of the time, but was instead a view fully justified by his own interpretation of the Whig tradition as well as of the teachings of Christianity. In one of his sermons he insists on the accidental character of 'distinctions of birth, fortune, or station' (Malthus 1997–2004, vol. 2, p. 6), by declaring it to be one of the New Testament teachings implied by the Golden Rule as enounced in Matthew 7.12. The idea that descriptive or de facto inequality is no inborn quality, but results mainly from environmental factors, was also a typical eighteenth-century assumption about human nature, one that Malthus, at the time he wrote the mentioned Sermon, may have already met with more than once, for example in Adam Smith's works. He may have read that:

> the difference of natural talents in different men is, in reality, much less than we are aware of; and the very different genius which appears to distinguish men of different professions, when grown up to maturity, is not upon many occasions so much the cause, as the effect of the division of labour.
>
> (Smith 1776, p. 28)

or also that the difference 'between a philosopher and a common street porter, for example, seems to arise not so much from nature, as from habit, custom, and education' (vol. 1, p. 28), since 'the understandings of the greater part of men are necessarily formed by their ordinary employment'.

(vol. 2, pp. 781–782)

Malthus did believe, at least in principle, in equality as a normative criterion, and he also believed in the possibility, at least to a point, of implementing it. He believed that 'the degree of proper pride and spirit of independence, almost invariably connected with education and a certain rank in life' (Malthus 1803, vol. 2, p. 150) is highly desirable, and that it would have been possible to spread such virtues among wider parts of society, or – I will argue in the following chapter – that it was possible to have a society with fewer people in the lowest ranks some day, and to keep even these above certain minimal standards that would make for a life at least compatible with human dignity. I mentioned that the primary polemical target was provided in 1798 by 'systems of equality'. With the end of the French Revolution and the re-definition of British political alignments, the target shifted, in 1803 and even more in following editions, largely from the left to the right, and the Tory-humanitarian supporters of the Poor Laws took the place of utopian egalitarians as the main target. To be more precise, the second *Essay* abounds in attacks on enemies both on the right and on the left. In Book 3, Chapter 1, after a short mention of Robert Wallace, the author of the *Dissertation of the Numbers of Mankind* (Malthus 1803, vol. 1, pp. 306–307; Wallace 1753),

Malthus discusses – in fact repeating what he had already written in the first *Essay* – the doctrine of Condorcet (vol. 1, pp. 307–315), the author of the *Sketch for a Historical Picture of the Progress of the Human Mind* (1795). In Book 3, Chapter 2 he closely follows his 1798 criticism of Godwin and in Chapter 3 he adds a counter-rejoinder to the latter's reply to the first *Essay* (Godwin 1801). In 1817, in Book 3, Chapter 3, he criticizes another enemy on the left, namely Richard Owen. On the one hand he declares his admiration for such a man of real benevolence and wishes him success in his campaign for an act of Parliament limiting working hours for children and preventing their employment at too early an age (Malthus 1803, vol. 1, p. 334). On the other hand, he adds that his two arguments against systems of equality – namely the needs for 'stimulants to exertion' in order to overcome the 'natural indolence of man' (p. 335) and the 'inevitable and necessary poverty and misery in which every system of equality must shortly terminate' (p. 335) from the tendency of populations to increase – also hold in Owen's case and, without some unnatural device for limiting the tendency of a population to grow, the latter's programme cannot work, either. It is precisely on the basis of an endorsement of equality as an ideal combined with a criticism of systems of equality that Malthus discusses poverty as the main moral and political issue of his time. The discussion will be reconstructed in Chapter 7.

Love of liberty

I have mentioned in Chapter 3 that the main reason for opposing paternalistic attitudes lying beneath the Poor Laws was, in the first *Essay*, allegiance to the principles of liberty and equality and that the only effective and humane alternative was assumed to be granting the poor more independence. In the second *Essay*, Malthus tries to single out virtuous examples in the real world. He claims that Scotland as a whole is a poorer country than England, and yet in this country there is less widespread poverty and more spirit of liberty and dignity. This – he contends – is a result of a different system of poor relief. The poor in Scotland, he writes:

> are in general supported by voluntary contributions, distributed under the inspection of the minister of the parish; and it appears, upon the whole, that they have been conducted with considerable judgment. Having no claim of right to relief, and the supplies, from the mode of their collection, being necessarily uncertain, and never abundant, the poor have considered them merely as a last resource in cases of extreme distress, and not as a fund on which they might safely rely, and an adequate portion of which belonged to them by the laws of their country in all difficulties.
>
> The consequence of this is, that the common people make very considerable exertions to avoid the necessity of applying for such a scanty and precarious relief.
>
> (Malthus 1803, vol. 1, p. 287)

In 1806, and in a modified form in 1807, he half-recanted the above claim in his customary clumsy way, admitting that it was true that the Poor Laws in Scotland were 'not materially different' from those established in England, and yet they had been 'very differently understood and executed', so that, whatever the law, 'the practice is generally as here represented' (vol. 1, p. 287 fn.; Waterman 2004, pp. 143–162).

The first *Essay*'s shocking novelty was the announcement that population growth was no unmixed blessing. Note that Malthus's conclusion did not depend on value premises different from those of his contemporaries, but on a proof the non-viability of goals suggested by such values without taking hard facts into account. An implicit assumption of all eighteenth-century pro-population doctrines – including Adam Smith's – was a perfectly elastic supply of land, that is, constant availability of more farmland. For example, Smith argues that the factor regulating population growth among the greater portion of society, that is, the labouring poor, is the scantiness of subsistence, and that 'it can do so in no other way than by destroying a great part of the children which their fruitful marriages produce' (Smith 1776, p. 98); and the 'liberal reward of labour' is the factor that, by enabling them to provide for their children, naturally tends to widen and extend the limits set 'to the further multiplication of the human species' (vol. 1, pp. 97–98); besides, the level of wages depends not on the absolute wealth of a nation but on its growing or declining condition and, as a consequence:

> the demand for men, like that for any other commodity, necessarily regulates the production of men; quickens it when it goes on too slowly, and stops it when it advances too fast. It is this demand which regulates and determines the state of propagation in all the different countries of the world, in North America, in Europe, and in China; which renders it rapidly progressive in the first, slow and gradual in the second, and altogether stationary in the last.
>
> (vol. 1, p. 98)

Smith's unspoken assumption is that in North America more men will be easily absorbed by the market and will create their own subsistence by putting more land to tillage. The circumstance that more land is available in America and not in China is what makes for the former's 'progressive' state and the latter's 'stationary' state. In 1803 Malthus qualifies his own previous conclusion while trying to pave objections. The main objection came from Paley's argument in his *Natural Theology*, where the principle of population was accepted and Paley's previous unqualified pro-population attitude was limited without giving up population growth as a valuable end on principle. Malthus's stratagem for defending himself is one of the most typical controversialist's moves, namely an insulating strategy, or creating a protective belt to one's claim (Dascal and Cremaschi 1999). He does so by introducing a distinction between two distinct desiderata: (i) a great actual population; (ii) a state of society in which 'squalid [abject] *poverty* and *dependence* are comparatively but little known' (Malthus 1803, vol. 2, p. 109). Two preliminary comments are in order before discussing how the stratagem works.

The first comment is that the former desideratum was shared by eighteenth-century political writers as almost a matter of course: first, on reasons of national power; second, on positive theological reasons based on the Biblical precept to grow and fill the earth interpreted as a precept requesting as much procreation as possible as a duty; third, on a natural theological argument based on the metaphysical plenitude Platonic argument (Malthus 1798, p. 9) in turn assumed to prove that filling the earth was a good in itself and perhaps a way of completing the task of Creation; and fourth, (Paley's case) on the basis of a total-sum utilitarian argument claiming that the numbers of population are a measuring rod for the total sum of happiness in a given country (Paley 1785, p. 587). Malthus had admitted in *The Crisis* that a growth in population is desirable in relation to the growth of the total sum of happiness (Empson 1837, p. 482) – that is, on the same value premises as Paley (1785, p. 588) – but then immediately reversing the argument's direction by contending that, contrary to what Paley assumed, since 'in the ordinary progress of human affairs, whatever, in any way, contributes to make a people happier, tends to render them more numerous' (p. 589) 'the actual population may be only a sign of the happiness that is past' (Empson 1837, p. 482). What Malthus, unlike Paley, had been able to understand and put to work, is Smith's dynamic argument according to which real wages are a function of population growth (or, the faster population growth is, the higher the real wages), and when population is stationary real wages are at subsistence level. Even after Paley had accepted the principle of population in the *Natural Theology*, there is no indication that he had been able to see the point in the Smith–Malthus argument. In fact, he seems to confine the principle's effects to some future state that will come about only after limits have been attained which are 'not yet attained, nor even approached, in any country of the world' (Paley 1802, p. 542). Perhaps, at the time young Malthus was writing *The Crisis*, he had such considerations already in mind as those he first spelled out in 1820 in the *Principles* concerning 'proportions' and 'middle points' (Cremaschi 2010). These considerations are that all factors, including population, best contribute to producing some given result when they are available in the optimal amount, whose level depends in turn on the proportion existing between the factor under discussion and other factors. Thus, partly in order to foster the progress of wealth, and accordingly population growth, and the mass of happiness and virtue, which is the real object to be wished for, since 'it is not the duty of man simply to propagate his species, but to propagate virtue and happiness' (Malthus 1803, vol. 1, p. 148), the right proportion is desirable between all required factors, including population. Thus – Malthus adds in his first *Essay* – the only efficient and morally acceptable way of fostering the goal of a more numerous population is making the provisions grow on which an increasing population may live decently, and any other way of increasing population 'is vicious, cruel, and tyrannical, and in any state of tolerable freedom cannot therefore succeed' (Malthus 1798, p. 50).

The second comment is that Malthus's second desideratum – namely less poverty and dependence – is twofold, including (i) reduction of poverty, (ii) reduction of dependence. The latter is distinguished from the former, and apparently neither reducible to nor negotiable with increasing amounts of it. This is no trifling distinction for, obviously enough, reduction of dependence or personal liberty is a legacy of the Whig tradition and it would have been hard to justify it as an independent goal for a Benthamite, for whom every desideratum should be comparable on the basis of one measuring rod.

Prudence

Clarification is again in order, concerning the various meanings of the word. Prudence is defined by Dr. Johnson as 'wisdom applied to practice' (Johnson 1755). The definition reflects a lack of two distinct words in English for denoting either theoretical or practical wisdom, and is vague enough to cover both the ancient and medieval philosophical idea of prudence as intellectual excellence and the modern idea of prudence as inductive knowledge referred primarily to one's private business. The meaning of Aristotle's term *phronesis* had been rendered in Latin, starting with Cicero, by the word *prudentia*. Aristotle understood *phronesis* as an intellectual excellence, but also as a constitutive part of all moral excellences, the disposition to use one's practical reason in the best way.

The Stoics introduced a distinction between superior and inferior prudence. The latter is the care of one's own interest – which cannot be, for the Stoics, a virtue, since virtue for them is undivided, but pertains to *adiaphora*, or to things indifferent. Middle Stoicism introduced a distinction between two different kinds of *adiaphora*, namely between the *rejected* ones and the *preferred* ones, as well as the idea of *kathekonta* – not real duties but rather those things that are convenient. As a result, taking care of oneself and then of one's immediate relations was classified as belonging to such kind of second-rank virtues, having little to do with the intellectual virtue of good deliberation. One more twist was added by Panætius and his follower Cicero, for whom prudence became a virtue governing intellectual as well as practical enterprises, in so far as our intellectual life should also be governed by a virtue directing us to worthy intellectual enterprises, while eschewing empty curiosity. Drawing on Cicero, Ambrose of Milan made prudence one of the four cardinal virtues. He thus modified the meaning of Plato's original catalogue, since for the latter *phronesis* was wisdom as such, having little to do with practice. Aquinas made *prudentia* the overarching virtue of practical reason or the 'mother' of virtues declaring, in *De Veritate* 14, 5 *ad* 11, that all other moral virtues are shaped by prudence (Thomas Aquinas V, p. 292).

A decisive turning point was in the sixteenth century. Prudence lost its Scholastic meaning of intellectual excellence regarding practical reason and, while becoming a more ubiquitous notion, it started to split into various levels and kinds. The Stoic distinction between superior and inferior prudence was widely accepted, and prudence as such became identified with inferior prudence, that is, the enlightened care of one's own interest. It is remarkable that in French the term *sagesse* won wide popularity as a name for practical wisdom, one less selfish and calculating than prudence but also more sceptical than Aristotelian *phronesis*. Prudence *qua inferior prudence* won a more detailed connotation also by contrast with the newly redefined idea of what we now call 'science'. Hobbes notes that wisdom is an English term that translates both *prudentia* and *sapientia* and claims that prudence is not philosophy, because it is not attained by reasoning, and is 'but a memory of successions of events in times past' (Hobbes 1651, p. 664), that prudence is 'much experience' and science is 'much sapience' (p. 37). In short, with Hobbes prudence becomes inductive, empirical knowledge, independent of theory and closer to Aristotle's *techne* than to *phronesis*.

Butler, in the framework of an attempt to reconcile self-love and benevolence, in a sense gives prudence pride of place, since all reasons for being moral are prudential reason. Prudence is clearly understood by him as inferior prudence for he writes that a 'due concern about our own interest or happiness, and a reasonable endeavour to secure and promote it, which is, I think, very much the meaning of the word *prudence*, in our language [...] this is virtue, and the contrary behaviour faulty and blameable' (Butler 1736, p. 311) and that conscience 'approves of prudent actions and disapproves imprudent ones' (p. 312) apart from any consideration of their consequences in terms of happiness and suffering. In more detail, being moral is an option that may be justified as a rational one if we assume that there is an after life and a God who may punish and compensate – note that this is an excellent summary of Kant's idea of a heteronymous ethics. Butler claims that 'pleasure and pain are the consequences of our actions: and we are endued by the Author of our Nature with capacities of foreseeing these consequences' (p. 167) and that, 'by prudence and care, we may, for the most part, pass our days in tolerable ease and quiet', and those who are not prudent 'follow those ways, the fruit of which they know [...] will be disgrace, and poverty, and sickness, and ultimately death' (pp. 167–168). From such a 'constitution of things', Butler adds:

> it cannot but follow, that prudence and imprudence, which are of the nature of virtue and vice, must be, as they are, respectively rewarded and punished.
>
> And thus, that God governs the world by general fixed laws, that he has endued us with capacities of reflecting upon this constitution of things, and foreseeing the good and bad consequences of our behaviour; plainly implies some sort of moral government, since from such a constitution of things it cannot but follow, that prudence and imprudence, which are of the nature of virtue and vice, must be, as they are, respectively rewarded and punished.
>
> (p. 176)

For Hume prudence is, as a matter of course, 'inferior prudence' and the virtues properly understood are other-regarding dispositions. What he adds is the claim that common sense has a tendency to blur the distinction between moral virtues and natural abilities, or better, argues that the distinction between the voluntary and the involuntary was what gave occasions to moralists for drawing the distinction between moral and non-moral qualities; but he adds that this is more a matter of curiosity than a practically relevant issue, since people in common life 'naturally praise or blame whatever pleases or displeases them [and] consider prudence under the character of virtue as well as benevolence' (Hume 1739–1740, vol. 1, p. 389). Prudence and industry are approved because of the spontaneous sympathy people feel with the benefits these qualities yield for their owners. In fact, ancient moralists 'made no scruple of placing prudence at the head of the cardinal virtues' (p. 389). For example, Aristotle ranks qualities useful to ourselves, such as courage and prudence, 'among the virtues', together with 'justice and friendship' (Hume 1751, p. 113), that is, qualities useful to others. Adam Smith made prudence one of the three private virtues, on the same level as justice and benevolence and under the supervision of the meta-virtue of self-command. Prudence as a private virtue is inferior prudence, the care of one's own interest (Smith 1759, p. 216), and yet it is compatible with morality, provided that the latter is not understood in the way of fanatical preachers. It is coldly esteemed, though not admired, by the impartial spectator, basically for the same reasons as those pointed out by Hume, namely because we tend to sympathize with what brings about a correspondence between means and ends (pp. 263–264).

Paley's moral epistemology is clearly a consequentialist one, but his normative ethics is an ethic of duty. Prudence for him carries out a subordinate role. According to one of the definitions proposed by moralists, it is the virtue that 'suggests the best means of attaining' (Paley 1785, p. 25) those good ends that have been pointed out by benevolence; according to another definition, it is the virtue that is 'attentive to our own interest' (p. 26), which has as its own end, no less than benevolence, the 'increase of happiness in nature' (p. 26), and takes 'equal concern in the future as in the present' (p. 26). 'There is always understood to be a difference between an act of prudence and an act of duty' (p. 36) but, given his consequentialist moral epistemology, such difference is just a matter of degree; in fact, while performing both an act of duty and an act of prudence, 'we consider solely what we shall gain or lose by the act', and the only difference is that 'in the one case, we consider what we shall gain or lose in the present world; in the other case, we consider also what we shall gain or lose in the world to come' (p. 40). So understood, private prudence is an important virtue in a well-ordered society, and its role cannot be substituted by the enlightened action of public rulers who are not in a position to provide a remedy for lack of 'domestic care and prudence' (p. 40).

Godwin's moral epistemology is – in so far as it is a consistent one – no less consequentialist than Paley's, to the point of defining morality as 'that system which teaches us to contribute, upon all occasions, to the extent of our power, to the well-being and happiness of every intellectual and sensitive existence' (Godwin 1793, vol. 4, p. 78). And yet his normative ethics is not an ethic of duty but a 'system of disinterested benevolence' (p. 195). He strongly opposes systems based on an opposition of self-love and beneficence, arguing – not unlike Butler – that beneficence is a motivation as basic as self-love (pp. 189–192). Virtue consists of those actions by an intelligent being proceeding from kind and benevolent intention, and having a tendency to contribute to general happiness, or 'a principle in the mind, by which we are enabled to form a true estimate of the pretensions of different reasons inviting us to preference' (p. 193). A vicious person is somebody who 'makes a false estimate, and prefers a trivial and partial good to an important and comprehensive one' (p. 193). The point is that it does not matter *whose* good the greater good is, for self-love is not an original principle and benevolence is at least as much an original disposition as the former; thus, it is *rational* to be moral, i.e. benevolent, on every occasion when a sufficiently comprehensive good is at stake. In this vein, Godwin constantly chides moralists who think of stimulating men to good deeds by considerations of 'frigid prudence' and 'necessary self-interest', and extols instead standards of magnanimity over those of 'personal prudence'.

Malthus warns the reader that, albeit a decent society is possible on principle, it is as well not to rejoice too much in any 'distant views of this kind' (Malthus 1803, vol. 1, p. 195) for such views may remain as impossible to bring about as Condorcet's and Godwin's dreams unless 'prudential habits' become widespread among the poor. The reason is that, without prudence, every benefit carried by justice and beneficence would be effaced. Prudence for Malthus is an attitude recommended by self-love, not by a wish for the general good, and it is useful not only to society at large when generally or widely practised, but also simply to those who practice it even though they live in a badly ordered society. In other words – as he notes in 1806 – it benefits society while benefiting the individual with no need for intention and design. It may play such a role thanks to the principle of unintended results, by which 'the most ignorant are led to promote the general happiness' (vol. 2, p. 214). All 'the greatest improvements' are effected thanks to each individual's effort in pursuing his own 'interest and happiness' (vol. 1, p. 105). Prudence is not only a 'natural', but also an 'artificial' virtue, since prudential conduct – as Malthus believes – is, while still being the sovereign private virtue, the basic civic virtue. The claim of such a coincidence is indeed one basic eighteenth-century paradox, the idea, defended by Adam Smith and, before him, by Montesquieu, that the good citizen's main virtue is identical with that of a good *pater familias*. For Malthus this familiar idea is construed within the context of his new discovery (the principle of population), so that a citizen's main virtue becomes the main virtue of a prospective husband, which may be on several occasions the virtue of refraining from hastily marrying. Spreading prudential habits among the population is thus the most valuable object for a wise man of government, a most effective way of promoting the improvement of human society, and indeed the way less dangerous to established rights and liberty. Note that to lay one's bet on the poor man's prudence is not tantamount to adopting a visionary project of making all the poor rational individuals with public spirit *before* they can be liberated from abject poverty, since prudence does not need to be recommended by any view of the public good and does not require as its precondition any general scheme of improvement.

It is because of such a multifarious role that prudence becomes the 'trump' in the social game, and Malthus's project of a decent society is based on the assumption of a possible spontaneous emergence of order, given a few preliminary 'artificial' inputs, namely education, law and order, civil liberties. This is made clear in 1806, when Malthus specifies that the requirements for growth of prudential habits are: (i) security of property; (ii) *respectability and importance* which are given to the lower classes. In order to foster this goal, a free constitution and good government are required, which are effective not so much because they yield good and equal laws, but because they give to everybody greater personal respectability and greater fear of personal degradation (vol. 1, p. 131). The 'main cause of very slow progress of freedom, so disheartening to every liberal mind, I should say that it was the confusion that had existed respecting the causes of the unhappiness and discontents which prevail in society' (p. 131). In fact, a diminished proportion of births 'invariably follows an improved government, and the greater degree of *personal respectability* which it gives to the lower classes of society' (p. 227).

Prudence, by recommending due care for our own interest, may on most occasions provide a stronger motive for right behaviour than a sense of duty alone would do. This holds, not surprisingly, for the moral restraint issue. Early marriage is dangerous to society and should be avoided, among other things, out of a sense of duty. But a kind of romantic pride would suggest sacrificing freedom and commodity to love while disregarding the consequences, and Malthus admits that there is something admirable in such an irresponsible attitude, for 'if all is to be sacrificed' – he writes – 'I do not know in what better cause it can be done' (vol. 1, p. 331). However, he adds that if we:

> were to remove or weaken the motive of interest [...] I fear that we should have but a weak substitute in a sense of duty. But if to the present beneficial effects, known to result from a sense of interest, we could super-add a sense of duty [...] it does not seem absolutely hopeless that some partial improvement in society should result from it.

> (vol. 1, p. 332)

Bibliography

Anderson, J. (1777) *An Enquiry into the Nature of Corn-Laws.* Edinburgh: Mundel.
Aristotle (*EN* [1956]) *The Nichomachean Ethics.* Ed. by Rackham, H. Cambridge, MA: Harvard University Press.

Augustine (*BC* [2001]) *De Bono Coniugali. De Sancta Virginitate.* Ed. by Walsh, P.G. Oxford: Clarendon.

Burke, E. (1790 [1981]) Reflections on the Revolution in France. In *The Writings and Speeches of Edmund Burke.* Volume 7. Ed. by Langford, P. Oxford: Clarendon Press.

Butler, J. (1726 [2006]) Fifteen Sermons Preached at the Rolls Chapel. In *The Works of Bishop Butler.* Ed. by White, D.E. Rochester: University of Rochester Press.

Butler, J. (1736 [2006]) The Analogy of Religion, Natural and Revealed, in the Constitution and Course of Nature. In *The Works of Bishop Butler.* Ed. by White, D.E. Rochester, NY: University of Rochester Press.

Cicero, Marcus Tullius (*LAE* [2006]) Laelius de Amicitia. In *De Republica, De Legibus, Cato Maior de Senectute, Laelius de Amicitia.* Ed. by Powell, J.G.F. Oxford: Clarendon.

Cicero, Marcus Tullius (*L* [2006]) De Legibus. In *De Republica, De Legibus, Cato Maior de Senectute, Laelius de Amicitia.* Ed. by Powell, J.G.F. Oxford: Clarendon.

Cicero, Marcus Tullius (*O* [1994]) *De Officiis.* Ed. by Winterbottom, R. Oxford: Clarendon.

Condorcet, J.-A.-N. de Caritat, Marquis de (1795 [1955]). *Sketch for a Historical Picture of the Progress of yhe Human Mind.* Introduction by Hampshire, S. London: Weidenfeld and Nicolson.

Cremaschi, S. (2002) 'Two views of Natural Law and the shaping of political economy'. *Croatian Journal of Philosophy* 2(5), pp. 65–80.

Cremaschi, S. (2006) The Mill-Whewell Controversy on Ethics and its Bequest to Analytic Philosophy. In *Rationality in Belief and Action.* Ed. by Baccarini, E. and Prijić Samaržja, S. Rijeka: University of Rijeka, Faculty of Arts and Sciences and Croatian Society for Analytic Philosophy.

Cremaschi, S. (2010) 'Malthus's idea of a moral and political science'. *The Journal of Philosophical Economics* 3(2), pp. 5–57.

Cumberland, R. (1672) *De Legibus Naturae Disquisitio Philosopica.* London: Flesher.

Dascal, M. and Cremaschi, S. (1999) 'The Malthus-Ricardo correspondence: sequential structure, argumentative patterns, and rationality'. *Journal of Pragmatics* 31(4), pp. 1129–1172.

Empson, W. (1837) 'Life, writings and character of Mr. Malthus'. *Edinburgh Review* 64(80), pp. 469–506.

Gisborne, T. (1789 [1798]) *The Principles of Moral Philosophy.* Fifth edn. London: Cadell.

Gisborne, T. (1794) *An Enquiry into the Duties of Men in the Higher and Middle Classes of Society.* London: J. Davis.

Godwin, W. (1793 [1993]) Enquiry Concerning Political Justice. In *Political and Philosophical Writings of William Godwin.* Volume 3. Ed. by Philp, M. London: Pickering and Chatto.

Godwin, W. (1801 [1993]) Thoughts occasioned by the perusal of Dr. Parr's Spital Sermon, preached at Christ Church, April 15, 1800, being a reply to the attacks of Dr. Parr, Mr. MackIntosh, the author of an Essay on Population, and others. In *Political and Philosophical Writings of William Godwin.* Volume 2. Ed. by Philp, M. London: Pickering and Chatto.

Hobbes, Th. (1646 [1961]) Elementa Philosophica de Cive. In *Opera Philosophica.* Volume 2. Ed. by Molesworth, Th .Aalen: Scientia.

Hobbes, Th. (1651 [1652]) The Leviathan. In *The English Works.* Volume 3. Ed. by Molesworth, Th. Aalen: Scientia.

Hole, R. (1989) *Pulpits, Politics and the Public Order in England 1760–1823*. Cambridge: Cambridge University Press.

Horne, T.A. (1985) 'The poor have a claim founded in the law of nature: William Paley and the rights of the poor'. *Journal of the History of Philosophy* 23(1), pp. 51–70.

Hume, D. (1739–1740 [2007]) *A Treatise of Human Nature*. Ed. by Norton, D.F. and Norton, M.J. Oxford: Oxford University Press.

Hume, D. (1751 [2003]) *An Enquiry concerning the Principles of Morals*. Ed. by Beauchamp, T.L. Oxford: Oxford University Press.

James, P. (1979) *Population Malthus. His Life and Time*. London: Routledge.

Jerome (*AI* [1883]) Adversus Iovinianum. In *Patrologiae cursus completus*. Series latina. Volume 23. Ed. by Migne, J.-P. Paris: Garnier.

Johnson, S. (1755) *A Dictionary of the English Language*. London: Klapton.

Locke, J. (1690 [1988]) *Two Treatises of Government*. Ed. by Laslett, P. Cambridge: Cambridge University Press.

Malthus, Th.R. (1798 [1986]) An Essay on the Principle of Population. In *The Works of Thomas Robert Malthus*. Volume 1. Ed. by Wrigley, E.A. and Souden, D. London: Pickering.

Malthus, Th.R. (1803 [1989]) *An Essay on the Principle of Population. The Version Published in 1803, with the Variora of 1806, 1807, 1817 and 1826*. Ed. by James, P. Cambridge: Cambridge University Press.

Malthus, Th.R. (1997–2004) *The Unpublished Papers in the Collection of Kanto Gakuen University*. Ed. by Pullen, J. Cambridge: Cambridge University Press.

Marcus Aurelius Antoninus (*SI* [1953]) *The Communings with Himself together with his Speeches and Sayings*. Ed. by Haines, C.R. Cambridge, MA: Harvard University Press.

McLean, M. (2003) Did Paley ignore Hume on the Argument from Design? In *Faith, Reason, and Economics: Essays in Honour of Anthony Waterman*. Ed. by Hum, D. Winnipeg: St. John's College Press, University of Manitoba.

Nicole, P. (1675 [1971]) De la charité et de l'amour propre. In *Essais de morale*. Volume 1. Genève: Slatkine.

Paley, W. (1785 [2002]) *The Principles of Moral and Political Philosophy*. Ed. by LeMahieu, D.L. Indianapolis, IN: Liberty Fund.

Paley, W. (1794 [1970]) *A View of the Evidences of Christianity*. Westmead: Gregg.

Paley, W. (1802 [1970]) *Natural Theology: or: Evidences of the Existence and Attributes of the Deity, Collected from the Appearances of Nature*. Westmead: Gregg.

Paul, Ch.K. (1876 [2002]) *William Goodwin: His Friends and Contemporaries*. 2 volumes. Whitefish, MT: Kessinger.

Plato (*G* [1953]) Gorgias. In *Lysis Symposium Gorgias*. Ed. by Lamb, W.R.M. Cambridge, MA: Harvard University Press.

Pope, A. (1734 [1978]) An Essay on Man. In *Poetical works*. Ed. by Davis, H. Oxford: Oxford University Press.

Pretyman, G. (1789) *A Sermon Preached before the Lords... January 30, 1789*. London: Cadell.

Smith, A. (1759 [1976]) *The Theory of Moral Sentiments*. Ed. by Raphael, D.D. and Macfie, A.L. Oxford: Clarendon Press,

Smith, A. (1776 [1976]) *An Inquiry into the Nature and Causes of the Wealth of Nations*. Ed. by Campbell, R.H., Skinner, A.S., and Todd, W.B. Oxford: Clarendon Press.

Southey, R. (1804) Review of An Essay on The Principle of Population. In *The Annual Review of History and Literature*. Second Volume for 1803 (30 April 1804), pp. 292–301.

Steuart, J. (1767 [1998]) *An Inquiry into the Principles of Political Economy.* Ed. by Skinner, A. London: Pickering.

Thomas Aquinas (*SCG* [1918–1930]) *Summa Contra Gentiles.* Rome: Commissio Leonina.

Thomas Aquinas (*V* [1964]) *De Veritate.* Taurini: Marietti.

Thompson, D.M. (2008) *Cambridge Theology in the Nineteenth Century.* Aldershot: Ashgate.

Turgot, A.-R.-J. (1767 [1972]) Sur le mémoir de Saint-Pérevy. In *Oeuvres de Turgot.* Volume 2. Ed. by Schelle, G. Glashütten im Taunus: Auvermann.

Wallace, R. (1753 [1969]) *Dissertation of the Numbers of Mankind in Modern and Ancient Times.* New York: Kelley.

Waterman, A.M.C. (1988) 'Hume, Malthus and the stability of equilibrium'. *History of Political Economy* 20(1), p. 85–94.

Waterman, A.M.C. (1991) *Revolution, Economics and Religion. Christian Political Economy, 1798–1833.* Cambridge: Cambridge University Press.

Waterman, A.M.C. (2004) Hey John. In *Oxford Dictionary of National Biography.* Volume 26 HAYCKOCK–HICHENS. Ed. by Matthew, H.C.G. and Harrison, B. Oxford: Oxford University Press.

Watson, R. (1818) *Anecdotes of the Life of R.W. Watson, Bishop of Llandaff.* Second edn. London: Cadell.

Wilberforce, W. (1797) *A Practical View of the Prevailing Religious System of Professed Christians, in the Middle and Higher Classes in this Country, Contrasted with Real Christianity.* Dublin: Dugdale.

6 Malthus's third normative ethics
A morality of humanity

Humanity

The '*gradual* abolition' of the Poor Laws, brought about in ways consistent 'with humanity' (Malthus 1803, vol. 2, p. 138) as suggested in the 1817 edition of the second *Essay*, marks the not inconsiderable way travelled in 19 years between the doctrine's original formulation and its next-to-final version. This is enough to reject the widespread opinion that Malthus's arguments in the following editions 'are no different' (Jensen 1999, p. 457 fn. 5) from those of the 1803 edition. The implications of the above mentioned qualification are that: (i) Malthus had come closer to Paley in 1803, but the ground of such rapprochement was more theodicy than ethics; (ii) and yet, around 1806 he started to feel uneasy with some of the implications of Paleyite theodicy and started to look around for ways of mitigating them; (iii) John Bird Sumner's new, and indeed post-Malthusian, theodicy offered him what he was looking for, namely a replacement of happiness with virtue as the element to be maximized by divine rational choice, and this helped him to avoid a number of unwished for consequences, all of them connected with the *general good particular hell* equation; (iv) Thomas Chalmers's contributions offered him one additional element for a more plausible solutions, namely a *practical* response to the theodicy challenge; (v) this implied, besides changes in the abstract subject of theodicy, also rather drastic changes in the real-world issue of anti-poverty policies, with a shift 'from punishment of the poor to investment in their human capital' (p. 450); (vi) this meant eventually turning almost everything Malthus had been contending for in 1798 upside down: in the next-to-final version, passions may be controlled by reason; education can change the original impulses; institutions, not just market mechanisms, do matter; and resources may grow *faster than population*, not only because the latter's growth may be slackened, but primarily because there is, besides the *soil*, which is limited in extension and of decreasing quality, one more resource, *man*, who is perfectible, not to an unlimited extent but at least to an unknown extent; (vii) and, strange as it may sound, Malthus did not only admit of almost everything Godwin had contended for – this after all happens almost invariably in controversies – but he did so by effect of an influence by people Godwin would have classified among his enemies, the Evangelicals.

The Malthusian controversy as applied theology

Critics from the right and from the left

I have already mentioned that the first *Essay* occasioned a number of reactions from different quarters. It is now time to examine the effects of those reactions on the gradual process of modification in Malthus's theory. The second *Essay* had a remarkably greater impact with reactions that grew in number by a snowball effect. Indeed a remarkable controversy developed between 1804 and 1830 through pamphlets, reviews and letters in influential journals such as the *Edinburgh Review*, the *British Critic*, the *Christian Observer*, the *Monthly Magazine*, the *Monthly Review*, the *Analytical Review* and the *Literary Journal*. The controversy, albeit recently reconstructed in some detail (James 1979, pp. 116–136, 382–406; Gilbert 1998), might still be the subject of further analysis, particularly trying to locate it within the framework of the history of moral doctrines. This would go beyond the scope of this book, and mentioning at least a few interesting aspects of the controversy itself may be enough here. One is a subdivision of conflicting parties into a multiform spectrum; orthodox Anglicans such as Simplex, the author of an anti-Malthusian pamphlet (Simplex 1808), and the *British Critic* reviewers; Whigs like 'Philander', the author of a letter to the *Monthly Magazine* (Philander 1804), and the *Edinburgh Review, Monthly Magazine* and *Analytical Review* reviewers; romantics such as Robert Southey and Samuel Coleridge, who attacked Malthus as an enemy of traditional values, and radicals such as William Cobbett and William Hazlitt, who attacked him as an enemy of the poor. Besides, there were Evangelicals like Thomas Gisborne, Richard Bird Sumner, Thomas Chalmers and the contributors to the *Christian Observer*, whom will be discussed in the present chapter.

Another aspect of the controversy is a recurrent feature in controversies (Cremaschi and Dascal forthcoming), that is, a holistic, and sometimes opportunistic, use of arguments in order to favour one given overall view. In this production of arguments – well or ill-adjusted either to the goal of attacking Malthus or to that of emphasizing the importance of his views – more than once sensible and competent remarks are made, and then these are taken up by the opposite camp at some later phase of the discussion. For example, James Mill in the *Literary Journal* raises a point that was taken up again by several commentators, not all of them so favourable to Malthus's principle. The point is that Malthus had:

> greatly over-rated the tendency in population to exceed; and that he has overlooked many things in the nature and situation of man, which have a tendency to keep provision on a level with population. Man consumes

food; but man too is the great creator of food; and when a man is produced, there is produced along with him the means of providing food [...] The great cause which hitherto has prevented the industry of man from producing much greater wonders than it has been seen to produce, are the shackles which have been placed upon it; the want of complete freedom to employ it always in the way most advantageous to the individual.

(Mill 1803, p. 587)

Here the *Gricean implicatures*, that is, those implications of an utterance that cannot be derived by entailment but may be grasped instead through its contextual interpretation (Grice 1989, pp. 22–40), are the following: (i) the discovery of the principle is important since it is a 'progressive' one and flies in the face of prejudice and received views; (ii) yet, it is the discovery of a *tendency*, which, like all tendencies, may or may not yield desirable or dangerous effects; (iii) in any event, it may provide one more argument for free trade, which is in turn good in itself, with or without the principle of population. In the course of the Malthusian controversy, the first among such implicatures was rejected by the more orthodox Christian critics because of its apparent irreligious implications, but at a certain stage it was domesticated by Sumner and Chalmers, the most devout among Malthus readers, and made the key stone of a new theological vision; the second implicature, in turn, was used by most of those who rejected the principle as such, shifting from Mill's qualification of the principle's actual scope to its reduction to a purely theoretical limiting condition. La Vergata (1990, pp. 93–123) starting with a different approach, has remarkably formulated the same suggestions with regard to this particular controversy, noting how the same arguments are used by critics from different sides in order to draw conclusions different from Malthus's while starting with the latter's own arguments, or to argue claims incompatible with those drawn by other critics from the very same assumptions. He writes that, for example, such a writer with radical tendencies as William Edward Hickson, publishing in the Benthamite *Westminster Review*, advances 'rather crude teleological arguments with some nonchalance' (p. 120).

The third aspect worth commenting is the controversy's 'closure'. It is marked by three facts: (i) repeated revision of the theory in subsequent editions of the *Essay*, incorporating objections into the restyled argument; effects of revisions are – *pace* Hollander's claim of Malthus's evolution towards more secularism – more explicitly presence of theological considerations, and a more clearly voluntarist view of natural laws; (ii) incorporation of the new theodicy worked out by Sumner and Chalmers, based on the principle of population and making the principle compatible with Anglican orthodoxy; (iii) design of a more detailed alternative to Poor Laws, one that, if read carefully, would have provided an alternative to the disastrous experiment in social engineering implemented shortly after Malthus's death.

I already suggested that analyzing the controversy as a whole would go beyond our present purpose and might be rather the subject for a distinct book. Here I will concentrate on three Evangelical critics who provided Malthus with the occasion for the deepest revisions in his doctrine qua applied moral theology.

Evangelicals: Gisborne

The first *Essay* – as noted in Chapter 3 – was the occasion for misgivings by the *British Critic*, the official voice of the Anglican establishment. The new theological doctrine of the second *Essay* yet soothed critics from this side, and in fact the journal added to its lengthy review the following 'recantation':

> It is but justice to this author to declare, that in this edition of his Essay, we do not find any trace of what we conceived to be intimated in the former; a notion that human minds were framed, by some natural process from inert matter. On the contrary, he seems here to write as impressed with a due sense of religious as well as moral truths.
>
> (*British Critic* 1804, p. 245)

In terms of biography, this recantation was for Malthus a kind of safe-conduct to the Anglican establishment, and Rashid (1982) has proved that in the following three decades Malthus himself contributed systematically to the journal. But as soon as troubles ended with the religious establishment they began with a new emerging current, Evangelicalism.

One among its leaders, Thomas Gisborne (1758–1846), was educated at St. John's College, Cambridge, graduated in 1780, received Orders in 1782 and was elected to the curacy of Barton under Needwood where he resided for the rest of his life. He became a central figure in the influential group of evangelical Anglicans known as the Clapham Sect, was a close friend of William Wilberforce and was involved in his anti-slavery campaign (Hole 2004). He is the author of the *Principles of Moral Philosophy* where he attacks Paley's *Principles*. The latter's alleged fault was having written one of those treatises of morals composed by 'professed believers in Christianity', where it is apparently 'the main purpose of the authors to prove themselves capable of extracting from the stores of Reason a complete code of human duty, *without being indebted for a particle of assistance to the revealed Word of God*' (Gisborne 1789, p. 4; italics added). Gisborne's alternative is a view of morality as a branch of religion, where the moral law amounts to God's will manifested through Revelation, even though the Scriptures, 'pre-supposing men to have acquired by the faculty of reason a general knowledge of the nature of moral duties [...] do not give the detail of moral information' (p. 90) and accordingly we may deduce subordinate rules for the direction of our conduct collecting the Divine will respecting our conduct on several fundamental points 'from the view of the situation and nature of man' (p. 92).

He was the author also of *An Inquiry into the Duties of Men in the Higher Ranks and Middle Classes* (1794), where he classifies *duties* according to different social positions, from the sovereign to naval and military officers, physicians, and 'private gentlemen'. In the same vein, *An Inquiry into the Duties of the Female Sex* (1797) expatiates on the middle-class married woman's duties, insisting on mildness, discretion and moderation, adding on top of that, that some amount of education is not too bad for a woman, and yet 'the more profound researches of philosophy and learning are not the pursuits most improving to the female mind' (Gisborne 1797, p. 285). All this seems to be able somehow to coexist with firm commitment to the anti-slavery campaign, yielding the mixture of humanitarianism and conservatism typical of Evangelicalism.

In 1805, in a letter to the Editor of the *Christian Observer*, the Clapham Sect's organ, Gisborne attacked the second *Essay* as a moral doctrine based on the system of 'expediency' and justified on the 'light of nature', that is, on argument pertaining to natural theology as opposed to Revelation (Gisborne 1805). The text is the following:

No one can read the elaborate Essay of Mr. Malthus on the Principle of Population, without admiring the extraordinary talent and laborious research which that work discovers; nor, I may add, without feeling the force of many of its general arguments. There can be little doubt that its effect will be widely felt, and that some growing evils will in future be materially repressed by its operation.

But there is hardly any work of which a sentiment perfectly uniform can be entertained; and although the present undoubtedly ranks high among the publications which have appeared on the subject of political economy, yet there are in it defects which ought not to be over-looked. Truth, and important truth, requires this exercise of impartiality. It is true, indeed, that in the larger edition of this Essay some passages are omitted which held a conspicuous place in the original outline. In the quarto volume we read no reflections upon the Christian doctrine of the ever-lasting punishment of the impenitent; nor are entertained by the theory of the grand operation of nature for exciting mind out of matter. The omission was just and prudent: but some rigid censor would be apt to insinuate that it was the duty of Mr. Malthus to retract as well as omit, unless he is still determined to afford to the world an example of the most acute intellectual powers joined with the imbecility of a visionary; an union of strength and weakness, which, for the mortification of the learned and the consolation of the million, has frequently been exhibited by men of unquestionable pre-eminence in literature.

There is no fault in this work with which I feel myself to have more right to quarrel, than the author's evident adoption of the principle of Expediency; a principle which, under favour of the fertility of human corruption, threatens to make far more extravagant advances, and to be attended with far more terrible consequences, in the moral world, than the principle of population in the natural. Expediency or utility, as the

foundation of morals, is as old a system as atheism and its natural produce. It has been revived in modern times by a work of Mr. Hume, as
inane and destructive in its whole texture, as any book which ever pre-
tended to the character of a philosophical discussion; although, probably,
not undeserving of the eulogium, bestowed upon it by himself, of being
of all his performances incomparably the best. This system has likewise
been adopted, much improved, and rendered by far more popular, by dr.
Paley, although that able writer has friends who deny that he makes
General Expediency the supreme rule of human duty, and contend, that
he assigns it only a collateral or subordinate place. Certain, however, it is,
at least as far as can be judged by the present work, that the principle, in
its genuine sense, has Mr. Malthus for a patron.

In a note, pp. 11, 12, Mr. Malthus asserts, that the circumstances of the
general consequence of vice being misery, 'is the precise reason why an
action is termed vicious'. In p. 493, he says, respecting moral restraint,
that 'our obligation to practise it will evidently rest exactly upon the same
foundation, as our obligation to practise any of the other virtues, – the
foundation of utility.' But it will be said, that, in these and other passages to
the same purpose, Mr. Malthus speaks only of morality as discoverable
by the light of nature. This is true. He quotes a passage from Dr. Paley, p. 521,
which speaks this language; and on p. 560, we meet with the following
passage: 'Though utility, therefore, can never be the immediate excitement to the gratification of any passion, it is the test by which alone we
can know, whether it ought, or ought not, to be indulged; and is, therefore, the surest foundation of all morality which can be collected from the
light of nature. All the moral codes which have inculcated the subjection
of the passion to reason, have been, as I conceive, really built upon this
foundation, whether the promulgators were aware of it or not.' But with
some writers the light of nature is the only acknowledged guide in these
matters, at least the supreme guide. That Mr. Malthus is of this class I
would not directly affirm. In speaking, however, of certain duties, he says,
that they 'are pointed out to us by the light of nature and reason, and are
confirmed and sanctioned by revelation' (p. 494). It should appear from
this mode of expression, to which as far as my recollection reaches, I can
find nothing which is opposed, that, however honourable a station this
author may assign to revelation, here, and in many other parts of his
work, she is brought forward rather as a handmaid than a mistress, rather
as a witness than a judge. If this be the case, utility is still the ultimate
foundation of morality; it is the supreme rule of right and wrong. Now by
utility, or general utility, I understand that system which brings the
greatest possible happiness to man. The duty of which God is immediately the object is left entirely out of question. But what is the happiness
of man, which is the professed end of this system? Is it the temporal or his
eternal happiness? With respect to most advocates of the system of
utility this is a question easily settled. Nothing can be more evident than

the happiness, to which they have respect, is the happiness of this world alone. But is this the true, is it the whole happiness of man? And can any system, which does not embrace the future as well as present, the spiritual as well as sensitive happiness of spiritual and immortal beings, be considered as a system of general utility, or as promoting the happiness of man in the greatest possible degree? It has been ably demonstrated, that the rule, to which this system refers, as the guide of human actions and the test of their moral character, is absolutely beyond the reach of our known limited faculties. According to the different progress of men in knowledge, some understand the happiness of man on a smaller, some on a larger scale; but on the most extended scale it falls almost infinitely below what we have reason to believe the general happiness of the human species. This indeed is certain that, in our present state, our views of utility must be particular: if they coincide with general or universal ones, this must be pure matter of accident. Not to urge, therefore, that this system is directly opposed even to the light of nature, there is a considerable degree of presumption in proposing such a view of things as belongs to God alone, as the rule of our conduct, to the exclusion of his declared will. This Jesuitical method of obtaining a dispensation from the divine commands is, indeed, peculiarly suited to the present relaxed sentiments concerning religion. Man is now strictly and literally considered as a double animal, denominated, from his better part, the animal: the spiritual, as the inferior part, obtains but little attention; it is well if its very existence is acknowledged. Religion, therefore, becomes irksome: it becomes hateful. And when the only true foundation of morality is discarded, it is no wonder that morality itself becomes radically defective and corrupt. It is certainly with a very ill grace, that the present age exclaims against the pious frauds of antiquity, or the preference of utility to truth, which is charged upon those, who, in moral worth, far exceeded their accusers. If an adequate temptation will justify a lie, it remains to be decided, whether the supposed advancement of religion, or the temporal convenience of an individual, has the best claim to that character.

Moral obligation can have no foundation but the will of an intelligent superior possessing supreme authority. If such a will has been declared, it is the duty of a man to obey it, in the face of consequences apparently the most inexpedient, in the face of any consequences whatever. The rule of the greatest possible utility, however, is not superseded in its proper subordinate province; that is, as falling under the general obligation to do good, and when it interferes with no cases of duty already prescribed.

I rejoice, Sir, that your valuable publication has taken so decided a part on this important question; and I trust, that in conjunction with other publications of similar views, it will open the eyes of Christians in general to an evil, which is so much the more formidable as it approaches under the disguise of moral excellence and moral obligation.

(Unus)

The importance of this letter could hardly be overrated. Gisborne's reasons for reaction against the *Essay* are not vague misgivings about what sounded impious or merciless, as was the case with Coleridge, Cobbett and Hazlitt. Here the point is a more precise one, and criticism more competent, namely that: (i) the foundation of the moral theory presented in the two ethical chapters of the second *Essay* is defective; (ii) a different foundation would yield a different standard of right action in general, namely the general obligation to do good; (iii) this would carry, first, a duty to comply with existing obligations whatsoever the consequences, and second, after such obligations have been complied with, also of a duty to pursue utility or general happiness. James aptly comments that Gisborne's main target was:

> Malthus's conception of right and wrong. Malthus, according to this writer, had adopted the noxious principle of Expediency or Utility, stating that the general consequence of vice being misery is the precise reason why an action is termed vicious [...] Unus quoted p. 560 of the quarto where Malthus had written:
> 'Though utility, therefore, can never be the immediate excitement to the gratification of any passion, it is the test by which alone we can know, whether it ought, or ought not, to be indulged; and is therefore the surest foundation of all morality which can be collected from the light of nature'. With this Unus most fundamentally disagreed, and went to some length to support his contention that 'Moral obligation can have no foundation but the will of an intelligent superior possessing supreme authority.'
>
> (James 1979, pp. 119–120)

While Gisborne's disagreement with Malthus on the foundation of morality is clearly spelled out, the reader may still ask what, in the *Essay*, seemed to him to hint at corruption of morality itself. The answer is not easy to give, for Gisborne is as reticent as it is possible to be. Clearly, what he may have found disturbing in the *Essay* is not justification of lying when it may serve beneficial purposes – it is the only example he gives, but it is typically a Benthamite one – in so far as in the *Essay* truthfulness is never discussed. A sensible suggestion may be that apparent overrating of benevolence sounded slightly impious to evangelical ears as implying downgrading God's love vis-à-vis love for His creatures; besides, postponement of marriage sounded as an intrusion in matters pertaining to religious discipline; also celibacy as a duty – albeit a temporary one – sounded offensive to Protestant ears because of its Popist echoes; and last, and worst, of all, an implication that occasional irregular gratification of the sexual drive may be a lesser evil than imprudent procreation sounded as libertine propaganda. All considered, it seems that it is in the light of Gisborne's criticism that a few changes in the 1806 edition make sense, in so far as they aim at stressing the *revealed* character of moral precepts recommending moral restraint.

Evangelicals: Sumner

John Bird Sumner (1780–1862) was educated at King's college, Cambridge, where he was a fellow from 1801 and, under the influence of Charles Simeon, the spiritual leader of Cambridge Evangelicals, became a convinced Evangelical. He was ordained a Priest in 1805 and was for a time an assistant master at Eton. From 1828 to 1848 he was the bishop of Chester, where he staged an aggressive pastoral strategy based on the building of new churches for the poorer neighbourhoods, encouragement to the clergy to avail themselves of lay helpers, and foundation of church-based day schools. In 1848 he was elected to the archbishopric of Canterbury, thus becoming the leader of the Anglican Church. He behaved with remarkable moderation in supporting causes not favoured by Evangelicals such as the Catholic emancipation bill, supported the Reform Bill of 1832, and helped shaping the new Poor Law Bill of 1834 (Scotland 1995; 2004; Waterman 1983; 1991a, p. 150–170).

In *A Treatise on the Records of Creation* (1816), which met with considerable success, he drew from the standard eighteenth-century analogy between the natural and the social world a basis for the familiar evangelical defence of social hierarchy, but – and this is novelty – adding to this basis the Malthusian doctrine, now made fully compatible with the Christian teaching. The main novelty in the work is a revision of Paley's theodicy incorporating the principle of population while emphasizing moral restraint. Such restyled Paleyite theodicy was bound to become the core of what was later called the 'Christian political economy' (Waterman 1991a, p. 169–170). Sumner's point is that not only the natural world appears to be organized according to an intelligent and benevolent design but also the social world, or better, modern British society at the dawn of the Industrial Revolution is the best possible contrivance for promoting virtuous habits, and accordingly the best scenario for our earthly existence understood as a state of 'probation':

> No single element in this – Waterman comments – is new and most are very familiar. But the whole is greater than the sum of its parts. For whereas Malthus himself and virtually all of his readers had looked on the principle of population as producing an uncommonly nasty case of the problem of evil to be reconciled as well as might be with the divine *goodness*, Sumner lifted it out of the icy realm of theodicy altogether, transplanting it to the genial soil of Paley's teleology, there to flourish as an example of divine *wisdom*.
>
> (p. 165)

In so far as a non-equalitarian society is 'the state best suited to excite the industry and display the most valuable faculties of mankind' (Sumner 1816, vol. 2, p. 191), and the Creator 'would devise a mean which should tend to bring the human race into such a situation' (p. 191), and indeed this is the principle of population's final cause, also 'inequality of fortunes and division of ranks' are eventually necessary.

Sumner has one correction to make, concerning the effect of moral restraint in the past, since he believes that it 'is incalculably the most universal and effectual' (p. 104) check to population, but 'it is a silent and unseen check, and, comparatively, makes no figure in the account' (p. 104). Thus, Malthus's theory is better understood in terms of a counterfactual model describing tendencies, not real-world empirical laws and, 'though none of its main facts can be disproved, is not to be taken as a representation of the actual state of human nature, but of the disorders to which it is liable' (p. 104). Yet, since we may assume that different degrees of fertility among animals proves the existence of divine design for the reasons illustrated by Paley, and may safely assume that the human race receives an attention by the Divinity at least equal to that reserved for brute animals, we may conclude that 'the ratio of increase among men, and its consequences' (p. 134) in terms of inequality, were clearly foreseen by the Creator.

The above reconstruction of the social order carries two moral implications: one is need for moral restraint or control over the passions, and the other is need for 'exertion of the human faculties' (p. 149). Once the effects of moral restraint have become so central a part of any proof of the well-ordered character of the world, also the link between theodicy and ethics becomes stronger. One question Sumner asks in the course of his revised argument in defence of hierarchical society, is whether equality or inequality of ranks and fortunes is the condition best suited to the exercise of virtue. His answer is that virtue is 'an active and energetic habit', exercised in the practice of real duties, so that as you increase the number and variety of those relations, you enlarge its sphere of action (p. 78), and independence is not a characteristic congenial to man, who tends instead to 'mutual dependence and connexion' (p. 89). He believes that poverty, understood as different from indigence, which is unnecessary, is 'not only the natural lot of many, in a well-constituted society, but is necessary, that a society be well constituted' (p. 92), for a hierarchical society offers moral advantages, among them the circumstance 'that every condition has a tendency to sink into the degree immediately below it, unless that tendency be countered by *prudence* and *activity*' (p. 92). The lowest ranks are those who, thanks to inequality of ranks, enjoy the greatest opportunities 'both for the trial of their virtue and the improvement of their reason' (p. 90). These are, first, the constant exertion of patient contentment, and second, the constant employment of reason in pointing out the advantage of 'a cheerful equanimity' and discovering 'what prospect there may be of meliorating, by successful industry, the difficulties' (p. 90). Equality would have had instead as its consequence 'a general inferiority of the rational faculties' (p. 95). The middle ranks are called to the special duty of practising a 'prudential restraint' over the passions aimed at checking 'the rapid growth of population' (p. 89), which Sumner believes to be a peculiar duty of these classes. In other words, the danger of backward social mobility is an occasion for cultivating prudence, industry and chastity for those who have some position to lose in the social ladder, since early and imprudent marriages, idleness, lack of application and foresight in running one's business and family are all occasions for loss of one's social status. What Sumner has to recommend to the opulent is liberality, that is, a disposition to spend one's money in pursuits that, even though not commonly defined as charitable, yet ultimately benefit the poor to whom they provide a source of revenue. Note that Sumner is adding up here Mandeville's argument in a domesticated version to Malthus's defence of unproductive consumption. Second, he recommends 'exercise of judicious charity', but even more he recommends contributing to planned philanthropic enterprises in such fields as education, since the 'charity which is often employed to wipe out the tear of distress, might, by a more prudent application, stop the source from which it flows' (p. 87).

The existence of social evil in present-day civilized society is no objection to the goodness of the Creator since – and this is Sumner's novelty, when compared with Paley and Malthus in 1803 – it is instead a proof of his wisdom (Waterman 1991a, pp. 162–163). Sumner's account of social evils is based on three kinds of considerations. The first is that, to some extent, evils 'arise necessarily from the law of nature', and suffering is necessary in order 'to make men look beyond the present day and the present state of things' (Sumner 1816, vol. 2, p. 258), but it is hard to know how great and how many such evils are; the main reason is that happiness is a baffling subject of study, and it is difficult to weigh or measure comparative happiness; for example, subjective reports yield results quite different from 'those produced by a survey of external circumstances' (p. 272). This happens because of the equalizing effect of habit as well as those of increased capacity for happiness conferred by education. Happiness, on the other hand, is not tantamount to real 'possession or enjoyment' (p. 272).

The starting point for the second kind of considerations is that evils are to a some extent the effect of ineffective institutions such as the Poor Laws, which is itself a mixture of good and evil: good in so far as the existence of such laws makes so that 'an infant family, deserted by profligate parents, or left orphans by the visitation of God, are not abandoned as if human life was of no value, and that the disabled or decrepit labourer has a sure resource' (p. 300), and evil in so far as, if they do not teach positively 'improvidence', at least are not an occasion for learning 'prudence' (p. 301).

The third kind of considerations starts with the idea that 'the fundamental cause of the greatest evil of the poor is ignorance' (p. 292), primarily that 'arising from want of intercourse with minds superior to their own [...] together with the scantiness of religious knowledge' (p. 292); neither is unavoidable, as recent improvements in educational systems may prove, and there is a possibility of great improvement in the human mind, nor the 'privileges of civilization, if granted universally, would throw down the ladder by which the eminence was reached and paralyze the industry' (p. 294) that keeps people from falling into indolence; on the contrary, somebody who is able to understand and foresee is a better and more active labourer. The conclusion is that ignorance:

> is not the inevitable lot of the majority of our community; and with ignorance a host of evils disappear [...] The only true secret of assisting the poor is to make them agents in bettering their condition, and to supply tem, not with a temporary stimulus, but with a permanent energy. As far as the standard of intelligence is raised, the poor become more and more able to co-operate in any plan proposed for their advantage, more likely to listen to any reasonable suggestion, more able to understand, and therefore more willing to pursue it [...] Indigence, therefore, will rarely be found in company with good education.
>
> (pp. 338–339)

To sum up, Sumner's three distinct considerations prove, on the one hand, that 'no preparatory dispensation could be more consistent with the divine goodness, than that which makes the general well-being of the members of society depend upon their right performance of their respective duties' (p. 324), while, on the other, perfect correspondence between virtue and happiness would be consonant to a perfect state, not to a state of trial, or an 'immediate distribution of rewards and punishments, could not be just, if it were not exact and universal; but [...] it would be inconsistent with the purpose of our existence in this world, as a state of preparation' (p. 375). The reason is that the subject matter of trial is moral character, and thus 'habit, not the action becomes the principal concern' (p. 375). This is required in order to keep the motivation pure since if a course of virtuous conduct were made 'the certain road to temporary prosperity [...] the springs of action would be deranged' (p. 379) and selfish motives would become the 'leading motive to virtue' (p. 379). Note that this argument based on the theme of the *veil of ignorance* – a theme showing up in Leibniz, Adam Smith, Kant and others – is the key to the problem of evil, natural and social. The basic idea is that not surprisingly our limited vision confines our prospect as regards both earthly affairs and eternal salvation. If:

> we search for the attributes of the Creator by the light which the natural world affords, we see the rays of goodness and justice emerging from his throne, though their lustre is partially obscured by clouds and darkness [...] This imperfection, instead of giving birth to a beneficial purpose, if it has its intended effect of reminding us, that the state we are now passing through is initiatory, not final, is a trial, a warfare, a pilgrimage; but that we must look upward, to an eternal habitation, for that unclouded light which may be one of the purest rewards of constant and victorious virtue.
>
> (pp. 292–293)

The main novelty is that the main goal pursued by the Creator is not for Sumner a positive balance of pain and pleasure but instead the *acquisition of virtuous habits*. That there should be room for the exercise of 'benevolence, a disposition of the mind, which, in fact, contains within itself more virtues, was undoubtedly in the contemplation of the Creator' (p. 323), and an unequal but strictly interdependent society as present-day society is, provides better ground for exercise of benevolence and related virtues than a more equal society would. Thus, morality becomes a key to theodicy, or better, it becomes equivalent to a *social* theodicy as opposed to a *cosmological* one. Such a conclusion had already been virtually achieved in Malthus's second *Essay* through adoption of Paley's theodicy, but in Sumner it is greatly amplified. His message is not only that we may come to terms with evil, since partial evils do contribute to universal good, but that evil is there as a teaching device, it is regularly connected with vice, and makes systematically room for mitigation. Indeed, the Creator:

> when he did not exempt us from the civil or physical disorders of an imperfect state, ordained also that each should have its alleviations; without which mankind would live miserably or perish prematurely.
>
> (p. 290)

Sumner was hailed by Malthus as the author of a 'masterly development and completion' (Malthus 1803, vol. 2, p. 250) of his own system. In the 1817 and 1824 editions of the second *Essay*, various changes and additions result from a reaction to Sumner's arguments, among them those verging on the foundations of morality, the role of prudence, humanity and other virtues, and also education as the main weapon for the war on poverty.

Evangelicals: Chalmers

Thomas Chalmers (1780–1842) was educated at the University of St. Andrews. After graduation he became the minister of Kilmany in Fife, while lecturing on chemistry at St. Andrews. In this phase of his career he displayed more interest for mathematics and natural philosophy than for divinity. He published *An Inquiry into the Extent and Stability of National Resources* (1808) where he rejects the idea that foreign trade was necessary to economic welfare by developing a path-breaking 'Ricardian' model of a self-standing agricultural economy and gradually introducing more realistic assumptions in order to come closer to the real economy of the day (Waterman 1991a, p. 225–229; 1991b). The pamphlet did not meet with success and this was the occasion for an existential crisis, which was resolved by a 'conversion' inspired by Wilberforce's writings. In 1813 he started systematic visiting at his parishioners' homes, took an active role in the distribution of poor relief, and started a Saturday school for the religious instruction of children. In 1814 he was appointed as minister at a parish in Glasgow where he enjoyed great success as a preacher. His *Series of Discourses on the Christian Revelation Viewed in Connection with the Modern Astronomy* (1817) sold 20,000 copies in nine months. In 1819 he obtained support by the municipality in founding a new parish in a poor district where he started his own experiment in re-establishing a sense of Christian community in modern city life. His goal was that the labouring poor would strive for independence by thrift, delayed marriage, and the ensuing limitation of family size. By careful investigations into the paupers' conditions, encouragement to self-sufficiency, and appeal to charity by neighbours, the new Parish managed by 1823 to reduce substantially the cost of poor relief with an improvement in the conditions of the poor. In 1823 he was elected to the chair of moral philosophy at St. Andrews and in 1828 to that of theology at Edinburgh. For several years he was the official leader of the Church of Scotland till, in rather tragic circumstances, after a rift on the issue of a right for congregations to appoint their ministers, he felt forced to lead a secession giving birth to the Free Church of Scotland (Brown 2004; Waterman 1991a, pp. 217–222).

Chalmers's ethics, such as it may be reconstructed from posthumously published lectures as well as from individual chapters in his works, consisted mainly in elaboration on ideas from Dugald Stewart, Thomas Reid, Adam Smith and Butler. His key idea is neat distinction between *mental* philosophy, an empirical or theoretical science of the mind dealing with facts, and *moral* philosophy, a discourse not on the *quid est* but instead on the *quid oportet*, or 'as distinct from the facts or principles which make up the actual constitution of the human mind, as Mathematical Truth is distinct from the actual laws and properties of the material world' (Chalmers 1848, p. 15). Chalmers's philosophy of morality is presented as an alternative to Paley's, whose alleged fault was his theological voluntarism, against which he repeats the familiar objection formulated, among others, by Richard Price that, did virtue consist in conformity to the Divine will, then 'nothing would be felt or apprehended as virtuous' (p. 412) besides what has been established by God's revelation. There is instead:

> a morality not constituted by the authority of law, however much it may prescribe our conformity to that will – a morality that, without the aid of any jurisprudence, will pronounce upon the rightness of all our justice and gratitude [...] and that, when a jurisprudence from heaven is made known to us, will also pronounce on the rightness of our submission thereunto.
>
> (p. 415)

On this basis, he stresses the role of conscience as an inner steering device that enables human beings to perceive intuitively the imperatives of prudence and virtue. The starting point is the fact that we are so constituted that 'the approving testimony of our hearts is the most pleasing of all gratifications' (p. 409). On the same basis, he attacks, besides Paley's system, also utilitarianism, insisting on the point that it is the moral constitution of man to provide the starting point for morality, and 'man does feel the moral rightness both of justice and truth, irrespective altogether of their consequences' (Chalmers 1833, vol. 2, p. 21). Utilitarianism rests upon an ill-founded, or imaginary, theory of human nature; for example, while we share the moral deference which is due to truth and justice, 'the utility of them is not in all our thoughts' (p. 21). Virtue and happiness are two related, and yet distinguished, elements; the 'utilitarians have confounded these two elements' (p. 66) while, on the opposite, 'Virtue is not right, because it is useful; but God hath made it useful, because it is right' (p. 66). Let me add that, obviously enough, Chalmers's contributions to ethics were published after Malthus's death and any influence by Chalmers on Malthus is out of question, but the circumstance is not irrelevant for our present concern that Malthus's best ally adhered to an ethical theory centred on conscience, owing much to Butler and the Scottish philosophy, and was a sharp critic of utilitarianism.

In *On Political Economy in its Relationship with the Moral State and Prospects of Society* his main claim is that, 'even for the economic well-being of a people, their moral and religious education is the first and greatest object of national policy' (Chalmers 1832, p. iv). There is a 'great resulting lesson' from Malthus's theory of population, namely 'the intimate alliance which obtains between the economical and the moral' (p. iv); the reason is that the goals at which political economy aims, cannot be brought about unless through dissemination of 'prudence and virtue among the common people' (p. iv). Delayed marriage is the key to balanced growth of population, virtue and wealth. In fact marriage is not a result of an instinct beyond human control, but it:

> may be a voluntary act, in the determination of which, prudence and foresight have had an influential share. It is evident, that the more we elevate man into a reflective being, and inspire him with self-respect, and give him a demand for larger and more refined accommodations, and, in one word, raise his standard of enjoyment – the more will the important step of marriage become a matter of deliberation and delay.
>
> (p. 24)

The implication is that the remedies fostered by the Ricardian School and a wide gamut of politically progressive currents, such as poor-law reform, emigration schemes, reduced taxation and expanded franchise are ineffective against poverty. Chalmers's solution is improvement of the character of the poor through moral instruction carried out by parish churches and schools run by the established church. He explains that:

> the change will be accomplished surely, though indirectly, and by insensible progress, though the means of general instruction, or by the spread of common, and more especially of sound Christian education over the

country. There is an indissoluble connection between the moral character and the economic comfort of a peasantry.

(p. 26)

Malthus's doctrine of population is what accounts for the link between moral character and economic comfort, but this does not imply that the common people should be schooled in Malthusian doctrine. He writes: 'let them only be a well-taught and moralized people; and, in that proportion, will they mix prudence and calculations and foresight, with every step in the history of their lives' (p. 26). And in fact – he argues – the effectiveness of moral restraint in the past is greater than Malthus had first admitted of, and in the Scottish lowlands such virtuous circle has already started being active before Malthus announced his new doctrine.

Chalmers has it clear in mind that there is no need that the poor be instructed in political economy to behave in a rational way; on the contrary, it is enough that they be schooled in religion and morality (Wilson and Dixon 2012, pp. 44–65). Repeating a simile that he may have found in Adam Smith, he claims that in:

> the mechanisms of human society, it needs not, that, to effectuate a given result, the people, who do in fact bring it about, should be able intelligently to view their own part in it. This is no more necessary in truth, than that, to fulfil the beneficent end of the planetary system, its various parts should be endued with consciousness.
>
> (Chalmers 1832, p. 27)

The physico-moral analogy, the same theme that played a central role for Sumner, had always been a recurrent topic in Chalmers's sermons, indeed a legacy of the eighteenth-century Scottish Moderate theology no less than of Cambridge theological rationalism. Here Chalmers fits Malthus's doctrine of population, a doctrine that in its 1798 version seemed precisely to substitute harmonious eighteenth-century world pictures with the fresco of a Dantesque *Inferno*, into a new version of the Cambridge Platonists' worldview, with one more doctrine of the correspondence between virtue and happiness. In *On the Power, Wisdom and Goodness of God*, he works out his own theodicy, roughly following Sumner and Paley. His main move, in order to fully immunize Malthus's doctrine from its apparent pessimist implications, is to substitute an empirical description of the world as it is with a counterfactual account of evil in the world. He contends that a fair assessment of God's goodness and wisdom should not be founded 'on the actual miseries which abound in the world, peopled with a depraved species – but on the fitness which abound in the world, to make a virtuous species happy' (Chalmers 1833, vol. 1, p. 220). After having made this move, the scope for morality is suddenly widened, for God wants for his creatures not just happiness, but happiness through virtue, and 'the miseries of life, in their great and general amount, are resolvable into moral causes' (vol. 2, p. 119). Thus, the main question now becomes:

Are we so constructed and so accommodated, that, in the vast majority of cases we, if morally right, should be physically happy [...] It were a very strong, almost an unequivocal testimony to the righteousness of Him, who framed the system of things and all its adaptations – if, while it secured a general harmony between the virtue of mankind and their happiness or peace, it has constantly impeded either the prosperity or the heart's ease of the profligate and the lawless.

(p. 113)

And he adds that political economy is one more example of such pre-established correspondence between morality and 'physical comfort'. For, however obnoxious it may have been 'to weak and limited sentimentalists' (p. 49), Malthus's doctrine of population:

is a pure case of adaptation, between the external nature of the world in which we live, and the moral nature of man, its chief occupier. There is a demonstrable inadequacy in all the material resources which the globe can furnish, for the increasing wants of a recklessly increasing species. But over and against this, man is gifted with a moral and a mental power by which the inadequacy might be fully countervailed; and the species in virtue of their restrained and regulated numbers, be upholden on the face of our world, in circumstances of large and stable sufficiency, even to the most distant ages. The first origin of this blissful consummation is the virtue of the people; but carried into sure and lasting effect by the laws of political economy, through the indissoluble connection which obtains between the wages and the supply of labour.

(p. 49)

The comment is in order here that Chalmers's theodicy was worked out in a cruder way than Sumner's, and he is 'crassly oblivious of the subtler difficulties of the subject and of the attempt of his predecessors and contemporaries to deal with them' (Waterman 1991a, p. 250).

Chalmers, no less than Sumner, was in constant touch with Malthus over many years, and they discussed first of all the Poor Laws and their alternatives. Malthus was an admirer of his practical achievements and even defined him his 'best ally'. While commenting on the first volume of the latter's *The Christian and Civic Economy of Large Towns* (1821–1826) in a letter to Chalmers of August 23, 1821 he confessed to Chalmers his own second thoughts about the feasibility of any plan for abolishing the Poor Laws. He writes that he had:

almost began to think that in a highly manufacturing state where so large a portion of the population must be subject to the fluctuations of trade, and the consequent sudden variation of wages, it might not be possible entirely to give up a compulsory provision *without the sacrifice of too many individuals to the good of the whole*.

(James 1979, p. 449; italics added)

Rashid (1982, p. 12) is right in stressing the importance of this letter, and I would add that it is important because it deals with the main problem still unsettled within his 1803 Paleyite theodicy, that is, the *general good particular hell* equation with which Malthus himself may have become increasingly uneasy as he was becoming increasingly an Evangelical. Now, the remarkable admission he makes is that Chalmers's practical experience has provided him with an answer for his theoretical conundrum, namely that it is possible to bring about the general good with no loss, and indeed with a net gain, in terms of individual happiness. In fact, Malthus had also written to Chalmers in the same letter:

> Your personal experience of the practicality of throwing the poor almost entirely on their own resources, with little risk of extreme distress, even in such a town as Glasgow and at so unfavourable a period, is of the highest importance.
>
> (James 1979, p. 449)

I have already illustrated how, a few years later, Malthus manifested disagreement with Chalmers's adoption of Jean-Baptiste Say's broad definition of wealth, including 'immaterial products' and therefore making the people's virtue, industry and frugality a part of national wealth and turning even clergymen into productive workers in so far as they directly contribute to produce national wealth. Malthus, in a letter of January 1827, objects that 'it is more correct in regard to common usage of language, and in accordance with all our common feelings to say that security, independence, moral and religious instruction, and moral and religious habits, are very superior in importance to what we usually mean by wealth, than to say that they ought to be included in the term' (Waterman 1991a, p. 243), and in another letter of March 1832 he writes that 'it is paying morals a very bad compliment to put them in the same category with cottons, and estimate their value by the money which has been given for them. We have always been told, and most properly, to prefer virtue to wealth; but if morals be wealth, what a confusion is at once introduced into all the language of moral and religious instruction' (p. 243).

There are also records of Malthus's reaction to Chalmers's *On the Power, Wisdom and Goodness of God* (1833). In a letter to Chalmers of 23 June 1833, he writes:

> The principal difficulty in the whole work is the impossibility of preventing the *constant recurrence to the mind of the pohen to kakon*; and everything that is said in treatises on such matters always suggest to me some difficulty in creation, and in the preparation of beings for a future state of happiness, which must ultimately resolve itself into a limitation of Power. This conclusion is equally forced upon me in natural theology, and in the old and new Testament; and I cannot think it is in any degree

inconsistent with the latter. In even some passages in Butler I think he had the same feeling though he does not like to dwell upon it.

(Waterman 1991a, p. 252)

This reaction proves that, as late as 1833, Malthus was still 'willing to incur the risk of heterodoxy rather than to assent to a theodicy which failed to exonerate the deity from the charge of creating evil' (p. 252), and that he was still interested in finding an answer to the question on evil, and besides was on balance dissatisfied with the three different solutions he had adopted, respectively in 1798, 1803 and 1817.

To sum up, in the 1820s and 1830s a comparatively well-documented interaction took place between Malthus and Chalmers and the former manifested awareness of having found in the latter his best ally. A few of the changes in the 1827 edition may be interpreted as reactions to Chalmers's ideas as well as to his practical experiments, and the increasing weight ascribed to education, and even more the increasing social function recognized to religion seem to echo Chalmers's arguments.

Malthus's third theodicy and his restyled ethics

Malthus's 1806 ethics

The idea that there should be a balance between benevolence and self-love, even though defended by such illustrious authors as Butler, might have sounded as not Christian enough to evangelical ears. This dissonance was the occasion for rather obvious criticism by Gisborne, to which Malthus's reaction consisted in careful rephrasing of his claims in the 1806 edition. The first important change concerns the doctrine of creation of mind, amounting to omission from the Preface of the already mentioned sentence from the 1803 edition where he affirmed that he believed the omitted parts might 'still have their use' and that he had omitted them not because he thought them 'of less value than what has been inserted, but because they did not suit the different plan of treating the subject' adopted there (Malthus 1803, vol. 1, p. 2).

A number of changes concern the foundation of morality. He modifies the passage quoted by Gisborne as a proof of Malthus's adoption of the pernicious 'system of expediency' in the following way:

Though utility, therefore, can never be the immediate excitement to the gratification of any passions, it is the test by which alone we can know, independently of the revealed will of God, whether it ought or ought not to be indulged; and is therefore the surest criterion of moral rules which can be collected from the light of nature.

(vol. 2, pp. 157–158)

James's comment on this change is particularly inept. She writes that she cannot 'imagine him, merely for respectability's sake, making these alterations in his text, and especially in his preface; he must have realised that they would pass almost unnoticed. That he must have done so for friendship's sake is more likely' (James 1979, p. 120). I would say, on the contrary, that such changes were important for Malthus himself, as they touched one central sore point in his system, namely the complex relationship between suffering, happiness, morality and religion. It is worth noting that the changes under discussion do not amount just to admissions confined in the Preface, but are instead introduced systematically wherever moral theory is treated, and besides that these points are the subject of further modification in 1817. A number of modifications make wider room for benevolence. He now writes that:

> though benevolence cannot in the present state of our being be our great moving principle of human actions, yet, as the kind corrector of the evils arising from the other stronger passion, it is essential to human happiness; it is the balm and consolation and grace of human life, the source of our noblest efforts in the cause of virtue, and or our purest and most refined pleasures.
>
> (Malthus 1803, vol. 2, p. 214)

And he goes on to make it clear that:

> though we have often reason to fear that our benevolence may not take the most beneficial direction, we need never apprehend that there will be too much of it in society. The foundations of that passion on which our preservation depends are fixed so deeply in our nature, that no reasonings or addresses to our feelings can essentially disturb it.
>
> (p. 215)

That is, he does *not* admit of having being mistaken in 1803, but nonetheless declares that *there never will be too much benevolence*, which blatantly contradicts what he had been arguing for until then. To be more precise, let us take a look back: in 1803 Malthus had declared that private charity is a *duty*, and indeed that we have a strong duty to rescue those who are in need without their fault, but the main point of his argument was that there is no *right* to subsistence, since a non-enforceable right is no right at all, and this was his decisive argument against the Poor Laws. This argument had more than one polemical target, first Paley and then Thomas Paine. The former had argued, indeed defending a traditional view shared by Aquinas and most Schoolmen, that 'the Poor have a claim founded in the Law of Nature' to subsistence (Paley 1785, p. 203). Malthus's counter-claim was that 'by the laws of nature [...] no person has any claim of right on society for subsistence' (Malthus 1803, vol. 2, p. 127). The point was that, once the justification for laws of nature has been made to rest on consequentialist arguments, as Paley had done, a contradiction arises in the doctrine of a right to subsistence, for no discrepancy is admissible between what is a duty and what is possible, and besides, a right may be such only when it is possible to establish the existence of a duty by somebody to grant its enjoyment by somebody else. Malthus, after Paley's doctrine of the right to subsistence, attacks also Paine's doctrine of the rights of man (Paine 1791), he insists that:

> there is one right which man has generally been thought to possess, which I am confident he neither does nor can possess – a right to subsistence when his labour will not fairly purchase it. Our laws indeed say that he has this right, and bind the society to furnish employment and food to those who cannot get them in the regular market; but in so doing they attempt to reverse the laws of nature; and it is in consequence to be expected, not only that they should fail in their object, but that the poor, who were intended to be benefited, should suffer most cruelly from the inhuman deceit thus practised upon them.
>
> (p. 128)

The ill-famed passage on the 'mighty feast of nature' was a *reductio ad absurdum* of arguments like Godwin's, based on *Nature* as a source for normative standards, by proving that Nature's standards are virtually the opposite. Malthus had written that:

> A man who is born into a world already possessed, if he cannot get subsistence from his parents on whom he had a just demand, and if the society do not want his labour, has no claims of *right* to the smallest portion of food, and, in fact, has no business to be where he is. At nature's mighty feast there is no vacant cover for him.
>
> (p. 127)

And he goes on to show how the compassion of a few of the guests may make room for him, but the result would be that immediately other intruders appear demanding the same favour, and the final consequence would be that the 'order and harmony' of the feast would be spoiled and plenty turned into scarcity. The lesson the guests should learn is their:

> error in counteracting those strict order to all intruders, issued by the great mistress of the feast, who wishing that all her guests should have plenty, and knowing that she could not provide for unlimited numbers, humanely refused to admit fresh comers when her table was already full.
>
> (p. 127)

Malthus's aim was one among the typical controversialist's pragma-rhetoric stratagems, namely *reversing the direction* of the opponent's argument (Dascal and Cremaschi 1999), by proving that Nature has been 'humane' precisely in *not* granting a right to subsistence. The argument makes sense if we assume that in the writer's intention it should have been read as a piece of irony, something that did not happen, since readers were led astray by the tragic story, not an appropriate subject for irony, and by an allegory whose main character was a cruel Goddess, not an appropriate character for any clergy-man. As mitigating circumstances, the considerations should be added that the rather cruel story told through the allegory makes things look even worse than Malthus's argument would have done if expressed literally. The fact is that, in Malthus's argument, those 'intruders' that Nature decides not to admit are *not* existing human beings to be sentenced to starvation, but just *potential* or *not yet conceived* human beings. Unfortunately, Malthus's intentions notwithstanding, the passage was read as an expression of sheer lack of humaneness. The critic hiding himself behind the name Philander, in a letter to the *Monthly Magazine*, after rather accurate remarks in matters of theory, adds the following on Malthus's language:

> Surely one who uses this language must forget that it is common to all mankind to come naked into the world; and that the heir of a princely opulence brings none of his provisions with him, but receives it all at the hand of that society of which rich and poor are all alike members. The table of nature is not full, though luxury and greediness may have sized on all her dainties, and excluded other guests, on the maxim 'The fewer the better cheer'. Nature can still keep a plentiful board of plain but wholesome fare; and shame on the man who would restrict her bounties! Worse than shame on him who can argue, that the rich man's horses have a better right to be fed than the poor man's children!
>
> Nothing can be more contrary to the spirit of our laws than this abandonment of such of our fellow-subjects as come into the world without property. The law instantly takes them under its protection, and in return claims from them all the duties of allegiance, upon the mere ground of being natives of the soil. Their country appropriates them to her service, and summons them from the remotest parts of the earth, when in need of their arms for her defence. Nay, she has made it a crime against herself for them to use the natural liberty of withdrawing from the world when life is a burden; for suicide is considered as felony, because 'it deprives the king of a subject'. If then the poor man has not a right to die, surely he has a right to live!
>
> (Philander 1804, p. 392)

Malthus's response to such reactions was suppression of the passage in the 1806 edition as being – as he admitted in 1817 – 'not sufficiently indulgent to the weaknesses of human nature and the feelings of Christian charity' (Malthus 1803, vol. 2, p. 250). Not unlike the story of other passages deleted because they sounded incompatible with charity, also this one illustrates something of Malthus's style. He suffered from a kind of *vis polemica* that made him too aggressive while attacking, and also of lack of candour that made him clumsy while retreating. It is fair to note, yet, that the source for the polemical spirit that induced him to publish such tactless passages was Whig contempt for a kind of Tory-humanitarian attitude that contented itself with praising the compassionate relationship between the rich and the poor while ignoring hard facts and aristocratically disregarding consequences. That is, precisely those passages that were promptly picked up by critics 'from the left' in order to prove that Malthus was an anti-poor reactionary, were instead a clumsy attack on idyllic Tory pictures of a non-existing social order. In fact, the chapter where the mentioned passage appeared in the 1803 edition discussed the relationship of poverty and civil liberty, and Malthus's pre-occupation was to separate the poor's interests from those of middle-class radicals who he believed were ready to exploit the former's grievances, and indeed he saw in the widespread fear of a combination of middle-class radicalism and the poor an obstacle to the advancement of reforms inspired by a Whig spirit of protection of liberties and limits to central government.

If we admit that *this* was Malthus's concern, a number of specifications and recantations made after 1803 turn out to be, if not explications of Malthus's true original intentions, or of 'what he always meant', at least admissions that clearly deny some of his earlier claims without sudden volte-face. For example, in the Letter to Samuel Whitbreadhe writes:

> The moral obligation of private, active, and discriminating charity, I have endeavoured to enforce in the strongest language of which I was capable; and if I have denied the natural right of the poor to support, it is solely [...] because it may be doubted whether 'any right, the gratification of which seems to be impracticable, can be said to exist'. I would instead be prepared to argue that, were it possible to fix the number of the poor [...] those who were actually in want should be most liberally relieved, and that they should receive it as a right and not as a bounty.
>
> (Malthus 1807, p. 8)

It may be worth comparing such cautious admissions with Paley's statements that had been drastically condemned by Malthus himself in 1798 and 1803. Right after his notorious argument to the fact that the poor have a claim founded in the law of nature, Paley had added that the relief of beggars, even though it is the lowest kind of exertion of benevolence and other more systematic and forward-looking exertions, for example subscription to public charity, should be recommended, should not be indiscriminately rejected, yet, on the ground that human beings 'are sometimes overtaken by distress, for which all other relief would come too late' (Paley 1785, p. 145).

The question may be raised whether Malthus in 1806 would have made room for Paley's second reason for not indiscriminately rejecting relief for beggars, namely that 'resolutions of this kind compel us to offer such violence to our humanity, as may go near, in a little while, to suffocate the principle itself' (p. 145). Paley's reason for his refusal to dismiss unconditionally the private exercise of charity is also one Malthus would probably have assented to. The reason is that 'many things are to be done and abstained from, solely for the sake of habit' (p. 27), and virtue consists, more than in doing the right kind of actions, in acquiring the right habits. The example Paley gives refers precisely to relief of beggars. Let us suppose that a beggar:

> with the appearance of extreme distress, asks our charity. If we come to argue the matter, whether the distress be real, whether it be not brought upon himself, whether it be of public advantage to admit such application, whether it be not to encourage idleness and vagrancy, whether it may not invite impostors to our doors, whether the money can be well spared, or might not be better applied; when these considerations are put together, it may appear very doubtful, whether we ought or ought not to give any thing. But when we reflect, that the misery before our eyes excites our pity, whether we will or not; that it is of the utmost consequence to us to cultivate this tenderness of mind; that it is a quality, cherished by indulgence, and soon stifled by opposition; when this, I say, is considered, a wise man will do that for his own sake, which he would have hesitated to do for the petitioner's; he will give way to his compassion, rather than offer violence to a habit of so much general use.
>
> (p. 27)

The passage may sound disgustingly condescending to twenty-first-century ears, but this should not blind our eyes to the main point, which is instead that Malthus himself more than once has recourse to such arguments in support of quite dubious moral rules, such as exclusion of contraception, which he argues – in absence of any proof of God's will – may be *assumed* to have been forbidden by him, and what justifies the assumption is the consideration that the contrary would be such as to encourage indolence!

It may be noted that another amendment in the 1806 edition seems to go in the general direction of more humanitarianism and less harshness, and more in detail of wider scope for the effects of charity. This is manifested by – or better, smuggled through – a tiny deletion. Malthus now admits that *the* 'partial evils' (that is, not *some of* them) 'arising from general laws' (Malthus 1803, vol. 2, p. 162) should be mitigated by our charity. In other words, partial evil is still accepted as an unavoidable counterpart to general good, but now what is still unavoidable evil is *mitigated* partial evil. Such evil is what is left in a society where there is still *a certain*, even though *reduced*, number of poor, and yet even these have an opportunity to be *respectable, virtuous, and happy*. Let me note that this is far from 'metaphysical' or 'theological' nonsense, that it does *not* amount to nothing, and is *not* – in Hollander's words – 'extraneous to analysis'. The fact is that the change carries also different policy advice. For example, an exception is proposed in 1806 for the disabled and the victims of war or bad harvest, or, in other words, for those whose 'best-founded expectations will sometimes be disappointed' (p. 161) and will be 'involved in unmerited calamities' (p. 161) or be the victims of 'those cases of urgent distress arising from disastrous accidents, unconnected with habits of indolence or improvidence' (p. 162).

Malthus's 1817 ethics

Malthus's 1798 theodicy was heterodox and pessimist. His 1803 theodicy was Paleyite and in a sense tragic. His 1817 theodicy seems to amount to either coming back to the Cambridge Platonists' optimism or adopting the Kantian claim of the failure of any kind of theodicy. This interpretation seems to be supported by the fact that inequality and poverty are no more accepted in a Paleyite fatalist spirit as well as by the introduction of the decisive – albeit generally overlooked – change according to which the de facto existing condition of society is now justified not by its being the happiest, but instead by its being the most favourable to moral development.

In fact, important innovations in the 1817 Appendix verged on God's benevolence and the world-order. Yet, these were not unrelated with both other points around which Malthus's amendments tend to crystallize, namely the criteria for moral judgement and anti-poverty policies. Malthus referred, as mentioned, to Sumner's doctrine as 'masterly development and completion' (Malthus 1803, vol. 2, p. 250) of his own system, and he went so far as to add that he 'had always considered the principle of population as a law peculiarly suited to a state of discipline and trial' (p. 250). Such a claim is clearly false, and reflects well Malthus's usual awkward way of retreating when defeated, sharply different from the mild attitude displayed whenever he was winning.

As already announced in Chapter 3, one point around which attacks concentrated was fn. 6 in Chapter 2. It was one among the passages where Malthus had spelled out his own hedonist, consequentialist and theological-voluntarist assumptions in more detail. As a belated response to critics, Malthus modified the footnote's third sentence, which in the 1803 version sounded:

> We want it particularly to distinguish that class of actions, the general tendency of which is to produce misery, but which, in their immediate or individual effect, may produce perhaps exactly the contrary.
>
> (vol. 1, p. 19)

Now, in the 1817 version, it sounds as follows:

> We want it particularly to distinguish those actions, the general tendency of which is to produce misery, and which are therefore prohibited by the commands of the Creator, and the precepts of the moralist, although in their immediate or individual effects they may produce exactly the contrary.
>
> (vol. 1, p. 19)

And he modified also the last sentence. In the 1803 version it sounded:

> But they are still evidently vicious, because an action is so denominated, the general tendency of which is to produce misery, whatever may be its individual effect.

(p. 19)

The sentence in the 1817 version reads as follows:

> But they are still evidently vicious, because an action is so denominated which violates an express precept, founded upon its general tendency to produce misery, whatever may be its individual effect.

(p. 19)

Both modifications seem to stress the voluntarist element in his view of the law of nature as *imposed* by God. The doubt may be raised whether there is no change in substance, or one might hint that the substance was already there, and Malthus was trying to appease Evangelical friends by adding a few more words without changing the substance. In fact, the idea that Revelation confirms the natural law was there in Gay, Brown, Hey, Watson, Paley and young Malthus himself. The difference between them is that the Cambridge rationalists, since they wanted to address a wider audience, were prepared to discuss moral issues in purely natural-law terms, while the Evangelicals tended to be horrified by any tendency to under-stress the divine origin of Christian Morality.

Yet, what was the sore point for the former group was hardly soothed in any effective way by the latter. The point was inability to justify the motivating force of a general law we must obey even in case it makes us unhappy. The reasons both groups were able to offer were either that: (i) it makes other people happy; or (ii) it pleases our Creator. To such scant reasons, Kant's and Whewell's criticism would have been that both consequentialist voluntarism and evangelical voluntarism were a kind of *heteronymous* (in Kant's jargon) or *dependent* (in Whewell's) morality.

Changes following similar lines were introduced in the definition of the test of utility. Let us compare the definitions as given in the 1803 and in the 1817 editions:

1803
An action is denominated vicious when its general tendency is to produce misery, whatever may be its individual effects (vol. 1, p. 19).

1817
An action is denominated vicious when *it violates an express precept, founded upon its* general tendency to produce misery, whatever may be its individual effects (p. 19; italics added).

At another point, that is Book 4; Chapter 10, he made a similar change:

1803
It is the test by which alone we can know whether it [a passion] ought or ought not to be indulged; and is therefore the surest *foundation* of all morality (vol. 2, pp. 157–158; italics added).

1817
It is the test by which alone we can know, *independently of the revealed will of God*, whether it [a passion] ought or ought not to be indulged; and is therefore the surest *criterion of moral rules which can be collected from the light of nature* (pp. 157–158; italics added).

The same is true for another change consisting in shift from 'foundation' to 'criterion':

1803
Any person, who acknowledges the principle of utility as the great *foundation* of *morals* (p. 104; italics added).

1817
Any person, who acknowledges *utility* as the great *criterion* of *moral rules* (p. 104; italics added).

A comment is in order here. The points stressed by the mentioned changes are:

i   the foundation of morality lies in God's will; by the light of nature we may just *discover* what its contents are, not *provide* a foundation for morality;
ii   so much concerns *natural* morality, as opposed to *revealed* morality;
iii   utility is a test or a *criterion*, not a *foundation*;
iv   utility as a *criterion* is not the *principle* of utility (possibly in its Benthamite, and accordingly atheist, version).

On balance, it is true that changes do stress points that were already there, but a need to defend himself from attacks by Evangelical fellow-travellers accounts fairly well for the kind of changes introduced, which are – *pace* James – something more than soothing words, for they reflect instead a search for solutions to theoretical troubles felt by Malthus to be his own.

As a whole, Malthus's newly formulated argument is far from being a scientific positive argument. It is instead a moral argument with political and theological corollaries. More than a 'Christian moral scientist', in Winch's description, Malthus in 1803, and even more in 1806, 1817 and 1826, is a moral philosopher who takes advantage of results afforded by experimental science in order to work out ways of applying moral precepts to practice, and who fixes a theological mess by transforming a theoretical issue into a practical or moral one. Besides, qua moral philosopher he is anything but a 'secular utilitarian'. The decisive proof is that he constantly refers to 'the laws of nature' as empirically observable signposts pointing to our happiness and to the 'partial evil' they unavoidably carry. For example, diseases are not an inevitable infliction of providence, but most of times an indication 'that we have offended against some of the laws of nature' (vol. 2, p. 89). This is as un-utilitarian as anything may be, in so far as no partial evil is conceivable for utilitarianism, provided that amounts of good and evil are to be summed up and we are left with the final result of a balance of pleasure and pain, 'well-being', which consists of nothing else than a magnitude or a pay-off.

To sum up: Malthus's *quod demonstrandum erat* is proved, once the proof has been given that:

i   the balance of evils and goods in the world would be in fact rather favourable in case mankind would not indulge to the satisfaction of the passions (in themselves good) in a disorderly way, and;
ii no trade-off between more happiness and less morality needs to take place.

Or, in Malthus's own words:

> If the prevalence of the preventive check to population, in a sufficient degree, were to remove many of those diseases which now afflict us, yet be accompanied by a considerable increase of the vice of promiscuous intercourse; it is probable that the *disorders and unhappiness*, the *physical and moral evils* arising from this vice, would increase in strength and degree; and, admonishing us severely of our error, would point to the only line of conduct approved by *nature, reason, and religion*: abstinence from marriage till we can support our children, and chastity till that period arrives.
>
> (p. 117)

Thus, Hollander is nearly right when he acknowledges that:

> a theological dimension thus certainly remains in 1803 and thereafter [...] Indeed, it is fair to say that the defence of the Deity is reinforced – though only if limited to an ideal rather than the real world, *considering the practical insignificance of restraint*.
>
> (Hollander 1997, p. 919)

Or better, he *would* be *nearly* right did he not miss one decisive point, namely that Malthus in 1803 still believed that the relevance of moral restraint *in the past* had been rather limited (which was contested by several of his critics including Chalmers), but his policy advice, namely equality, dignity, self-reliance, generalized education, higher wages, higher standards of consumption, pointed at a *possible*, not just *ideal*, world where the 'moral restraint' would be practised, the lottery of society will yield fewer blanks, and this will allow for *respectability, virtue* and *happiness*.

Bibliography

British Critic (1804) 'Review of: An Essay on the Principle of Population'. 23(1–2), pp. 59–63.

Brown, S.J. (2004) Chalmers, Thomas. In *Oxford Dictionary of National Biography*. Volume 10 CAPPE–CHANCELLOR. Ed. by Matthew, H.C.G. and Harrison, B. Oxford: Oxford University Press.

Chalmers, Th. (1808) *An Enquiry into the Nature and Stability of National Resources*. Edinburgh: Moir.

Chalmers, Th. (1817 [2009]) *A Series of Discourses on the Christian Revelation Viewed in Connection with the Modern Astronomy*. Cambridge: Cambridge University Press.

Chalmers, Th. (1821–1826) *The Christian and Civic Economy of Large Towns*. Glasgow: Chalmers and Collins.

Chalmers, Th. (1832 [1968]) *On Political Economy in its Relationship with the Moral State and Prospects of Society*. New York: Kelley.

Chalmers, Th. (1833 [2009]) *On the Power, Wisdom and Goodness of God, as Manifested in the Adaptation of External Nature to the Moral and Intellectual Constitution of Man*. Cambridge: Cambridge University Press.

Chalmers, Th. (1848) *Sketches of Moral and Mental Philosophy*. Edinburgh: Constable.

Cremaschi, S. and Dascal, M. (forthcoming). *The Malthus-Ricardo Controversy. From a Pragma-Rhetoric Point of View*. The Hague: Benjamins.

Dascal, M. and Cremaschi, S. (1999) 'The Malthus-Ricardo correspondence: sequential structure, argumentative patterns, and rationality'. *Journal of Pragmatics* 31(4), pp. 1129–1172.

Gilbert, G. (1998) Introduction. In *T.R. Malthus. Critical Responses*. Volume 1. Ed. by Gilbert, G. London: Routledge.

Gisborne, T. (1789 [1798]) *The Principles of Moral Philosophy*. Fifth edn. London: Cadell.

Gisborne, T. (1794) *An Enquiry into the Duties of Men in the Higher and Middle Classes of Society*. London: J. Davis.

Gisborne, T. (1797) *An Inquiry into the Duties of the Female Sex*. London: T. Cadell.

Gisborne, T. [Unus] (1805) Letter to the Editor. *The Christian Observer* 45(9, vol. 4), pp. 539–541.

Grice, H.P. (1989) *Studies in the Way of Words*. Cambridge, MA: Harvard University Press.

Hole, R. (2004) Gisborne, Thomas. In *Oxford Dictionary of National Biography*. Volume 22 GIBBES–GOSPATRIC. Ed. by Matthew, H.C.G. and Harrison, B. Oxford: Oxford University Press.

Hollander, S. (1997) *The Economics of Thomas Robert Malthus*. Toronto: University of Toronto Press.

James, P. (1979) *Population Malthus. His Life and Time*. London: Routledge.

Jensen, H.E. (1999) 'The development of T.R. Malthus's institutionalist approach to the cure of poverty: from punishment of the poor to investment in their human capital'. *Review of Social Economy* 57(4), pp. 450–465.

La Vergata, A. (1990). *Nonostante Malthus. Fecondità, popolazioni e armonia della natura, 1700–1900*. Torino: Bollati Boringhieri.

Malthus, Th.R. (1803 [1989]) *An Essay on the Principle of Population. The Version Published in 1803, with the Variora of 1806, 1807, 1817 and 1826*. Ed. by James, P. Cambridge: Cambridge University Press.

Malthus, Th.R. (1807 [1986]) Letter to Samuel Whitbread Esq. M.P. on his proposed bill for the amendment of the poor laws. In *The Works of Thomas Robert Malthus*. Volume 4. Ed. by Wrigley, E.A. and Souden, D. London: Pickering.

Mill, J. (1803) 'An essay on the principle of population'. *The Literary Journal* 2(10), pp. 578–587.

Paine, Th. (1791 [1993]) *Rights of Man*. Ed. by Bigsby, C.W.E. London: Dent.

Paley, W. (1785 [2002]) *The Principles of Moral and Political Philosophy*. Ed. by LeMahieu, D.L. Indianapolis, IN: Liberty Fund.

Philander (1804) 'Letter to the editor'. *Monthly Magazine* 18 (December), pp. 381–382.

Rashid, S. (1982) 'Malthus and the British Critic'. *History of Economics Society Bulletin* (3), pp. 11–16.

Scotland, N. (1995) *John Bird Sumner: Evangelical Archbishop*. Leominster: Gracewing.

Scotland, N. (2004) Sumner, John Bird. In *Oxford Dictionary of National Biography*. Volume 53 TONSON–USHER. Ed. by Matthew, H.C.G. and Harrison, B. Oxford: Oxford University Press.

Simplex (1808) *An Inquiry into the Constitution, Government and Practices of the Church of Christ… with Strictures on… Mr. Malthus on Population*, Edinburgh 1808; partial reprint in: T.R. Malthus. *Critical Responses*. Volume 1. Ed. by Gilbert, G. London: Routledge.

Sumner, J.B. (1816) *A Treatise on the Records of Creation, and on the moral attributes of the creator; with particular reference to the Jewish history, and to the consistency of the principle of population with the wisdom and goodness of the deity*. London: Hatchard.

Waterman, A.M.C. (1983) 'The ideological alliance of Christian theology and political economy, 1798–1833'. *The Journal of Ecclesiastical History* 34(2), pp. 231–244.

Waterman, A.M.C. (1991a) *Revolution, Economics and Religion. Christian Political Economy, 1798–1833*. Cambridge: Cambridge University Press.

Waterman, A.M.C. (1991b) 'The canonical classical model of political economy in 1808, as Viewed from 1825: Thomas Chalmers on the 'National Resources''. *History of Political Economy* 23(2), pp. 221–241.

Wilson, D. and Dixon, D. (2012) *A History of Homo Economicus. The Nature of the Moral in Economic Theory*. London: Routledge.

7 Malthus's applied ethics

War on poverty as moral reform

Inequality as evil

Malthus was persuaded that the first point in any agenda for either public or private morality in his time should have been poverty. In the 1817 Appendix he insists on the idea that, whether his work be read with alterations introduced in later editions or instead without them, it would have appeared to 'every reader of candour' that the writer's 'practical design' was 'to improve the condition and increase the happiness of the lower classes of society' (Malthus 1803, vol. 2, p. 251). The need he felt to insist on this point obviously depended on controversy that had been raging between 1803 and 1817. It is worth reminding, yet, in the face of the die-hard tradition about ogre Malthus, that these are Malthus's own words, albeit written 19 years after the first *Essay*, and accordingly deserve examination before being discarded as nonsense. It is as well to add that the same concern is what lies behind even the most infelicitous statements in both Essays, including the one on the 'mighty feast of Nature' discussed in Chapter 6.

In the first *Essay* he writes that the inevitability of the existence of a class of landowners and one of labourers is proved, but also that we cannot by no means infer from such inevitability that 'the present *great inequality* of property, is either necessary or useful to society. On the contrary, it must certainly be considered as an evil, and every institution that promotes it, is essentially wrong and impolitic' (Malthus 1798, p. 102 fn.; italics added), and besides, a better lot for the working classes is a necessary wish for 'every friend of humanity' (p. 49). In 1826 he adds:

> If all could be completely relieved, and poverty banished from the country, even at the expense of three-fourths of the fortunes of the rich, I would be the last person to say a single syllable against relieving all, and making the degree of distress alone the measure of our bounty.
>
> (Malthus 1803, vol. 2, p. 369)

That is, he is still insisting on the idea that the claim he has been defending all the time is not the legitimacy of property as such, but a weaker one, namely the impossibility of eliminating poverty as such.

For Malthus there is one more reason why the condition of the poor should be the moral and political philosopher's main concern, namely that his subject of enquiry is not just *the wealth* of a nation, as Adam Smith allegedly believed – in fact he *did not* – but *the mass of happiness* allotted to its members, which is, 'after all, the legitimate end even of its wealth, power, and population' (Malthus 1798, p. 116). Needless to say, this reading is mistaken. It seems to reflect faintly a climate of opinion emerging in the 1790s, when it seemed important to draw a sharp distinction between 'political economy', a name that precisely at this time was adopted for the discipline, and political discourse, as a means of protecting Adam Smith's followers from the suspicion of sympathy with Jacobinism (Rothschild 2001, p. 55–61). The fact is that Smith had it clear in mind that the end of all the economy is the consumer's needs, and that the labouring poor, who is the one who provides for the needs of the whole of society, should be at least 'decently fed and clothed' (Smith 1776, p. 96; cf. Cremaschi 1984, p. 118–126, p. 155–165; Fleischacker 2005, p. 203–226). What Smith was careful to avoid was mention of *happiness*, but this happened because of his own sophisticated and slightly sceptical views on happiness itself, which he believed to be comparatively easily available in any permanent state granting safety and some minimal enjoyment. Instead, he would have made the ironical suggestion that the real end of that 'operose machine', which is the economy in a civilized society and is kept in motion by individuals struggling hard in their delusory quest for happiness, is providing more effectively for the necessities and commodities of life of the 'meanest labourer' than primitive societies can do even for kings.

Since the working classes make for the bulk of society – as Malthus contends, in what is precisely Adam Smith's spirit – it is their condition that should be our main concern. Thus – he repeats 22 years later – 'it is most desirable that the labouring classes should be well paid, for a much more important reason than any that can relate to wealth; namely the happiness of the great mass of society' (Malthus 1820, vol. 1, p. 472). In this spirit, Malthus declares once more that every friend of humanity would find that to make a better life possible for the greatest part of society is a desirable object, while noting that 'unfortunately the working classes, though they share in the general prosperity, do not share in it so largely as in the general adversity' (p. 522).

More swings than ratios

Costabile and Rowthorn (1985) complained of 'the cavalier way in which Malthus's work is treated and some of its most fundamental features are ignored, such as, for example, his theory of value and real wages' (p. 418). Now, 30 years after, the situation has changed to a remarkable extent, with the help of Samuelson's decisive contribution (1978) that marked a line of

enquiry followed by others, yielding a massive exercise in rational reconstruction of Malthus's theory by Hollander (1997) as well as several contributions on individual aspects by Waterman (1987; 1988; 1998; 2012),
Costabile (1983) and others. One important result of such a revision process is
dismissal of the *anti-classical Malthus* myth, not to mention Malthus the
'vulgar' economist. Malthus the economist came out of Hollander's reconstruction in a new shape, much closer to Ricardo than economists used to
believe, and it is precisely because of such closeness that the 12-year controversy between them could start making sense, and the mystery of how
Ricardo could waste his time with such a nullity as Malthus could be dis-
pelled (Cremaschi and Dascal 1996; 1998a; 1998b; Dascal and Cremaschi
1999). Another important result was dismantling the *two Malthuses* thesis
formulated first by McCulloch, according to which Malthus's demographic
theory was scientific and progressive while his non-Ricardian economic
theory was non-scientific and reactionary. The point is that Malthus's population theory is his 'total' population theory (Spengler 1945), where political
economy and demography cannot be separated.

But, classic as he is, there is one element making for the difference between
Malthus and most of his contemporaries. This is basically the fact that his
political economy is on principle economic sociology or socio-economics, and
cannot be reduced to a kind as economic theory – as it is possible to do, to
some extent, with Ricardo, Say, John Stuart Mill. The point is that Say's law
does not hold for Malthus, and effective demand is what makes for value, but
also, unlike Ricardo, the existence of effective demand is not always granted
by some basic characteristic of human nature such as a desire for accumula-
tion (Cremaschi and Dascal 1998a, p. 11), and permanent unemployment is
for Malthus, unlike the other classics, a constant possibility. This is what
makes Malthus's theory of economic *growth* more a theory of *development*
(Maccabelli 1997, p. 262–270), or, to put it more bluntly, population theory
and the various branches of political economy, far from being self-contained
empirical disciplines, are auxiliary sciences of the 'moral and political science'
(Cremaschi 2010).

One among the sources of confusion has been the constant evolution in
Malthus's ideas between 1798 and his death. This was a side-effect of controversies in which he was willy-nilly involved for decades, those on the principle
of population with its theological, moral and political implications, and
those – mainly with Ricardo – on general gluts, effective demand, value. The
present writer's contributions on these controversies, as referred to above,
have yielded a couple of lessons. Apart from individual 'style' in a weaker
sense, that is, preference for certain kinds of arguments or a tendency to be
more or less generous when attacking and more or less clumsy while retreating, both Malthus and Ricardo do constantly what every philosopher or scientist has always being doing, that is engaging in controversy for a number of
motives different from disinterested love for truth. This is the reason why they
claim victory when conceding the opponent whatever he contends for, hedge

and modify their own claims by ad hoc distinctions, escaping into abstraction or into practice, creating protective belts, moving one claim to the very centre of one's theory with the consequence that it does no more directly influence any observable consequence. This is what happened also with Malthus's demographic and economic theory from 1798 to his death. As regards population and poverty, an astonishing effect of evolution is that what was the central thesis in 1798, namely the opposition of geometric and arithmetic ratio applying respectively to population and resources, at the end is as valid as ever in theory and it becomes at once irrelevant for the real world. What Malthus admits in the 1820s is that this would apply in an 'ideal' state such as Godwin's equalitarian society (with a number of additional conditions such as no emigration, no international trade, no technological change, etc.), but the real world is not made of permanent states, but rather of transitional periods, and this would imply that what we may observe are swings between phases where food may grow for a time faster than population and other phases where unavoidably population tends to take the lead (Waterman 1987). He writes to William Nassau Senior on 23 March 1829:

> It is no doubt true that, in every stage of society, there have been some nations, where, from ignorance and want of foresight, the labouring classes have lived very miserably, and both the food and population have been nearly stationary long before the resources of the soil had approached towards exhaustion. Of these nations, it might safely have been predicted, that in the progress of civilization and improvement, a period would occur when food would increase faster than population. On the other hand, if, from favourable circumstances at any time, the people of a country were very abundantly supplied, it might as safely be predicted that, in their progress towards a full population, a period would occur when population would increase faster than food. It is absolutely necessary, therefore, to know the actual condition in which a people is living, in regard to subsistence, before we can say whether food or population is likely to increase the fastest [...] There is some reason, indeed, to think [...] that population is now increasing faster than food. It appears, then, that it cannot safely be assumed as a fact, that food *has* generally increased faster than population.
>
> (Malthus 1829a, p. 75)

Senior's objection was that, since for Malthus the solution may be brought about not by 'exertions to increase food, but by the moral restraint which will diminish the misery and vice constantly occasioned by the tendency of population to press against subsistence' (Senior 1829, p. 77), Malthus's admission that food may have at some time a *tendency* to increase faster than population appears to be open to the objection that it leads 'to direct the attention towards means which must of necessity be inefficient' (p. 77), since the only efficient means of contending with the difficulty are provided by moral restraint. Malthus answers in a letter of 31 March that:

> It does not by any means follow from these principles, that we should not use our utmost endeavours to make two ears of wheat grow where one grew before, or to improve our commercial code by freeing it from restraints. An increase of population is in itself a very decided advantage, if it be not accompanied by an increased *proportion* of vice and misery. And the period during which the pressure of population is lightened, though it may not be of long duration, is a period of comparative ease, and ought by no means to be thrown out of our consideration. It is further to be observed, that the experience of such a period may sometimes operate in giving to the labouring classes a taste for such a mode of living as will tend to increase their prudential habits. But it is obvious, that without this latter effect, the pressure of poverty cannot be permanently lessened. And when the principal question is distinctly respecting the *permanent* condition of the great mass of the labouring classes [...] imperiously require that we should not call off their attention to the chances of a great increase of food, but endeavour by every proper means to direct their view to the important and unquestionable truth, that they can do much more for themselves than others can do for them, and that the *only* source of an essential and permanent improvement of their condition, is the improvement and right direction of their moral and religious habits.
>
> (Malthus 1829b, p. 86)

It is such a kind of softer theory – a version where nothing of the 1798 version is denied, and yet nothing is left as it was – that makes room for active intervention in the chain of causes and effects and gives pride of place to moral restraint and reduction of misery and vice. This is how tendencies may coexist with a course of events going the opposite direction and the threat of catastrophe may always be there and yet leave room for an imperfect but decent world (Waterman 2012; Hofman 2013).

Policies of self-reliance

The practical consequences of Malthus's revised total population theory are that the desired goal cannot be reached neither by the traditional means prompted by Tory-humanitarians nor by those advocated by radicals, that is, either indiscriminate private charity, or worse, public assistance that would include the able-bodied among its beneficiaries or, even worse, abolition of private property and family. The reason is that such measures yield or would yield results opposite to the intended ones, for any attempt to reverse the laws of nature implies 'not only that they should fail in their object, but that the poor who were intended to be benefited, should suffer most cruelly from this inhuman deceit' (Malthus 1798, p. 127, cf. p. 33; 1803, vol. 2, p. 192; Jensen 1999, pp. 453–457). Also those less unpalatable declarations that did not contribute much to Malthus's popularity fit well in this strategy. For example, a need for generalized blame accompanying dependent poverty is justified with regard to general consequences in terms of happiness; it should be noted that what is justified by such a line of argument is need for praise or blame, not a judgement on the acts blamed or praised as such. Malthus writes in 1798: 'hard as it may appear in individual instances, dependent poverty ought to be held disgraceful. Such a stimulus [is] necessary to promote the happiness of the great mass of mankind' (Malthus 1798, p. 33), and he repeats in 1803 that 'disgrace' ought to be attached to dependent poverty 'for the best and most humane reasons' (Malthus 1803, vol. 1, p. 360). Malthus's moral is that, even though a society with no inequality is just a visionary dream, yet a society with less inequality is a viable goal. In such a society the distance between the top and the bottom would be lesser and the positions at the bottom would be less crowded, while more individuals would be in middle positions. He adds:

> The structure of society, in its great features, will probably remain unchanged. We have every reason to believe that it will always consist of a class of proprietors and a class of labourers; but the condition of each, and the proportion which they bear to each other, may be so altered as greatly to improve the harmony and beauty of the whole.
>
> (p. 203)

In other words, the 'unhappy persons who in the great lottery of life have drawn a blank' (p. 325) will be at least fewer in number and '[1806: the lottery of] human society would appear to consist of fewer blanks and more prizes; and the sum of social happiness would be evidently augmented' (p. 195), that is, the degree of inequality and the mass of unhappiness will be greatly reduced, even though some amount of both will unavoidably remain. The importance of this conclusion could be hardly overemphasized, since it contradicts in general the widespread idea of Malthus's *unqualified* pessimism, and more specifically Hollander's claim that according to Malthus moral restraint has not only played no relevant role in past history (which is roughly correct) but also will play no relevant role in the future (which is clearly mistaken since it contradicts Malthus's line of argument as reconstructed above).

Malthus's argument for gradual abolition of public relief is that a trade-off is unavoidable between more dependence and relief on the one hand and more freedom and higher wages on the other. The measuring rod adopted seems to be *comfort and happiness*. He writes:

> if we weight on the one hand the great quantity of *subjection and dependence* which the poor laws create, together with the kind of *relief* which they afford, against the greater degree of *freedom* and the *higher wages*

which would be necessary consequence of their abolition, it will be difficult to believe that the *mass of comfort and happiness* would not be
greater on the latter supposition, although the few that were then in distress
would have no their resource than voluntary charity.

But though I think that the difficulties attending this state of things would
be more than compensated by its advantages [...] till the poor themselves
could be made to understand that they had purchased their right to a
provision by law, by too great and extensive a sacrifice of their *liberty and
happiness.*

(Malthus 1807, pp. 6–7; italics added)

Important features of Malthus's redefined agenda are that the Poor Laws
should not only be abolished in a *gradual* manner, that some kind of support
might be kept indefinitely for the disabled and victims of bad harvest, that
education of the poor should be considered an important and, from a certain
stage on, even a preliminary and necessary, task to carry out in order to make
them able to rely on themselves. The example he has in mind is Scotland, and
in more detail Chalmers's experiments. Besides, he may have discovered
Adam Smith's argument on the role of education as investment in human
capital. He writes that 'the practical good effects of education have long been
experienced in Scotland; and almost every person that has been placed in a
situation to judge, has given his testimony that education appears to have a
considerable effect in the prevention of crimes, and the promotion of industry,
morality and regular conduct' (Malthus 1803, vol. 2, p. 200). And in a passage added in 1817, he argues that even though the 'errors of the labouring
classes of society are always entitled to great indulgence and consideration', since
they 'are the natural and pardonable results of their liability to be deceived by
first appearances, and by the arts of designing men, owing to the nature of
their situation, and the scanty knowledge which in general falls to their share'
(Malthus 1803, vol. 1, pp. 334–335), these mistakes are to be corrected 'by
spreading knowledge of the true causes of poverty, rather by patience and the
gradual diffusion of education and knowledge, than by any harsher methods'
(p. 335). The 'mere knowledge of these truths' would improve the prudential
habits of the poor with regard to marriage and, as a result of apt combination
of duty and interest, the natural check to population may be expected to
become 'still more effective, as the lower classes of people continue to improve
in knowledge and prudence' (p. 338).

He adds that the tool for making 'the operation of the prudential check to
marriage' effective among the poor as much as among the upper classes is
a plan for general education similar to the one proposed by Adam Smith,
consisting in:

> establishing in every parish or district a little school, where children may
> be taught for a reward so moderate, that even a common labourer may
> afford it; the master being partly, but not wholly paid by the publick [...]

In Scotland the establishment of such parish schools has taught almost the whole common people to read, and a very great proportion of them to write and account. [...] If in these little schools the books, by which the children are taught to read, were a little more instructive than they commonly are, and if, instead of a little smattering of Latin [...] they were instructed in the elementary parts of geometry and mechanicks, the literary education of this rank of people would perhaps be as complete as it can be.

(Smith 1776, p. 785)

General education would have a threefold effect: first, it would contribute to gentrify the lower classes, by instilling not just habits of prudence and industry but also new tastes, for example for tea and sugar, that would make the customary standard of living higher; second, it would contribute – he writes in 1803 – in 'correcting the prevailing opinions respecting marriage, and explaining the real situation of the lower classes of society' (Malthus 1803, vol. 2, p. 154), or – as he more prudently writes in 1806 – in 'explaining the real situation of the lower classes of society' (p. 155 fn. 16) as depending 'almost entirely' or 'principally' upon themselves 'for their happiness or misery' (p. 155); third, it would bring about an investment in human capital along the lines described by Adam Smith, understood as 'a capital fixed and realized, as it were, in his person' (Smith 1776, p. 282).

Thus, Malthus has reasons to expect, not just a growth in the mass of human happiness through reduction of the relative number of the poor but also a growing chance for each poor person of rising beyond the threshold of poverty. We might even, he suggests:

venture to indulge a hope that at some future period the processes for abridging human labour, the progress if which has of late years been so rapid, might ultimately supply all wants of the most wealthy society with less personal labour than at present; and if they did not diminish the severity of individual exertion, might, at least, diminish the number of those employed in severe toil. If the lowest classes of society were thus diminished, and the middle classes increases, each labourer might indulge a more rational hope of rising by diligence and exertion into a better station; the rewards of industry and virtue would be increased in number.

(Malthus 1803, vol. 2, pp. 194–195)

As Jensen aptly summarizes:

Malthus was now of the opinion that the gradual abolition of the poor laws was an ideal policy of the future which should not be implemented until education had implanted moral restraint so firmly in the personalities of the poor that the parish laws had become functionless and obsolete and, therefore, institutionally ripe for relegation to the dustbin of history. In other words, investment in human capital was Malthus's final solution of the population problem.

(Jensen 1999, p. 463)

In fact, changes in Malthus's theodicy and ethics did carry implications for policy advice. A policy which would foster independence, dignity and responsibility would now include not just *gradual* abolition of public assistance granted under the Poor Laws, but also the establishment of a system of liberties and rights as well as generalized primary education. Besides, there would be new institutions such as saving banks that would contribute to raise a sense of foresight and responsibility among the poor. And, last but not least, it will be only under 'the prevalence of habits of prudence' that 'the whole of this vast mass might be nearly as happy as the individuals of the other two classes' (Malthus 1820, vol. 1, p. 423), and thus the key to the whole issue of poverty lies in promoting circumstances that would tend to:

> elevate the character of the lower classes of society, that would make them approach the nearest to beings who 'look before and after' and who consequently cannot acquiesce patiently in the thought of depriving themselves and their children of the means of being *respectable, virtuous and happy.*
>
> (p. 251; italics added)

From sexual morality to procreation ethics

It is commonplace that the Victorian age was obsessed with sex. This was an aspect of a mass campaign aimed at spreading control over the passions. The sexual drive was felt as a ubiquitous enemy, and religion, education and manners were all meant to conspire in keeping it under control and confining it to a space reserved for its proper function, so as to make it virtually invisible. The diffusion of Victorian morality was to a wide extent the Evangelicals' masterpiece, and among Evangelical ammunitions there was a whole battery of doctrines about the family, marriage, procreation, industry, thriftiness and self-control deriving, among other sources, also from Malthus. But how far was he responsible for this obsession with sex? One may say that sexual morality is indeed one important, and perhaps the most important, chapter in Malthus's view of *private* morality, but this depends on the relationship he discovered between procreation and poverty (Cremaschi 2012). On the other hand, the tone of Malthus's treatment of most of the topics related with the subject – making exception for contraception, whose mention he is as careful as any of his contemporaries to avoid – is far from sanctimonious, and, for example, pregnancy outside wedlock is deemed to be the result of 'so natural a sin' (Malthus 1803, vol. 2, p. 143).

How did sex turn out to be so important? He believed that *the* problem of his time was, as illustrated above, poverty, and this was the central issue in the first *Essay*. The main difference between his 1798 and his 1803 outlook is the role that prudence may play in allowing for a tolerable individual existence and a decent society. This implies that the problem of theodicy may be settled now not exclusively taking an afterlife into account but both in inner-worldly and in other-worldly perspective.

I have illustrated how vice, misery, and the prudential restraint were already mentioned on one occasion in the first *Essay* as the three factors contrasting the population principle, but the third element was declared irrelevant in accounting for past history, was declared to be irrelevant for 'technical' reasons in designing a future society, and eventually reduced, on moral reasons, to the first of the three factors, that is, vice. The reasons for irrelevance are the following: 'among plants and animals' the effects of the 'imperious and all-pervading law of nature of necessity' are 'waste of seed, sickness, and premature death, among mankind, misery and vice. The former, misery, is an absolutely necessary consequence of it. Vice is a highly probable consequence, and we therefore see it abundantly prevail; but it ought not, perhaps, to be called an *absolutely necessary* consequence' (Malthus 1798, p. 9; italics added). The prudential check to population growth 'almost necessarily, though *not absolutely* so, produces vice' (p. 14; italics added). This consists in the action of reason, which interrupts the effects of a powerful instinct that would urge man to pursue the dictate of nature in an early attachment to one woman. The clause '*not absolutely* so' seems to hint at the possibility of 'moral restraint'. This would have been envisaged by Malthus as a possible, albeit remote, solution as soon as in 1798, but it seems also to be confined to pure speculation, since Malthus seems to believe that, in practice, checks to population are 'resolved into misery and vice' (p. 38).

I mentioned that the decisive change in 1803 was systematic introduction of the third element in the list of checks to population, now constantly modified so as to include 'moral restraint, vice, and misery' (Malthus 1803, vol. 1, p. 23). *Moral* restraint is expressly declared to be different from what had been previously defined as the *preventive* check. The latter seems to consist, in fact, in postponement of marriage possibly accompanied by 'irregular gratification', whereas the former means postponement of marriage *with pre-marital chastity*, which does not exclude virtuous attachments, which are enjoyable in themselves without ceasing to be chaste, with marriage coming at the end of the story as a longed for prize. It is fair to say that Malthus owes the idea basically to Godwin himself, that is, to his main opponent. Let me add that this is no strange circumstance, and it is instead a recurrent feature in controversies, where the best contributions in carrying out a research programme, by filling out blanks or solving puzzles come most of the time more from the opponents than from the followers of any new theory (Cremaschi and Dascal 1998a). This was also the case with Godwin, who may be credited with one among the most important contributions to Malthus's modified theory. In Chapter 3 of Book 3 in the second *Essay*, Malthus, while replying to Godwin's *Thoughts occasioned by the perusal of Dr. Parr's Spital Sermon*, does in fact acknowledge Godwin's innovation, consisting in admitting of a kind of check to population which is morally acceptable and fits such innovation in his own solution. After arguing that in the past no check has ever contributed to keep down the population to the level of the means of subsistence, that does not fairly come under some form of vice or misery, he mentions the check of 'moral restraint' (Malthus 1803, vol. 1, p. 329) and admits that it has been recommended by Godwin as 'that sentiment whether *virtue, prudence, or pride*, which continually restrains the universality and frequent repetition of the marriage contract' (p. 331). To be fair, what Godwin had written in 1801 was something more precise and less fabulous than former claims about a spontaneous tendency of the sexual drive to lose its force as human nature is improved by better education and rising standards of civilization. Practical effects pointed at in 1801 are the same, but made less utopian and more practical. Godwin argues in fact that there is an already effective restraint on population depending on the effect of rational considerations on individual behaviour. He writes:

Another check upon increasing population which operates very power-fully and extensively in the country we inhabit, is the *sentiment*, whether *virtue, prudence, or pride*, which continually restrains the universality and frequent repetition of the marriage contract. Early marriages in this country between a grown up boy and girl are of uncommon occurrence. Every one, possessed in the most ordinary degree of the gift of foresight, deliberates long before he engages in so momentuous a transaction [...] It is needless to remark that, where marriage takes place at a later period of life, the progeny may be expected to be less numerous.

(Godwin 1801, p. 203)

Malthus, once more claiming victory while retreating, admits that this may be highly effective within the context of his own system, while in Godwin's system it is bound to remain ineffective. The reason is that, in order to have a powerful enough motivation, we need 'a sense of duty, superadded to a sense of interest' (Malthus 1803, vol. 1, p. 331) and if 'we were to remove or weaken the motive of interest, which would be the case in Mr. Godwin's system', we would be left with a sense of duty alone, which would be 'a weak substitute' (p. 332).

Yet, it was not to Godwin alone that Malthus owed his new solution. The other half of the job had been done by the Scandinavian population. After intensive reading of 'the best authenticated accounts we have of the state of other countries' (Malthus 1803, vol. 2, p. 18) about the effects of the principle of population on the past and present state of society, he undertook a jour-ney, with the company of Jesus fellows William Otter and Edward Daniel Clarke, in turn followed by his pupil John Martin Cripps, in the Scandinavian countries and Northern Russia. During this journey he did field-work observing everyday life and collecting information about institutions while interviewing local scholars – having recourse to Latin as a *Lingua Franca* in case the latter did not speak French – who provided him with data about births, marriages and deaths, and local institutions (James 1979, pp. 69–76; Jensen 1999, pp. 457–459). Remarks in his travel journal include the information that sons of Danish farmers were 'not liable to be call'd upon' (Malthus 1966, p. 59) for military service after 28 years of age and that, as a result, marriage was generally delayed until this age; besides, that in Norway no son of a peasant usually married until he was free from military duties, which did not apply until he was 40, and this 'has hitherto operated as a strong preventive check to population in Norway, and accounts for their increasing slowly, tho the people live so long' (p. 89).

Thus, Malthus shortly after 1798 was convinced that there was a third element besides vice and misery acting as a preventive check. And yet he declares, in 1803 and after, that 'whatever hopes we may entertain of its prevalence in future, has undoubtedly in past ages operated with very inconsiderable force' (Malthus 1803, vol. 1, pp. 329–330). Note that Malthus is – as always – reticent about the fact that the first *Essay*, far from acknowledging only an 'inconsiderable' influence to the action of this check in the past, did not make any room for it in the future, apart from the cryptic clause 'not absolutely so' about which I have commented above. In 1806, in a footnote added, he specifies that this diagnosis about the past turns out clearly to be true if one recollects that by moral restraint he means 'a restraint from marriage from prudential motives, which is not followed by irregular gratifications' (p. 330 fn.) and in another he admits that it is true that the *moral* restraint has been seldom practised in the past (p. 18 fn. 4) and one should not be too naïvely hopeful also about future prospects. Yet, it is fair to add that Malthus is less naïve about human nature than the last sentence may seem to suggest, since he is explicit enough about the idea that sex outside marriage is not the worst sin and that it is not true that 'the vices which relate to the sex are the only vices which are to be considered in a moral question; or that they are even the greatest and most degrading to the human character' (vol. 2, p. 111). In the 1806 Appendix he argues that a greater degree of sexual promiscuity accompanied by the practice of contraception, an evil that may be carried as a side-effect by widespread 'prudential check to marriage', is still 'better than premature mortality' (p. 222). And thus, once we may prove that the world at large is not, at least on principle, an evil place in so far as a decent society would be possible on the basis, first, of prudence and, second, of other virtues, and that a more humane world is a viable prospect, Malthus manifests a belief that we must dare to face also the unpalatable implication that we should confront first the greater evils carried by an excessive birth-rate, and only after that lesser evils. Nonetheless, he has it clear in mind that 'if every man were to obey at all times the impulses of nature in the gratification of this passion, without regard to consequences, the principal part of these important objects [those fixed by nature as the ends promoted by sexual instinct] would not be attained, and even the continuation of the species

might be defeated by a promiscuous intercourse' (p. 156). As a consequence, he believes that sexual promiscuity 'ought always strongly to be
reprobated', since such sins 'can *rarely or never* be committed without producing unhappiness somewhere or other' (vol. 1, p. 156; italics added), and
besides have the effect 'to weaken the best affections of the heart' (vol. 2,
p. 97), as well as an obvious tendency 'to degrade the female character' (vol. 1,
p. 18) and to spread real distress and aggravated misery among 'unfortunate
females'.

I have illustrated how, according to Malthus, starting with observation of
the workings of the laws of nature we may conclude that chastity is a virtue
and that it implies not only avoidance of casual sex, homosexual intercourse,
and sexual intercourse before marriage, but also of contraception within
marriage. He writes that '[p]romiscuous intercourse, unnatural passions, violations of the marriage bed, and improper arts to conceal the consequences of
irregular connections' (p. 18) are incompatible with this virtue and accordingly 'clearly come under the head of vice' (p. 18). Another virtue, prudence,
enjoins also a duty not to contract marriage before one is in condition to
support a family. No matter how probable and how direct the evils carried by
the contrary vice may be, the existence of such evils is a clear proof of the
existence of this virtue, for also in other instances 'it has not been till after
long and painful experience that the conduct most favourable to the happiness of man' (vol. 2, p. 99) has been recognized to be such, and thus the
'delayed consequence of particular effects does not alter their nature, nor our
obligation to regulate our conduct accordingly' (p. 99). It is worth noting once
more that a consequentialist-voluntarist foundation of virtue opens the way to
a kind of functionalist view of the latter (with the above-mentioned deadlocks
concerning the relationship between general good and individual unhappiness). Malthus's view of the origins and nature of existing social sanction of
female chastity may have been derived from various eighteenth-century sources where proto-functionalist views of law and customs are sketched. He
reports the conjecture advanced by the Abbé Raynal (1770) that customs such
as approbation of celibacy and the consecration of virginity, as well as other
more cruel ones may have had their origin in islands as a consequence of a
superabundance of population (Malthus 1803, vol. 1, p. 46). Considerations
of a similar kind regarding female chastity may be found in Hume, who
writes:

> Men are induc'd to labour for the maintenance and education of their
> children, by the persuasion that they are really their own; and therefore
> 'tis reasonable, and even necessary, to give them some security in this
> particular. This security cannot consist entirely in the imposing of severe
> punishments on any transgressions of conjugal fidelity on the part of the
> wife; since these public punishments cannot be inflicted without legal
> proof, which 'tis difficult to meet with in this subject. What restraint,
> therefore, shall we impose on women, in order to counter-balance so

strong a temptation as they have to infidelity? There seems to be no restraint possible, but in the punishment of bad fame or reputation; a punishment, which has a mighty influence on the human mind, and at the same time is inflicted by the world upon surmises, and conjectures, and proofs, that wou'd never be receiv'd in any court of judicature. In order, therefore, to impose a due restraint on the female sex, we must attach a peculiar degree of shame to their infidelity, above what arises merely from its injustice, and must bestow proportionable praises on their chastity.

(Hume 1739–1740, p. 365)

Also Adam Smith may have been a direct source. He had written:

Treachery and falsehood are vices so dangerous, so dreadful, and, at the same time, such as may so easily, and upon many occasions, so safely be indulged, that we are more jealous of them than of almost any other. Our imagination therefore attaches the idea of shame to all violations of faith, in every circumstance and in every situation. They resemble in this respect, the violations of chastity in the fair sex, a virtue of which, for the like reasons, we are excessively jealous [...] Breach of chastity dishonour irretrievably. No circumstances, no solicitation can excuse it; no sorrow, no repentance atone for it.

(Smith 1759, p. 332)

Malthus's attitude is connected with his general views on penal law and punishment, another rather hot issue at the time, as shown by the echo met by Cesare Beccaria's *An Essay on Crimes and Punishments* (1767). Malthus seems to have his own peculiar theory in mind according to which the principal objects which human punishments have in view, are: (i) *restraint*, or 'removal of an individual member whose vicious habits are likely to be prejudicial to the society' (Malthus 1798, p. 91); and (ii) *example*, which 'by associating crime and punishment' provides 'a moral motive to dissuade others from the commission of it' (p. 91); its effect is that of generating that sentiment that the author of a murder will sooner or later will be detected, and the 'horror in which murder is in consequence held' (p. 92). Imperfections in a system of punishment may be: (i) lack of accurate proportion of punishment to crime, and this is 'absolutely impossible' to avoid because of 'the inscrutability of motives' (p. 92) that makes so that no human judge may fully appreciate the circumstances of a crime; (ii) the fact of having made examples too impressive and terrible with the ensuing barbarous cruelties; this is an abuse that should be avoided but 'no argument against the practice of punishment in general' (p. 92). There are limits to the scope of punishment, depending on the existence of boundaries between the private and the public. Every act that does damage mainly the agent is not a proper subject-matter for punishment. This applies to the case of imprudent marriage. Also Adam

Smith's theory of punishment accounts for such an irregularity in our senti-ments that makes so that, while in principle we are prepared to judge of actions according to intentions, in real-world cases we tend to give a great importance to actual consequences albeit dependent on chance (Smith 1759, p. 92–108). Similar considerations had been developed also by Paley who had written that the:

> loss which a woman sustains by the ruin of her reputation, almost exceeds computation [...] By a rule of life, which it is not easy to blame, and which it is impossible to alter, a woman looses, with her chastity the chances of marrying at all.
>
> (Paley 1785, p. 175)

Malthus, not unlike Hume, Smith and Paley, believes that, as the children born of irregular unions may either fall upon the society for support or starve, there is 'a very natural reason why the disgrace which attends a breach of chastity should be greater in a woman than in a man' (Malthus 1803, vol. 1, p. 324). And, to prevent the frequent recurrence of such an inconvenience, as it would be highly unjust to punish 'so natural a sin' by some penalty, society might agree to punish it with disgrace. Malthus notes that males and females are de facto not treated in the same manner in so far as this virtue is concerned and women are subject to 'superior disgrace' when they perpetrate a breach of chastity. He admits that such inequality is a breach of '*natural* justice' and yet it has a *natural* origin since the offence is 'more obvious and conspicuous in the woman, and less liable to mistake'. He concludes that the fact:

> that a woman should at present be almost driven from society, for an offence, which men commit nearly with impunity, seems to be undoubt-edly a breach of natural justice. But the origin of the custom, as the most obvious and effectual method of preventing the frequent recurrence of a serious inconvenience to a community, appears to be natural, though not perhaps perfectly justifiable.
>
> (Malthus 1798, p. 73)

Indeed the society would punish also the man, were the offence obvious and easy to establish. Since it is not so, the result is that 'the largest sum of blame' (p. 73) falls where 'the evidence of the offence was most complete and the inconvenience to the society at the same time the greatest' (p. 73). Such a custom is not *justifiable* and yet it is *natural*, for it has the same 'very natural origin' as the artificial institutions of property and marriage, in turn carrying their own artificial virtues. It originates in the state of scarcity which inevi-tably arises from the combined effect of the tendency of population to grow and the impossibility of a parallel growth in the production of supplies. Since we should not expect that a woman has resources sufficient to support her own children, once a woman has intercourse with a man 'who had entered into no compact to maintain her children' and 'has deserted her' (p. 73), these children will be a burden to society. Thus, in order to:

> prevent the frequent recurrence of such an inconvenience, as it would be highly unjust to punish *so natural a fault* by personal restraint or infliction, the men might agree to punish it with disgrace.
>
> (p. 73; italics added)

Note the distinction between what is *natural*, understood as 'spontaneous' or 'not artificial', and what is *justifiable*, in the sense of what is conforming to impartiality and conducive to the greatest mass of happiness. Such a distinction, hardly a utilitarian one, corresponds to those we may find in Adam Smith with regard to corruption of natural sentiments deriving from habit, from the tendency to sympathize with the more powerful and from that to appreciate 'utility' more than impartiality (Cremaschi 1989, p. 98–102).

Malthus elaborates on this point in the second *Essay*. The general theory on laws of nature and virtue that has been presented in the previous chapter provides the background for discussion of chastity. Physical evils, such as disease and death, by the fixed laws of nature, are unavoidable consequences of vice. This seems to have been a 'benevolent dispensation', since the unhappy lot of the vicious one carries out the function of 'a beacon to others' (Malthus 1803, vol. 2, p. 89). This holds for such vices as intemperance in eating and drinking, followed by ill-health, as well as for those carrying the consequence that 'we increase too fast for the means of subsistence' (p. 89) and are followed by squalid poverty and all its consequences. Not unlike desire for food, which is a necessary passion but must be limited by a corresponding virtue, so also the passion between the sexes is not only necessary for the survival of the species but also 'one of the principal ingredients of human happiness' (p. 92), and yet 'much evil flows from the irregular gratification of it' (p. 92).

Nonetheless, Malthus reaffirms also in 1803 his sympathy with the woman who has committed 'so natural a sin' and a severe judgement on the man involved in the affair, while admitting of the tragic contrast between the dictates of fairness and the laws of nature. He writes that it may appear to be:

> hard that a mother and her children, who have been guilty of no particular crime themselves, should suffer for the ill conduct of the father; but this is one of the *invariable laws of nature*; and, knowing this, we should think twice upon the subject, and be very sure of the ground on which we go, before we presume systematically to counteract it.
>
> (p. 143, italics added)

He adds that the kind of self-respect that may inspire female chastity may be learned and cultivated only when a person is respected first by others, what seldom happens among the poorest members of society. Abject poverty, he remarks:

particularly when joined with idleness, is a state the most unfavourable to chastity that can well be conceived. The passion is as strong, or nearly so, as in other situations; and every restraint on it from personal respect, or a sense of morality, is generally removed. There is a degree of squalid poverty, in which, if a girl was brought up, I should say, that her being really modest at twenty was an absolute miracle. Those persons must have extraordinary minds indeed, and such as are not usually formed under similar circumstances, who can continue to respect themselves when no other person whatever respects them. If the children thus brought up were even to marry at twenty, it is probable, that they would have passed some years in vicious habits before that period.

(p. 114)

And yet, punishment inflicted to the man, though fair in principle, would be ineffective, productive of greater evils, and would imply more moral mischief. It describes as not uncommon the practice of endeavouring, 'when the father of an illegitimate child can be seized [...] to frighten him into marriage by the terrors of a jail' (p. 142), but adds that 'such a proceeding cannot surely be too strongly reprobated' (p. 142). One reason is that the consequence would be starting one more family living in squalid poverty and accordingly 'having three or four children to provide for, instead of one' (p. 142). Another reason, of a different nature, is that this would imply 'a gross and scandalous profanation of a religious ceremony' (p. 143). He concludes that if:

a man deceive a woman into a connexion with him under a promise of marriage, he has undoubtedly been guilty of a most atrocious act, and there are few crimes which merit a more severe punishment; but the last that I should choose is that which will oblige him to affirm another falsehood, which will probably render the woman that he is to be joined to miserable, and will burden the society with a family of paupers.

(p. 143)

The virtue opposite to irregular gratification of the sexual drive is chastity, and 'virtuous love' is the only admissible gratification of this passion. Thus there is a 'law of chastity', which:

cannot be violated without producing *evil*. The effect of anything like a promiscuous intercourse, which prevents the birth of children, is evidently *to weaken the best affections of the heart*, and in a very marked manner to degrade the female character. And any other intercourse would, without *improper arts*, bring as many children into the society as marriage, with a greater probability of their becoming a burden to it.

(p. 97)

All this implies the assumption that contraception is as such vicious. It may sound strange that Malthus neatly rules out birth control within marriage without second thoughts. In fact he lists 'unnatural' practices that 'would prevent breeding' (vol. 1, p. 310) or 'improper arts' that 'prevent the birth of children' (vol. 2, p. 97) among such evils as sexual promiscuity and abortion (vol. 1, p. 18). He insists, under pressure from critics, that he has always opposed the kind of restraints prompted by Condorcet, that is, he has always reprobated 'any artificial and unnatural modes of checking population, both on account of their *immorality* and their tendency to remove a necessary *stimulus to industry*' (vol. 2, p. 235; italics added). Since the discussion here concerns married couples, it is clear that the 'immorality' in question does not consist in promiscuous intercourse but in contraception as such. In the 1817 Appendix he adds an account of the reason why contraception is vicious. This is that:

> if it were possible for each married couple to limit by wish the number of their children, there is certainly reason to fear that the indolence of the human race would be very greatly increased.
>
> (p. 235)

This is quite in tune with the general consequentialist-voluntarist approach and its *general good particular hell* equation. In fact, Malthus never explains what is *intrinsically* immoral in birth control within marriage, but his general outlook exonerates him from the burden of detecting any intrinsic moral quality in actions, for moral qualities are by definition *superimposed* on kinds of actions and the general, albeit remote, tendency to produce evils is enough as a *mark* of the vicious character of a category of actions. On the other hand, he may have never felt a need to explain the sources of immorality in contraception because it was something simply obvious for his readers, and even discussing it was likely to arouse strong reactions. In order to understand what precisely was so obvious, it is important to avoid mixing together different lines of thought that to the present-day reader may seem vaguely similar, while in fact they are not. Malthus, while alluding to the inherently immoral character of contraception within marriage, does not have recourse to the argument of *conformity to nature* (typical of Catholic, or better Thomist, theology with regard to contraception) because he is a voluntarist and believes general laws to have been proclaimed by God not respecting the *essence* of things he had created but instead keeping the *general consequences* of such general laws in mind.

It may be a temptation for the modern reader to dismiss all this as mere hypocrisy. It is true that Malthus was pleading what was far from being a popular cause, and the last thing he needed was arousing more opposition by contrasting also rooted prejudices in matters of sexual morality. This is probably part of the story, but assuming it was all of it would contrast with Malthus's courage, or even lack of any diplomacy, in fighting prejudice in other fields. James (1979, p. 121–126) suggests that in this case Malthus was talking about possibilities that seemed as unrealistic as travels to the Moon. This is not false, and yet it seems to be too much charitable. If we take the circumstance into account that contraception was not unknown in Britain at the time and it was widely practised in France (Gilbert 1993, p. 3–5) some more reasons appear to be required. One is that contraceptive techniques were rudimentary and the most advanced one (the sponge, imbibed with some mildly acid liquid such as lemon juice) was even dangerous for women (sponges tended to lose pieces that were the sources of dangerous infections), and that another, the condom, had been used by soldiers and sailors in intercourse with prostitutes and accordingly was sanctioned by a social stigma as something associated with immorality. Another, and more important, reason is that the Christian churches had always taken refusal of contraception as a matter of course, partly because in the first centuries of Christianity in the Roman-Hellenistic society it was customarily associated with other obviously immoral practices such as prostitution and extra-marital sex, partly because potions used for contraceptive purposes were not clearly distinguished from abortive potions, partly because the practice was associated with one doctrinal tendency, the Gnostic 'left' – the libertine tendency in Gnosticism as opposed to the ascetic Gnostic 'right' – that favoured contraception precisely *because* it favoured sexual freedom. In this context, the adoption by Clemens of Alexandria of the Stoic view that marriage is justified by procreation seemed plausible enough. The influence of Augustine (BC, pp. 10–15) was heavier in the following centuries and had more extreme implications. In the context of his own tract on marriage he insisted that chastity for married people does not consist just in mutual faithfulness among spouses but also in limiting contacts to those strictly required for procreation, since those going beyond this point are sinful. Aquinas and the other scholastics taught a slightly milder doctrine according to which marital sexuality practised with a barren wife or with one no longer able to procreate was admissible for the sake of the other two ends of marriage, but ruled out contraception on a different ground, namely the requirement that sexual intercourse should not violate an order of nature implying that the male seed be deposited in the wife's vagina (Noonan 1965). The practical teaching of all Christian denominations did not depart from this doctrine, even when – as it happened with the Reformation – the superior moral value of virginity was universally denied and the natural-law approach was virtually rejected. This lasted well into the twentieth century, when the 1930 Lambeth conference of the Anglican Church cautiously admitted other methods besides complete abstinence. This was sharply condemned by Pope Pius XI in his encyclical *Casti Connubi* of the same year (Curran 1995). Indeed this was in tune with the campaign, at the practical pastoral level, against contraception and for bigger families that began in the nineteenth century, superseding the milder 'don't ask don't allow' attitude that had been taught by Alfonso de' Liguori and had been prevailing in the Catholic Church until then. The Protestant Churches aligned themselves quickly with the Anglican and a prevailing position emerged in Orthodox Churches based on their traditional refusal of nature as a source of normativity, and accordingly of the Catholic distinction between natural and artificial means, leaving details to the spouses' conscience.

Malthus mentions contraception once more in 1817 while discussing Owen's views as presented in his *A New View of Society* (1813–1816). He speaks in highly respectful tone of Owen's experiment of an industrial community at Lanark run on a socially minded basis. Yet, while not trying to deny those facts that contradicted a few of his own basic assumptions, he resorts to a typical limiting clause used by social scientists when their theories are refuted by facts: conceding the validity of the adversary's claim and then proceeding to show that such validity is limited to one particular domain (Dascal and Cremaschi 1999), in this instance to one comparatively small community where there was no communion of goods in Godwin's sense, in so far as 'the whole of every man's earnings is his own' (Malthus 1803, vol. 2, p. 177) and where individual members could be under the threat of being expelled for, 'if any workman be perseveringly indolent and negligent if he get drunk and spoil his work, or if in any way he conduct himself essentially ill, he [...] may at any time be turned off, and the society be relieved from the influence and example of a profligate and dangerous member' (p. 177). Owen's experiment could not work as a model for bigger communities of millions of people where 'the produce of all the labour employed would go to a common stock' (p. 177) and expulsion would be impossible. In such cases, instead of dismissal 'recourse must be had to a system of direct punishment of some kind or other [...] which is always painful and distressing, and generally inefficient' (p. 177). Besides, he adds that Owen's project suffers from the very crucial difficulty which undermined Godwin's utopia, namely the fact that the natural check to population in a state of equality and community of property could only be replaced by some artificial regulation of 'a very different stamp' and a much more 'unnatural' character. He admits that Owen is aware of that and in fact had taken the principle of population into account, advancing the claim that the growth of necessaries may keep pace with the growth of population, 'for man knows not the limit to his power of creating food' (Owen 1813–1816, p. 96). In Britain – Owen adds – this power has been lately increased to an unforeseeable extent, chemistry is daily adding to our knowledge of the original elements out of which food is compounded, and it cannot be told yet to what this knowledge may lead, or where it may end, and the sea also affords an inexhaustible source of food, and thus it may be safely asserted that 'the population of the world may be allowed naturally to increase for many thousand years', and yet 'the whole may continue to live in abundance and happiness, without one check of vice and misery' (p. 96). What is required is that, by judicious and proper laws and training, the population would acquire knowledge and habits which will enable them to produce far more than they need for their support and enjoyment. Owen concludes that:

Mr Malthus is, however, correct, when he says that the population of the world is ever adapting itself to the quantity of food raised for its support; but he has not told us how much more food an intelligent and industrious people will create from the same soil, than will be produced by one ignorant and ill-governed. It is, however, as one to infinity.

(p. 96)

Malthus comments on Owen's 'absolute inability' to suggest any way of reaching this goal that would not be 'unnatural, immoral, or cruel in a high degree' (Malthus 1803, vol. 1, p. 338), and adds that, even in case the most complete success were attained, 'the system would, without some most unnatural and unjust laws to prevent the progress of population, lead to a state of universal poverty and distress' (p. 177–178). It is unclear where Owen suggests any 'unnatural' or 'immoral' way of preventing the progress of population, and thus Malthus's charge with immorality seems to be based just on implication. The fact is that there were rumours that Owen in Lanark had been spreading knowledge of contraceptive techniques. This is reflected in a letter from Ricardo to Malthus where the former comments on a manuscript by Francis Place. Ricardo notes that Place 'speaks of one of Owen's preventives to an excessive population' (Ricardo 1821, p. 118), while commenting that he doubts 'whether it is right even to mention it' (p. 118).

Malthus's basic reason for ruling out the morality of contraception was backed by his natural theology, and based on his voluntarist-consequentialist view of the moral law. Malthus's inference starts with the assumptions that contraception has to be *either* moral or immoral and that, in order to find out which is the case, we have to look at consequences, and he then goes on to prove that, were contraception allowed, the general outcome would be discouragement of habits of 'sobriety, industry, independence, and prudence' (Malthus 1803, vol. 2, p. 155), and that, since the latter are virtues, contraception should be assumed by implication to be vice, and thus we may safely assume that it has been forbidden by the Deity. When read this way, Malthus's argument is not that contraception is immoral and *besides* it discourages the virtues of sobriety, industry, independence and prudence, but that it is immoral precisely *because* it may be assumed to discourage those virtues. Let me comment that on this issue two dark spots in Malthus's approach are evident. One point is an inherently authoritarian view of morality, according to which the *moral* law is rather moral *law*. Another is an extrinsic consideration of human action that makes so that the option is not even envisaged that the use of scientific methods to prevent conception might be neither moral nor immoral, but may simply be morally neutral until we do not take goals, intentions and circumstances under consideration. The third is that the recurrent conundrum of general laws shows up again, namely that the alleged beneficial effect of prohibiting contraception in general is the only reason given for sacrificing individual happiness on the altar of general good. Finally let me add – this time in defence of Malthus – that the standard of *six* children adopted by Malthus may have not sounded so absurd at a time when infant mortality was enormously higher than now, when the effort required for education of children was lesser because of less demanding standards for lower classes and availability of cheap domestic help for middle and upper classes, when a son at the age of 12 already used to become more an asset than a burden for the lower classes, and thus a two-children family – nowadays generally believed to carry 25 years heavy *corvée* for any couple – could then be thought to be an encouragement to 'the indolence of the human race'!

Malthus also mentions infanticide while responding to Godwin's apologia. The latter had boldly argued that Malthus's own view was that a fixed amount of misery and vice was required at every stage in history in order to check the growth of population, and that instead there were remedies different from misery and vice that had been practised in the past. One among these expedients, alternative to misery and vice, is – according to Godwin – infanticide. He writes:

> What was called the exposing of children prevailed to a very extensive degree in the ancient world. The same practice continues to this hour in China.
>
> I know that the prejudices and habits of modern Europe are strongly in arms against this institution. I grant that it is very painful and repulsive to the imagination of persons educated as I and my countrymen have been.
>
> (Godwin 1801, p. 199)

And yet – Godwin adds – if we compare it with 'misery and vice, the checks pleaded for in the Essay on Population', no doubt this is a more appealing practice. Besides, even if Hume's argument to the ineffectiveness of this practice in checking the population of China were true, yet 'the exposing of children is in its own nature an expedient perfectly adequate to the end for which it has been cited' (p. 66). Godwin adds that 'other expedients' may be found in use in other parts of the world, one of them being abortion.

In the island of Ceylon for example, it appears to be a part of the common law of the country that no woman shall be a mother before she is 30, and they accordingly have their methods for procuring abortions, which, we are told, are perfectly innoxious (p. 66).

Godwin doesn't even ask the question whether such methods were 'innoxious' to foetuses, showing that he had no idea of what could have been a shared premise from which to argue. He concludes admitting that these are 'harsh and displeasing remedies' but – typically begging the question – adds that 'they are better than misery and vice' (p. 66). Malthus's response is, obviously enough, that he had always meant such practises to be examples of misery and vice. Besides the moral argument, he insists on Hume's argument that proves that its permission, instead of checking, tends to encourage the growth of population. Hume had written in 'Of the Populousness of Ancient Nations' that:

CHINA, the only country where this practice of exposing children prevails at present, is the most populous country we know of; and every man is married before he is twenty. Such early marriages could scarcely be general, had not men the prospect of so easy a method of getting rid of their children.

(Hume 1742, p. 396)

Note that, even though Adam Smith is not quoted here, Hume's remark had been repeated by him, noting that marriage 'is encouraged in China, not by the profitableness of children, but by the liberty of destroying them. In all great towns several are every night exposed in the street, or drowned like puppies in the water. The performance of this horrid office is even said to be the avowed business by which some people earn their subsistence' (Smith 1776, p. 90). Malthus adds that permission of infanticide is 'bad enough, and cannot but have a bad effect on the moral sensibility of a nation' (Malthus 1803, vol. 1, p. 330 fn.) but also that, in order to be effective it must be done by the magistrate, as it happened in ancient Greece and was recommended by Plato and Aristotle, and not left to the parents, and this would be not only bad, but 'detestable or shocking to the feelings' (p. 330) more than anything one could conceive of.

On balance, the exchange was a remarkable exercise in cross-purpose. In fact, Godwin deviously attributes to Malthus promotion of misery and vice as remedies, then he argues that there are alternatives to misery and vice, meaning *purposeful*, albeit 'painful and repulsive', practices such as infanticide and abortion (he seems to ignore the possibility of contraception) that are 'perfectly adequate to the end', as opposed to poverty, diseases, war, famine and prostitution which only *inadvertently* contribute to check the population. Malthus, on his side, tacitly expands his own previous description of 'misery and vice' so as to include abortion and infanticide, although it is fair to acknowledge that, even he did not have those practices in mind in 1798, yet he would have considered them as immoral. Then, when Godwin advances the proposal of postponement of marriage as a solution, he suddenly subtracts it from the category of 'misery', under which it was clearly enough classified in 1798, and starts arguing that it would be more a source of happiness than of misery – forgetting to add that he had *not* always meant what he is contending for now.

Individual Rights

Malthus, the son of a country gentleman, was some kind of Whig by birth. Besides, he had been taught a political philosophy that tried to justify traditional Whig claims on a 'philosophical' basis, as opposed to those mythological paraphernalia as the Magna Charta or the Saxons' pristine liberties. He had accordingly an approach to political issues that was quite the opposite of – in present-day terminology – 'political realism', but viewed instead politics as – again in present-day jargon – 'morality in the public domain'. Malthus's reasons for adopting such an approach are, first, a belief that political power is some kind of dangerous entity. He assumes as 'an incontrovertible truth' that there is 'in all power a constant tendency to encroach' (Malthus 1798, p. 125). Thus he sees power as unavoidable evil, something that has to be accepted to a point, but with the proviso that the 'degree of power to be given to the civil government […] must be determined by general expediency' (p. 125). That is, government should not have too much power, and the scope of its action should have fixed limits.

He believes that one basic mistake that is constantly made is that of attributing 'all want of happiness' to government, whereas there are 'evils which do not depend by the action of government' (p. 127). For example, Malthus's doctrine of population, since it ascribes the greater part of the sufferings of the lower classes of society exclusively to their lack of prudence as a cause, seems at a first glance to be 'unfavourable to the cause of liberty' (p. 122), but this is a mistaken appearance. On the opposite, the claim that the cause of all evils of the lower classes depends on government is 'the great error under which Mr Godwin labours […] the attributing almost all the vices and misery that are seen in civil society to human institutions' (p. 65; cf. Malthus 1803, vol. 1, p. 317). The fact is that, even under the best government, 'the most squalid poverty and wretchedness might universally prevail from the principle of population alone' (Malthus 1798, p. 130), and government 'can do little on the basic cause', yet its influence 'is great in giving the best direction to those checks which […] must necessarily take place' (p. 130).

In the light of the principle of population, Malthus reinterprets one eighteenth-century familiar doctrine, that of public happiness as the object of government. Public happiness – he says – is a distinct entity, not to be reduced to the wealth of a nation (as Adam Smith had allegedly done), or to the size of its population (as Paley had in fact done). The inquiry into the causes of the wealth of nations should be carefully distinguished from that into the causes 'which affect the happiness of nations, or the happiness and comfort of the lower classes of society, which is the numerous class in every nation' (p. 107), and Adam Smith has considered these two inquiries as still more nearly connected than they really are. His mistake has been, according to Malthus, assuming 'every increase of the revenue or stock of a society as an increase of these funds' (p. 108), those by which more labour may be maintained; instead, an increase in provisions is needed in order that the lower classes may be better fed, unless an increase in the total revenue would simply turn into a rise in the price of food. Thus, countries are *populous* according to the quantity of food which they produce or can acquire; and they are *happy* according to the way in which distribution of food is carried out, or according to 'the quantity which a day's labour will purchase' (Malthus 1803, vol. 1, p. 303). The happiness of nations:

> does not depend either upon their being thinly or fully inhabited, upon their poverty or their riches, their youth or their age; but on the proportion which the population and the food bear to each other.
>
> (p. 303)

Thus, politics is a matter of morality, since its goals are neither the state's greatness, glory or power, nor the nation's wealth or population, for:

> Wealth, population and power are, after all, only valuable, as they tend to improve, increase and secure the mass of human virtue and happiness.
>
> (Malthus 1814, p. 102)

But politics as morality is not moralizing about public issues, since different moral objects should be balanced with each other on criteria dictated by prudence. Factors at play in human society are always variable and often unknown, and there is a point where one additional share of one factor starts yielding opposite effects. Thus the desirable amount of any factor has to be assessed on the basis of 'general expediency'. The overarching criterion for dealing with political issues is prudence. This applies to such issues as the reform of the representative system, which he approved on principle, while fearing some of its possible consequences for contingent reasons, or the Corn Laws, which he disliked on principle while arguing that they should not be abolished on grounds of expediency, and even the Poor Laws, which he detested on reasons of both expediency and principle, but whose abolition he proposed to carry out gradually. Note that prudence is also the overarching virtue in private morality. As the main virtue of the politician, its importance depends, not unlike Adam Smith's polemics against the 'man of system' (Smith 1759, pp. 233–234) and drawing inspiration from the Cambridge *via media* in its aversion to 'system', on awareness of the non-artificial character of society. Prudence has for Malthus a more decisive role to play precisely because he is aware that social change always carries costs, and meets with constant limits. His idea – a ubiquitous one in the eighteenth century after Jean-Jacques Rousseau – is that what are called social evils are just the price paid for abandoning the savage state. This is a state of comparative innocence but lacking those chances of development in human capabilities that the civilized state provides. In turn, the 'civilized state' is an obliged path to such development, but a division of society into classes and the prevalence of self-love are its unavoidable drawbacks. Malthus writes in the first *Essay* that, first, evil does not originate only from institutions, second, that the noblest exertions of human nature are made possible precisely but what we call evil, and third, that improvement of the human condition, besides paying such price, cannot go beyond pre-established limits (Malthus 1798, pp. 95–103). In his famous letter to Godwin he adds:

> Great improvements may take place in the state of society; but I do not see how the present form or system can be radically and essentially changed, without a danger of relapsing into barbarism.
>
> In speaking of the present structure of society, I do not in the least refer to any particular form of government, but merely to the existence of

a class of proprietors and a class of labourers, to the system of barter and exchange, and to the general moving principle of self-love.

(Paul 1876, vol. 1, p. 325)

Thus also promotion of improvements should be governed by prudence. This is dictated by two distinct kinds of considerations. Those of the first kind are that, even though it were true, that 'man is susceptible of perpetual improvement' (Malthus 1798, p. 94), as Godwin claims, this would not mean much more than that 'man is always susceptible of improvement'; in other words, not that 'our efforts to improve man *will always succeed*' but just 'that the precise limit of his improvement cannot possibly be known' (p. 96), and what we can accordingly foresee is not 'an *unlimited* improvement', which is not applicable to man 'under the present laws of his nature', but merely 'an improvement *the limit of which cannot be ascertained*' (p. 97; italics added). The second kind of considerations has to do with the costs to pay for any change. An experiment with the human race is different from an 'experiment upon inanimate objects', and 'the bursting of the bonds of society is such a separation of parts as cannot take place without giving the most acute pain to thousands: and a long time may elapse, and much misery may be endowed, before the wound grows up again' (p. 97).

Malthus's call for combination of *strict justice* and *good policy* should be kept in mind when considering his stance on the Corn Laws, assumed by a few commentators to be a proof of his pro-landed-interest attitude. In fact his argument consists once more in balancing rights-based reasons against expediency-based ones, or *strict justice* against *good policy*. He starts arguing from a Free Trader's viewpoint and then introduces several limitations to this viewpoint in the name of reasons of national security, such as risks of aggressive commercial policies by other nations, costs carried by change as such, and side-effects of the change under discussion on other valuable policy-goals such as the preservation of the English Constitution (Malthus 1814; 1815; cf. Collini, Winch and Burrow 1983, pp. 75–77; Winch 1987, pp. 48–55; Gascoigne 1989, pp. 187–236; Waterman 1991). The discovery that he did revise his position concerning agricultural protectionism as soon as he felt the situation had changed (Hollander 1992; 1997, pp. 846–855) is an important one, but it is also a proof that his statements on respective weight to be recognized to value-judgements and to considerations of expediency should be taken at their face-value, and Hollander draws the wrong conclusions from his own findings when defining Malthus's policy advice as 'utilitarian' (p. 830). On the contrary, precisely a non-utilitarian distinction between considerations of justice and considerations of expediency lies constantly at the basis of Malthus's changing assessments, and what is modified is only his appreciation of the weight of political and social factors. Against this background, Malthus's endorsement of a number of what were considered in his time to be 'progressive' causes, coexisting with a number of more conservative attitudes, ceases being surprising even though it flies in the face of the still surviving image of a 'reactionary' or 'ogre' Malthus. Let us examine a few of these causes endorsed by Malthus.

Reform

The issue of so-called 'Reform' started being on the British agenda with the debate about the so-called 'Crisis' in the last decade of the eighteenth century and became an urgent practical issue in the aftermath of the Napoleonic wars. The young Malthus's first contribution meant for publication was entitled *The Crisis* precisely because it was a rejoinder to other pamphlets published in those years discussing this keyword. The word itself was a neologism, since it was introduced into the language of politics precisely in those years, coming from the language of Hippocratic medicine where it had the meaning of 'turning-point'. The issue of Reform in British political institutions comes to the fore in the first *Essay*, where the issue of poverty is located within discussion of reform of representative institutions, the peculiar character of the English constitution, and 'rational freedom' (Malthus 1798, p. 132).

The inherent danger Malthus sees in current discussion of poverty is that discourse on its causes tends to be couched in terms of naïve radicalism, or of lip-service to such radicalism motivated by concealed middle-class interest. Malthus forecasts that no good will come out of inflamed speeches about the poor's rights in so far as 'the poor serve ambitions of men in the middle classes' (p. 128) who have an interest not so much in improving the formers' lot as in a share in political power. Malthus's antidote is spreading knowledge of the 'true causes' of social evils, to be found not in bad governance but instead in fixed laws of nature whose effects may just be softened by good government and private prudence, but never completely removed. This would not give an advantage to government, but instead, in so far as it would prevent waste of energies in trying to attain impossible goals, it would give 'a great additional weight to the popular side of the question' (p. 132).

This is what he thought of projects of social reform publicized, in the years after the French Revolution, by radicals of the Thomas Paine and William Goodwin kind. But Malthus was wary also of 'Reform,' as it was understood in political discourse between 1815 and 1832. This was a programme cherished by 'philosophic radicals' such as Jeremy Bentham, James Mill, Francis Place and David Ricardo, and half-heartedly supported by Malthus and many others, among them Ricardo's religious and philosophical mentor Thomas Belsham. It implied restyling representative institutions with a comparatively wide extension of the franchise, and nothing less than separation of Church and State, which may both sound rather obvious to twentieth-century readers but were perceived as real Revolution in early nineteenth-century Britain (Clark 1985, p. 501–564). Malthus believed that change in itself would carry costs, that giving a share in power to people who do not own enough as to have an interest in the common good was dangerous, that the latter would be tempted by projects of radical redistribution of wealth, that the story of the

English liberties was the result of a combination of institutional and socio-logical factors, among which the role of the country gentlemen appeared to have been decisive. Malthus's fear that a majority made of educated middle-class voters would use political power in order to expropriate private property on a mass scale now sounds rather odd. But we had in the last two decades of the twentieth century the opportunity of enjoying the spectacle of right-wing governments elected by a majority of lower-class voters allied with the top of the social pyr-amid against the 'conservative' middle class and industrial workers combina-tion. Malthus had the example provided by the French Revolution in mind, and thus his fears, even though refuted by later events, were not totally absurd.

It was because of this role of the gentry that Malthus is prone to sacrifice considerations of other nature, that is, not only of wealth, as he is proud to admit, but also of equality, as he is rather reluctant to admit, to political considerations prompting not only a limitation of franchise but also an insti-tution as incompatible with Malthus's own ideal of equality as primogeniture, mentioning 'higher considerations [...] than those which relate to mere wealth' (Malthus 1820, vol. 1, p. 437). And yet, in the 1830s Malthus did revise his former moderate position on Reform. In fact, in a footnote in the 1836 edition of the *Principles* he approves of the 1832 Reform Act, albeit 'a reform of a more sudden and extensive nature than prudence would have perhaps suggested' (vol. 2, p. 270), as a dictate of 'imperious circumstances'. Even though somewhat risky in practice – he admits – the Reform is fine on principle, since 'all which has been done, is to bring the practical working of the constitution nearer to its theory' (p. 270).

Catholic emancipation and the Irish issue

Malthus was strongly in favour of equality among citizens, and believed this should apply to those belonging to religious communities different from the established Church. He was aware that lack of full equality for Roman Catholics implied, in the given circumstances, a semi-colonial regime in Catholic Ireland, and that this carried a sequel of social evils as well as dan-gers to political freedom and peaceful coexistence. Catholic emancipation was a cause supported, besides Roman Catholics, by a composite 'progressive' front of Whigs, Philosophic Radicals and Dissenters. Malthus on this issue was decidedly on the side of the above alignment, something that was not so much a matter of course for a member of the clergy, who was supposed to belong automatically to the pro-establishment party. This cause – he believed – was justified not only in terms of values, but also in terms of national interest. In his review of Thomas Newenham's *A Statistical and Historical Inquiry into the Progress and Magnitude of the Population of Ireland,* published in the *Edinburgh Review,* he writes that if:

> the middling and lower ranks of society in this country are by no means prepared to consider the Irish Roman Catholics as fellow Christians

worshipping the same God, and fellow subjects entitled to the same civil privileges; if they are really so bigoted as to which to deny the benefits of the British constitution to above a fourth part of the population of the empire, and so ignorant as to imagine they can do it with safety [...] they are not only violating the genuine spirit of Christianity, but blindly endangering their own security, and risking the subjugation or dismemberment of the empire.

(Malthus 1808, p. 24)

In another review in the same journal, namely of Newenham's *A View of the Natural, Political and Commercial Circumstances of Ireland* as well as of another two books about Ireland, he invites his fellow-citizens to 'a great and generous act', namely giving the Irish Catholics 'all that they have demanded', that is, no more than what '*strict justice* and *good policy*' (Malthus 1809, p. 67) should concede to them, namely, full citizenship, that would make them 'enjoy all the civil advantages of the British Constitution' (p. 67), and full recognition for the Catholic Church in Ireland, in the same terms as for the Presbyterian Church in Scotland, that is, those of 'a Church establishment' (p. 67).

In his correspondence with Henry Parnell, a Whig MP from Ireland, he discusses the causes of oppression and misery among the Irish peasants, supporting a battle for drastic reform of the Irish tithes system that made the burden fall entirely upon the poor peasants leaving landlords exempt (James 1979, pp. 142–159). In a letter to Parnell of 4 May 1808, he suggests, as the most effective parliamentary tactic, avoiding any detailed plan for substitution of tithes and dwelling only on the 'extreme oppression and distresses to which the lower classes of the Irish are subject in the present mode of levying them' (p. 158), in order 'to get, if possible, an assent to the absolute necessity of some change' (p. 158) before discussing the specific mode of doing it.

War as evil

On the evils of war, Malthus seems to have shared in the concerns of the most enlightened writers at the time of wars with revolutionary France. His tutor Gilbert Wakefield had heavily paid for manifesting such concerns in print; in fact, in 1798 he responded to the *Address to the People of Great Britain* by Richard Watson, the Cambridge Professor mentioned in Chapter 2, who had described war against France as a just war, for 'under whatever circumstances the war was began it is now become just; since the enemy has refused to treat, on equitable terms, for the restoration of peace' (Watson 1798, p. 11), denounced the French as the bearers of revolutionary ideas inimical to religion, and added that victorious defence from French invasion was a quite feasible prospect, and that fear of defection to the invader by Dissenters, Irishmen and political radicals was unrealistic, since no more than the scum of British society would have been able to sympathize with the enemy, adding, as a final sundry, mention of 'that silly system of democratic liberty and equality, which never has had, nor ever can have a permanent establishment amongst mankind' (p. 34). Wakefield argued that there had already been 250,000 dead since the beginning of war, that 'in every county, by commencement of war, commerce is interrupted, trade declines, manufactures cease; thousands are deprived of their subsistence [...] manufacturers necessarily become soldiers [...] They are led into the field to the deliberate destruction of men, against whom they have not conceived the least emotion of resentment' (Wakefield 1798, p. 13) and, as a final truism, that the precept to defend religion by weapons is not included in the Gospel. As a result, he was sentenced to two years imprisonment for seditious libel, and died shortly after serving the sentence. Watson gives a rather awkward account, according to which he 'took some pain to prevent this prosecution, thinking the liberty of press to be the palladium of the constitution; but' – he adds – 'I did not succeed in my endeavours' (Watson 1818, p. 309). What he actually did was politely refuse to give evidence for Wakefield's character at the trial, on the reason that he had never met him personally before, and this did not help him in obtaining acquittal.

Also Malthus's Cambridge tutor, William Frend, had written that patriotism does not justify hostile aggression and that, even though Christianity 'does not prohibit arms in defence of the country or in self-defence, every war of hostile aggression is indefensible by its precepts' (Frend 1793, p. 183).

Malthus, writing a few years later, seemed to share such feelings as he writes that 'the commission of war is vice, and the effect of it, misery' (Malthus 1798, p. 22), that war was included among the positive checks to population arising either from vice or misery (Malthus 1803, vol. 1, p. 18), that it is morally repugnant, and that the argument on 'positive checks' to population in the *Essay* could not be appealed to in defence of the morality of war, since the latter is 'a voluntary act, tending to foster the more malignant passions of the soul, and to produce the worst effects upon the human character' and accordingly 'must ever be considered a vice' and man 'can never be justified in recurring to vice in order to avoid misery' (Malthus 1799, pp. 135–136); besides:

> war is in itself an evil in no respect inferior to any that it might be supposed to prevent. If it were probable that ten thousand people would die of a pestilence or famine, it would certainly be a strange mode of proceeding, to massacre these ten thousand, in order to prevent such an event [...] you would only have exchanged one species of distress for another not inferior in degree, and you still have the crises of the orphan and the widow, and the groans of the dying.
>
> (p. 136)

Abolition of the slave trade

The slave trade was a hot issue during Malthus's lifetime. Slavery had been an institution tolerated during the early centuries of Christianity and the Middle

Ages, but with a declining importance vis-à-vis its role in the Roman Empire. Yet, in the sixteenth century, that is, at a time when slavery had become of tiny relevance in Europe, the slave trade won suddenly an enormous weight in connection with colonial expansion in America and the growth of the plantation system. The French Revolution had abolished slavery and this had repercussions on the other side of the Channel. An anti-slave trade campaign began, supported by a composite front of Quakers, Evangelicals and Radicals. William Wilberforce, an Evangelical MP, became the leader of the campaign until he succeeded in 1807 in having the Slave Trade Act approved by Parliament. It implied abolition of the slave trade but not of slavery as an institution in the Colonies. The discussion kept raging for decades, until the Slavery Abolition Act was approved in 1833.

John Locke had argued in the *Second Treatise* par. 27 that 'every man has property in his own person' (Locke 1690, p. 287). Adam Smith argued that slavery is irrational in economic terms and is an application of the 'vile maxim' of the masters of humankind: 'All for ourselves and nothing for other people' (Smith 1776, p. 418), and the reason for persistence of such an unjust and irrational institution was that the:

> pride of man makes him love to domineer, and nothing mortifies him so much as to be obliged to condescend to persuade his inferiors. Wherever the law allows it, and the nature of the work can afford it, therefore, he will generally prefer the service of slaves to that of freemen. The planting of sugar and tobacco can afford the expence of slave-cultivation. The raising of corn, it seems, in the present times, cannot.
>
> (Smith 1776, p. 388)

William Paley defined slavery as 'an obligation to labour fort the benefit of the master, without the contract or consent of the servant' (Paley 1785, p. 135) that may be justified on three grounds: crimes, captivity, debt, but the 'slave-trade upon the coast of Africa is not excused by these principles' (p. 136), that is, even though slavery is admitted of by the laws of nature under quite specific conditions, the present slave trade from Africa lacked any justification. He expressed his wish that the fact of a revolution in France, a colonial power that admitted of the slave trade, 'may probably conduce [...] to accelerate the fall of this abominable tyranny' (p. 137) as well as his hope that as the 'knowledge and authority' of Christianity 'advance in the world, they will banish what remains of this odious institution' (p. 138).

Malthus was an opponent of the slave trade. He was upset by malicious insinuations by William Cobbet that the *Essay* was meant to support the slave trade as one more way of checking population and met Wilberforce in order to 'furnish him the data' (James 1979, p. 125) required in order to rescue his own character from the imputation of being a friend to the slave trade, and in the 1806 Appendix he declared that it is 'perfectly clear that a consideration of the laws which govern the increase and decrease of the human species tends to strengthen, in the most powerful manner, all the arguments in favour of the abolition' (Malthus 1803, vol. 2, p. 232). In other words, he argues that the population theory plays against slavery both on grounds of humaneness and on grounds of efficiency. In fact:

> abolition of the slave trade is defended principally by the two following arguments:
> 1st. That the trade to the coast of Africa for slaves, together with their subsequent treatment in the West Indies, is productive of so much human misery, that its continuance is disgraceful to us as men and as Christians.
> 2d. That the culture of the West-India islands could go on with equal advantage, and much greater security, if no further importation of slaves were to take place.
>
> (p. 231)

And the population theory may contribute to prove, first, that since so great is the tendency of mankind to increase that the fact that 'in the West India islands a constant recruit of labouring negroes is necessary' only proves that 'the immediate checks to population operate with *excessive* and *unusual* force' (p. 231). Besides, it proves that, since population everywhere in the world 'has been able to keep herself up to the level of the means of subsistence' (p. 231), if the slaves in the West Indies 'were placed only in a *tolerable* situation, if their civil condition and moral habits were only made to *approach* to those which prevail among the mass of the human race in the worst-governed countries of the world, it is contrary to the general laws of nature to suppose that they should not be able, by procreation, fully to supply the effective demand for labour' (pp. 231–232). He adds that the supposition is plausible that the underdeveloped state of African society depends heavily on the slave trade on the coast, as one would expect in a society where the capture of men is made a more advantageous employment than agriculture or manu-factures and that, as long as 'the nations of Europe continue barbarous enough to purchase slaves in Africa, we may be quite sure that Africa will continue barbarous enough to supply them' (p. 232).

Bibliography

Augustine (*BC* [2001]) *De Bono Coniugali. De Sancta Virginitate*. Ed. by Walsh, P.G. Oxford: Clarendon.

Beccaria, C. (1767) *An Essay on Crimes and Punishments*. London: Almon.

Clark, J.C.D. (1985) *English Society, 1688–1832*. Cambridge: Cambridge University Press.

Collini, S., Winch, D. and Burrow, J. (1983) *That Noble Science of Politics. A Study in Nineteenth Century Intellectual History*. Cambridge: Cambridge University Press.

Costabile, L. (1983) 'Natural prices, market prices and effective demand in Malthus'. *Australian Economic Papers* 22(4), pp. 144–170.

Costabile, L. and Rowthorn, B. (1985) 'Malthus's theory of wages and growth'. *Economic Journal* 95(378), pp. 419–437.

Cremaschi, S. (1984) *Il sistema della ricchezza. Economia politica e problema del metodo in Adam Smith.* Milan: Angeli.

Cremaschi, S. (1989) Adam Smith. Sceptical Newtonianism, disenchanted republicanism, and the birth of social science. In Dascal, M. and Gruengard, O. (eds) *Knowledge and Politics: Case Studies on the Relationship between Epistemology and Political Philosophy.* Boulder, CO: Westview Press.

Cremaschi, S. (2010) 'Malthus's idea of a moral and political science'. *The Journal of Philosophical Economics* 3(2), pp. 5–57.

Cremaschi, S. (2012) Malthus dalla morale sessuale all'etica della procreazione. In Mordacci, R. and Loi, M. (eds) *Etica e genetica. Storia, concetti e pratiche.* Milan: Bruno Mondadori.

Cremaschi, S. and Dascal, M. (1996) 'Malthus and Ricardo on economic methodology'. *History of Political Economy* 28(3), pp. 475–511.

Cremaschi, S. and Dascal, M. (1998a) Persuasion and Argument in the Malthus-Ricardo Correspondence. In Samuels, W.J. and Biddle, J.E. (eds) *Research in the History of Economic Thought and Methodology.* Volume 16. Stamford, Conn.: JAI Press.

Cremaschi, S. and Dascal, M. (1998b) 'Malthus and Ricardo: two styles for economic theory'. *Science in Context* 11(2), pp. 229–254.

Cremaschi, S. and Dascal, M. (2002) 'The unitarian connection and Ricardo's scientific style'. *History of Political Economy* 34(2), pp. 505–508.

Cremaschi, S. and Dascal, M. (forthcoming) *The Malthus-Ricardo Controversy. From a Pragma-Rhetoric Point of View.* The Hague: Benjamins.

Curran, Ch.E. (1995) Fertility Control: Ethical Issues. In Reich, W.Th. (ed.) *Encyclopedia of Bioethics.* Volume 2 DE–HY. New York: Macmillan.

Dascal, M. and Cremaschi, S. (1999) 'The Malthus-Ricardo correspondence: sequential structure, argumentative patterns, and rationality'. *Journal of Pragmatics* 31(4), pp. 1129–1172.

Fleischacker, S. (2005) *On Adam Smith's Wealth of Nations: a Philosophical Companion.* Princeton, NJ: Princeton University Press.

Frend, W. (1793) *Peace and Union Recommended to the Associated Bodies of Republicans and Anti-republicans.* London: Robinson.

Gascoigne, J. (1989) *Cambridge in the Age of the Enlightenment. Science, Religion and Politics from the Restoration to the French Revolution.* Cambridge: Cambridge University Press.

Gilbert, G. (1993) Why Did Malthus Oppose Birth Control? In Samuels, W.J. and Biddle, J.E. (eds) *Research in the History of Economic Thought and Methodology.* Volume 11. Stamford, Conn.: JAI Press.

Godwin, W. (1801 [1993]) Thoughts occasioned by the perusal of Dr. Parr's Spital Sermon, preached at Christ Church, April 15, 1800, being a reply to the attacks of Dr. Parr, Mr. MackIntosh, the author of an Essay on Population, and others. In *Political and Philosophical Writings of William Godwin.* Vol. 2. Ed. by M. Philp. London: Pickering.

Hofmann, K. (2013) 'Beyond the principle of population: Malthus's Essay'. *The European Journal of the History of Economic Thought* 20(3), pp. 399–425.

Hollander, S. (1992) 'Malthus's abandonment of agricultural protectionism: a discovery in the history of economic thought'. *American Economic Review* 82(3), pp. 650–659.

Hollander, S. (1997) *The Economics of Thomas Robert Malthus.* Toronto: University of Toronto Press.

Hume, D. (1739–1740 [2007]) *A Treatise of Human Nature.* Ed. by Norton, D.F. and Norton, M.J. Oxford: Oxford University Press.

Hume, D. (1742 [1992]) Of the populousness of Ancient Nations. In *Essays and Treatises on Several Subjects.* Volume 1. Ed. by Green, Th.H. and Grose, Th.H. Aalen: Scientia Verlag.

James, P. (1979) *Population Malthus. His Life and Time.* London: Routledge.

Jensen, H.E. (1999) 'The development of T.R. Malthus's institutionalist approach to the cure of poverty: from punishment of the poor to investment in their human capital'. *Review of Social Economy* 57(4), pp. 450–465.

Locke, J. (1690 [1988]) *Two Treatises of Government.* Ed. by Laslett, P. Cambridge: Cambridge University Press.

Maccabelli, T. (1997) *Il progresso della ricchezza. Economia, politica e religione in Thomas Robert Malthus.* Milan: Giuffré.

Malthus, Th.R. (1798 [1986]) An Essay on the Principle of Population. In *The Works of Thomas Robert Malthus.* Volume 1. Ed. by Wrigley, E.A.and Souden, D. London: Pickering.

Malthus, Th.R. (1799) Letter to the Monthly Magazine. In Rashid, S. (1984) 'Malthus' theology; an overlooked letter and some comments'. *History of Political Economy* 16(1), pp. 135–138.

Malthus, Th.R. (1803 [1989]) *An Essay on the Principle of Population. The Version Published in 1803, with the Variora of 1806, 1807, 1817 and 1826.* Ed. by James, P. Cambridge: Cambridge University Press.

Malthus, Th.R. (1807 [1986]) Letter to Samuel Whitbread Esq. M.P. on his proposed bill for the amendment of the poor laws. In *The Works of Thomas Robert Malthus.* Volume 4. Ed. by Wrigley, E.A. and Souden, D. London: Pickering.

Malthus, Th.R. (1808 [1986]) Review of: Thomas Newenham *A Statistical and Historical Inquiry into the Progress and Magnitude of the Population of Ireland* 1805; H. Dudley *A Short Address to the Most Reverend and Honourable William, Lord Primate of All Ireland, Recommendatory of Some Commutation or Modification of the Tithes of that Country* 1808; J. W. Croker *A Sketch of the State of Ireland Past and Present* 1808. In *The Works of Thomas Robert Malthus.* Volume 4. Ed. by Wrigley, E.A. and Souden, D. London: Pickering.

Malthus, Th.R. (1809 [1986]) Review of: Thomas Newenham *A View of the Natural, Political and Commercial Circumstances of Ireland* 1808. In *The Works of Thomas Robert Malthus.* Volume 4. Ed. by Wrigley, E.A. and Souden, D. London: Pickering.

Malthus, Th.R. (1814 [1986]) Observations on the Effects of the Corn Laws, and of a Rise or Fall in the Price of Corn on the Agricultural and General Wealth of the Country. In *The Works of Thomas Robert Malthus.* Volume 3. Ed. by Wrigley, E.A. and Souden, D. London: Pickering.

Malthus, Th.R. (1815 [1986]) Grounds of an Opinion on the Policy of Restricting the Importation of Foreign Corn Intended as an Appendix to Observations on the Corn Laws. In *The Works of Thomas Robert Malthus.* Volume 3. Ed. by Wrigley, E.A. and Souden, D. London: Pickering.

Malthus, Th.R. (1820 [1989]) *Principles of Political Economy.* Ed. by Pullen, J. Cambridge: Cambridge University Press.

Malthus, Th.R. (1829a) To Nassau William Senior March 23 1829. In Senior, N.W. (1829) *Two Lectures on Population [...] to which is Added a Correspondence* between the author and the Rev. T. R. Malthus. London: Saunders and Oatley. Available at: babel.hathitrust.org/cgi/pt?id=hvd.32044011469707;view=1up;seq=85 (accessed 18 November 2013).

Malthus, Th.R. (1829b) To Nassau William Senior March 31 1829. In Senior, N.W. (1829) *Two Lectures on Population [...] to which is Added a Correspondence between the author and the Rev. T. R. Malthus.* London: Saunders and Oatley. Available at: babel.hathitrust.org/cgi/pt?id=hvd.32044011469707;view=1up;seq=85 (accessed 18 November 2013).

Malthus, Th.R. (1966) *The Travel Diaries of Thomas Robert Malthus.* Ed. by James, P. Cambridge: Cambridge University Press.

Noonan, J.T. (1965) *Contraception: A History of its Treatment by the Catholic Theologians and Canonists.* Cambridge, MA: Harvard University Press.

Owen, R. (1813–1816 [1993]) A New View of Society: or, Essays on the Principle of the Formation of the Human Character, and the Application of the Principle to Practice. In *Selected Works.* Volume 1. Ed. by Claeys, G. London: Pickering.

Paley, W. (1785 [2002]) *The Principles of Moral and Political Philosophy.* Ed. by LeMahieu, D.L. Indianapolis, IN: Liberty Fund.

Paul, Ch.K. (1876 [2002]) *William Goodwin: His Friends and Contemporaries.* 2 volumes. Whitefish, MT: Kessinger.

Philp, M. (ed.) *William Godwin.* Volume 2. London: Pickering and Chatto.

Raynal, G.-Th. (1770) *Histoire philosophique et politique des établissemens et du commerce des Européens dans les deux indes.* Amsterdam Genève: Pellet.

Ricardo, D. (1821 [1951]) Ricardo to Malthus 10 Sept. 1821. In *The Works and Correspondence of David Ricardo.* Volume 9. Ed. by Sraffa, P. with the collaboration of Dobb, M.H. Cambridge: Cambridge University Press.

Rothschild, E. (2001) *Economic Sentiments. Adam Smith, Condorcet, and the Enlightenment.* Cambridge MA: Harvard University Press.

Samuelson, P.A. (1978 [1986]) The Canonical Classical Model of Political Economy. In *The collected scientific papers of Paul A. Samuelson.* Volume 5. Ed. by Crowles, K. Cambridge, MA: MIT Press.

Say, J.-B. (1803 [1972]) *Traité d'économie politique.* Ed. by Tapinos, G. Paris: Calmann-Levy.

Senior, N.W. (1823) To Th. Robert Malthus March 26 1829. In Senior, N.W. (1829) *Two Lectures on Population [...] to which is Added a Correspondence between the Author and the Rev. T. R. Malthus.* London: Saunders and Oatley. Available at: babel.hathitrust.org/cgi/pt?id=hvd.32044011469707;view=1up;seq=85 (accessed 18 November 2013).

Smith, A. (1759 [1976]) *The Theory of Moral Sentiments.* Ed. by Raphael, D.D. and Macfie, A.L. Clarendon Press, Oxford.

Smith, A. (1776 [1976]) *An Inquiry into the Nature and Causes of the Wealth of Nations.* Ed. by Campbell, R.H., Skinner, A.S., and Todd, W.B. Oxford: Clarendon.

Spengler, J.J. (1945) 'Malthus's total population theory: a restatement and reappraisal'. *The Canadian Journal of Economics and Political Science/Revue canadienne d'Economique et de Science politique* 11(1), pp. 83–110.

Wakefield, G. (1798) *A Reply to some parts of the Bishop of Llandaff's Address to the people of Great Britain.* London: Cuthell.

Waterman, A.M.C. (1987) 'On the Malthusian theory of long swings'. *The Canadian Journal of Economics/Revue canadienne d'Economique* 20(2), pp. 257–270.

Waterman, A.M.C. (1988) 'Hume, Malthus and the stability of equilibrium'. *History of Political Economy* 20(1), pp. 85–94.

Waterman, A.M.C. (1991 [2004]) A Cambridge 'via media' in late Georgian Anglicanism. In *Political Economy and Christian Theology since the Enlightenment*. Houndsmills: Palgrave & MacMillan.

Waterman, A.M.C. (1998) 'Malthus, mathematics, and the mythology of coherence'. *History of Political Economy* 30(4), pp. 571–599

Waterman, A.M.C. (2012) 'Adam Smith and Malthus on high wages'. *The European Journal of the History of Economic Thought* 19(3), pp. 409–429.

Watson, R. (1818) *Anecdotes of the Life of R.W. Watson, Bishop of Llandaff*. Second edition. London: Cadell.

Watson, R. (1798) *An Address to the People of Great Britain*. London: Faulder.

Winch, D. (1987) *Malthus*. Oxford: Oxford University Press.

8 Conclusions

Strengthening the theological foundation

Malthus did *not* believe his own work to be that of a 'demographer' and an 'economist'. This is the reason why he was not primarily the 'great economist' mentioned by Bonar and accordingly did *not* go *'beyond his province'* when he confronted the problem of evil. On the contrary, he went beyond his own original province, namely natural theology, when trying to make his work in the 'moral and political science' more empirical than what his predecessors had been able to provide, and when tracing the consequences of a well-known principle in order to prove the impossibility of perfectionist political designs. He did so by the hypothetico-deductive Newtonian method while working out a new population theory and improving on several among Adam Smith's theories, on value, price, demand and consumption. These developments are *at once* contributions to the newly born research programme or discipline of political economy and auxiliary disciplines to the science of natural law. In other words, by the fact of being decisive contributions in the history of the social sciences, his contributions do not cease being also *applied ethics.*

Malthus believed that his work belonged to the wider field of the 'moral and political science'. He had inherited the commonplace eighteenth-century view that human knowledge is divided into two fields, *natural* philosophy and *moral* philosophy. He believed, like almost everybody else in his time, that the former had recently made extraordinary advances, while the latter was just trying to keep pace. He believed also that this goal was highly desirable, since so much, in terms of human happiness, depended on progress in the moral and political science. He writes in the *Principles* that it is a sad remark to make that:

> while the views of physical science are daily enlarging [...] the science of moral and political philosophy should be confined within such narrow limits, or at best be so feeble in its influence, as to be unable to counteract the increasing obstacles to human happiness arising from the principle of population [and albeit we] cannot expect that the virtue and happiness of mankind will keep pace with the brilliant career of physical discovery yet [...] hope that, to no unimportant extent, they will be influenced by its progress and will partake in its success.
>
> (Malthus 1820, vol. 1, p. 203)

Thus he apparently believed, on the one hand, in scientific progress and the unity of method between the natural and the moral science and, on the other, in virtue and happiness as the inbuilt goal of the moral science. The fact is that he did not understand the latter in terms of social engineering or value-free science, but as some kind of unified discourse encompassing the disciplines of ethics, politics, demography and economics such as they are presently understood.

In fact, what matters in political economy is not only 'the physical qualities of the materials which are acted upon' (p. 381), and commodities are not just figures and numbers (p. 355). What matters are instead 'the moral as well as the physical qualities of the agents' (p. 381), and differences in customary standards regarding work, leisure, consumption make so that the same market mechanisms yield different results in different social contexts, such as England, where the comparative difficulty of producing food has acted as a stimulus to industry, and Ireland or Mexico, where the high productivity of the soil in terms of bananas, maize, or potatoes, through a typical perverse effect, has contributed in perpetuating poverty (Cremaschi 2010, pp. 46–48).

Bonar's conclusion on Malthus's theodicy was, as mentioned, that:

> perhaps the great economist went beyond his province in attacking the problem of evil.
>
> (Bonar 1885, p. 38)

And Hollander's was that his own reconstruction:

> supports Lord Robbins's position that Malthus's explanation of 'dis-harmonies' by reference to Divine Wisdom is 'extraneous to analysis' and without influence on the theory of policy [...] the two last chapters in the 1798 essay turn out to be an embarrassment, and the apologia for a benevolent Deity is radically altered in later editions [...] Malthus's efforts to reconcile dogma and utility [was] a process involving effectively the undermining of the theological foundation.
>
> (Hollander 1997, pp. 918–921)

We are now in a position to see why both conclusions are mistaken, and how the theological foundation was not *undermined*, but instead *strengthened*. The reasons for that are the following:

1　Utilitarianism properly understood was Bentham's own invention; this resulted from secularization of a theological argument as well as from transfer of a meta-ethical argument to normative ethics, yielding the Benthamite 'new morality'.
2　The argument gradually developed by Cumberland and his followers up to Paley was not a gradual, albeit incomplete, discovery of a truth waiting to be revealed in full only to secular thinkers (i.e. to Utilitarians), but

was rather the discovery and refinement of a consequentialist argument for settling two meta-ethical issues, and besides one purely theological question, namely: (i) the nature of motivation; (ii) the criterion of rightness; and (iii) the reasons for existence of evil.

3 The kind of normative ethics supported by the meta-ethical approach described was not utilitarian, it did not come close to utilitarianism, was no confused formulation of a utilitarian normative ethic; on the contrary, it was basically the same normative ethics as the one proposed by Samuel Clarke, Richard Price, Thomas Reid and Dugald Stewart, namely a rather traditional ethics of duties, with Aristotelian, Stoic or natural-law elements blended together with Platonic virtue ethics. Such a blend was justified by Cumberland, Gay, Paley and Malthus on the basis of meta-ethical arguments different from both Clarke's and Price's rationalist claims and Reid's and Stewart's common-sense theory. Their meta-ethics depended in fact on a natural theology combining voluntarism with non-arbitrariness of the moral law. The 'test of utility' is for them the key stone or the link connecting normative ethics with meta-ethics. This circumstance led two or three generations of commentators into the conceptual trap of 'theological utilitarianism', a label as innocent as any name may be when used as a token for a better word, but poison for intellectual history when used as a description of alleged *Benthamite utilitarianism in disguise* uneasily coexisting with Christian theology (while waiting for divorce). The important difference to keep in mind is that, according to the consequentialist voluntarist, utility does not grant the agent a standard for right action, but just provides for the legislator's benefit general standard for right classes of actions. Human agents may resort to such a test in their quality of enquirers into God's will, that is, they are entitled to apply it *a posteriori* to sets of laws in order to find out whether they have been really promulgated.

4 The test of utility plays a central role in Malthus's meta-ethics, but one different from the one played in Bentham's ethics. Reasons are, first, that the test applies to sets of rules, not individual rules; second, that benevolence, unlike Bentham, is not unconditionally a virtue, but only an instinctive impulse and a law of nature, limited by other stronger impulses and other laws; third, that benevolence – contrary to Hollander's suggestion – is not the unique criterion for appraisal of policies, and the latter, although connected with happiness, is not carried out on a utilitarian basis. In more detail, Malthus's policy advice (i) assumes a distinction between wealth and happiness as a starting point; (ii) includes virtue besides happiness into states of affairs to be appraised; (iii) makes room, within the global sum of happiness and virtue, for such priorities as rights, equality, liberty, security, among which some are non-negotiable priorities.

5 Malthus was – his friendship with Ricardo notwithstanding, and apart from the formally correct terms in which his relationship with Mill took

place – the object of suspicion by the latter and his group. The reasons were that the latter felt he was the spokesman for the landed gentry, a lukewarm fighter for science against prejudice, and disliked him as a member of the Anglican clergy, and besides a supposedly insincere clergyman in so far as no rational person could *really* profess the 39 articles. John Ramsey McCulloch, Ricardo's Scottish adept, gave a theoretical formulation to such mixed feeling by the 'two Malthuses' theory, according to which there are the good and progressive Malthus, who in his youth invented the principle of population and the bad and reactionary Malthus, who in his old age introduced such strange ideas as effective demand and unproductive consumption.

6   Bonar's mentioned conclusion that 'the great economist went beyond his province in attacking the problem of evil' (Bonar 1885, p. 38) results from pure anachronism. On the contrary, Malthus was not yet an 'economist' at his birth time, and indeed 'economics' had not been invented yet as a separate science, while 'political economy' established itself as the name of a 'science' precisely during Malthus's lifetime. His Cambridge education was meant to teach him natural philosophy and natural theology, and the problem of evil was accordingly precisely his original 'province', in so far as it had been the eighteenth-century philosophers' and divines' obsession. On the other hand, his unusually enlightened education had exposed him from the times of Warrington Academy to Adam Smith's work and 'commerce' as a subject. His attack on Godwin was waged with an item of economic theory, namely the recently discovered idea of diminishing returns, as its main weapon, and this forced him to face the dismal fact of scarcity as a basic feature of the real world. This finding implied in turn some kind of U-turn in political economy as it had been codified by Adam Smith, in so far as the discipline was transformed into a discourse, more than on the wealth of nations, on the poverty of the labouring classes, and something we may fairly well name 'social theodicy' became its central issue. But this highlights precisely how far social science was still intrinsically theology (even when it was meant to be, like for Bentham and Mill, *a-theology*). And this is the reason why Bonar's picture of Malthus as some kind of twentieth-century professional economist who starts to fumble with theology in his spare time without due academic training in the subject is the purest specimen of anachronism.

7   Hollander is right when he contends that there was indeed an evolution in Malthus's ideas. It is true that moral restraint as a *real* possibility for the future is a novelty showing up in 1803 and that at this stage vice ceases being *absolutely* necessary as it was in 1798. It is true that the final 'tragic' or 'sublime' 1798 picture, echoing Dante's *Inferno*, of a process of creation of mind out of matter gives way to some kind of harmonious picture of a Christian society resembling more the Cambridge Platonists' worldview, not to say Godwin's utopia. It is true that there are increasingly radical changes concerning partial evil, in so far as widespread

virtue would, to a remarkable extent, free the world from evil. It is also true that the evil of inequality is unavoidable but it may be gradually reduced, at least up to an unknown point and in an improved society even the degree of misery to which the idle and improvident are damned may be reduced, and such reduced degree may be alleviated by private charity. To sum up, it is true that, albeit society will always be composed of two classes, 'the condition of each, and the proportions which they bear to each another, may be so altered, as greatly to improve the harmony and beauty of the whole' (Malthus 1803, vol. 2, p. 203).

8 Whether theodicy is 'extraneous to analysis' is probably an ill-framed question, since the answer is positive, but it is so by definition. In fact, we may extract bits of 'analysis' out of any text (starting with Aristotle, Aquinas, Azpilqueta, Azór, etc.), once we know what we are looking for in the text itself. As Waterman aptly comments, 'we must take the theological content of the first *Essay* [I would add: and of the second as well] as seriously as its political economy. More precisely, we must recognize that what we now presume to identify as 'political economy' and 'theology' respectively are abstractions that we ourselves have made [...] from the undifferentiated texture of Malthus's argument' (Waterman 1991, p. 61). A question framed in more historical and justified terms is whether the 1803 model of a society in equilibrium requires assumptions on ideal moral behaviour and whether such model is viable. If the question is framed in these terms, the answer may be that ethics and social theodicy are not *extraneous* to the argument as a whole, but are the very points around which Malthus's overall argument turns.

9 Between 1798 and 1803 no shift from *philosophy* (or worse, theology, or metaphysics) to *science* took place; theodicy remained stably where it had always been, albeit in a somewhat different shape; what was dropped is just a few theological speculations about the process of Creation, mind and body, the immortality of the soul, but this is not tantamount to dropping theodicy as such, even less to dropping philosophy, theology, or metaphysics. The fact is that such speculations are not indispensable for theodicy, which consists in discussion of the reasons for existence of evil in the world. The reason for dropping them is that their place was taken in 1803 by ethical theory, since the missing link in the chain reconciling God's goodness with our experience of evil had become morality, and moral improvement, not creation of mind out of matter, is now the goal served by partial evils resulting from the principle of population. Thus, besides being unorthodox, these speculations became useless for the new overall design. What is really new in the second *Essay* is not so much its *scientific* or *empirical* character as the fact that a systematic treatment of morality is added, and indeed granted pride of place. For this reason, the second *Essay* is a *more*, not a less, *philosophical* work than the first.

10 Malthus never attempted to reconcile 'dogma' with 'utility', nor did he ever undermine any theological foundation he had laid before for his

work. He just modified on a number of points his 1798 theological views, thus yielding different, albeit no less, and indeed even *more*, theological views. The real novelty was wider scope for morality and the related possibility of some kind of 'worldly' harmonious design of human society, a picture that does rest on a theological foundation (or on 'dogma', as Hollander would prefer to say). The alleged counterpart of dogma, 'utility', in turn, was just one element in Malthus's ethics, going with others, which for Bentham were pure nonsense, such as *laws of nature* and *rights*. And ironically enough, utility, far from being a strange Benthamite erratic stone lost in the wasteland of dogma and theology, was itself the most markedly theological element in Malthus's system of ideas.

My reconstruction suggests a way out of familiar conundrums created *ex nihilo* by the Bonar–Hollander reading, namely, how could Malthus be both a utilitarian and the target of Mill-and-co.'s condescendence; how could an alleged utilitarian be biased in favour of established institutions on the ground of their being already there; how could a utilitarian admit of a mix of factors on whose basis policies such as agricultural protectionism or defence of primogeniture might be justified; how could a utilitarian keep a distinction between such distinct elements of the good as respectability, virtue and happiness; and finally how could a utilitarian be a proponent of natural law and innate rights? My suggestion is that none of these questions is worth answering since Malthus was just the member of a different school of thought that had its own answers to theological, moral and political questions, and all his attempts to solve theoretical questions and to provide policy advice fit in this framework.

One important element of discontinuity in Malthus's train of thought, yet, is the increasing influence of evangelical ideas, carrying increasing stress on *revealed*, as opposed to *natural*, theology, increasing room for benevolence or charity as opposed to justice and liberty, and increasing optimism as to a possible transformation of existing social conditions in the sense not only of more political liberty and personal independence, but also of more equality, more self-respect, and a combination of material welfare with intellectual and moral development. The change in Malthus's views from, say, 1798 to 1820, albeit not a conversion to a new and incompatible view, was a remarkable one. But let me stress once again that such a change went in a sense quite opposite to the one suggested by the Bonar–Hollander reading. It was a turn towards more philosophy, more theology, more ethics, that is, towards all those factors that nineteenth-century positivists and their grandchildren hastily labelled under the catch-all word Dogma. Or, if theology is tantamount to 'Dogma', we can safely conclude that, at the end of Malthus's career, Dogma was still safely installed, holding hands with Utility, at the core of his system of ideas. Thus, *malgré* Bonar and Hollander, what Malthus was doing step-by-step between 1803 and 1834 was not weakening, but instead *strengthening* the theological foundations of his work.

Bibliography

Bonar, J. (1885) *Malthus and his Work*. London: Macmillan.

Cremaschi, S. (2010) 'Malthus's idea of a moral and political science'. *The Journal of Philosophical Economics* 3(2), pp. 5–57.

Hollander, S. (1997) *The Economics of Thomas Robert Malthus*. Toronto: University of Toronto Press.

Malthus, Th.R. (1803 [1989]) *An Essay on the Principle of Population. The Version Published in 1803, with the Variora of 1806, 1807, 1817 and 1826*. Ed. by James, P. Cambridge: Cambridge University Press.

Malthus, Th.R. (1820 [1989]) *Principles of Political Economy*. Ed. by Pullen, J. Cambridge: Cambridge University Press.

Waterman, A.M.C. (1991) *Revolution, Economics and Religion. Christian Political Economy, 1798–1833*. Cambridge: Cambridge University Press.

Index

For Product Safety Concerns and Information please contact our EU
representative GPSR@taylorandfrancis.com
Taylor & Francis Verlag GmbH, Kaufingerstraße 24, 80331 München, Germany